Buzz for *Knock 'em Dead Resun*

"Two recruitment firms both gave me compliments on my resume. At Volt the recruiter said, 'This is the best resume regarding format that I have seen in a long time.' At Robert Half they stated the same thing, that the format was easy to read and very professional. Your *Knock 'em Dead: The Ultimate Job Search Guide* and *Knock 'em Dead Resume Templates* have been life-savers for me!"

—P.K., Operations Administration, San Diego

"I was sending out hordes of resumes and hardly getting a nibble—and I have top-notch skills and experience in my field. I wasn't prepared for this tough job market. When I read your book, however, I immediately began applying some of your techniques. My few nibbles increased to so many job interviews I could hardly keep up with them!"

—C.S., Chicago, Illinois

"This book is as good as it gets. Put the time into following step by step and you will have a dramatically different view of your own skills. Plus, you'll end up with a fantastic resume."

—J.A., Boise, Idaho

"After I sent my new resume and cover letter, I got four interviews in one week and refused two interviews. I want to say thank you: thank you for doing this for millions of professionals who work hard, and thank you for changing our lives—job seeking is life, it is for everyone who takes their life seriously."

—N.P., Chicago, Illinois

"First of all, thank you soooo much! It was YOU who helped me move from under-evaluating myself to accurately presenting who I truly am on my resume [and, thus, at interviews]. As a result, this brought my salary up by a giant leap."

—E.A. (no address given)

"I bought all three of your books: *Knock 'em Dead Resumes, Knock 'em Dead Cover Letters*, and *Knock 'em Dead: The Ultimate Job Search Guide*. I read each book cover to cover. I went for the interview yesterday with a mental health center. They said they would call me by the end of the week. Soon as I got home I wrote a follow-up letter; I mailed it express to get there noon next day. I got the call from the hiring manager within the hour letting me know that I have the job. I think he called me as soon as he put the letter down."

—K.G. (no address given)

"This book was wonderful! I've been in a management role for multiple years and the ideas in this book helped me determine what I should be looking for. The information in the book was spot on and spoke to the reader in volumes in just a few short pages."

—K.W., St. Louis, Missouri

"For job hunters of all ages this book is valuable. It provides a comprehensive guide to thinking about your experience, defining your personal brand and translating it into a resume that will get attention. The text and 100 sample resumes are up to date and should help the majority of searchers find a style and sample text in their field."

—T.K., Carmel, Indiana

"After reading your book, *Knock 'em Dead Resumes*, I rewrote my resume and mailed it to about eight companies. The results were beyond belief. I was employed by one of the companies that got my new resume and received offers of employment or requests for interviews from every company. The entire job search took only five weeks."

—J.V., Dayton, Ohio

"You resonated through your understanding of the realities of our current job climate and practical approaches, especially the resume Target Job Deconstruction Process. Awesome."

—M.M., Chicago, Illinois

"I re-jigged my resume exactly as you outlined in your book and one employer said, 'You can tell this person has a real love of PR from his resume.' Within three weeks I had three job offers and was able to pick and choose the perfect job for myself."

—M.W., Detroit, Michigan

"I am very grateful for your *Knock 'em Dead* series. I have read the trio and adopted the methods. In the end, I get a dream job with a salary that is almost double of my previous! By adopting your methods, I got four job offers."

—C.Y., Singapore

"Your book is simply fantastic. This one book improved my yearly income by several thousand dollars, and my future income by untold amounts. Your work has made my family and myself very happy."

—M.Z., St. Clair Shores, Michigan

"I cannot tell you what a fabulous response I have been getting due to the techniques you describe in your books. Besides giving me the tools I needed to 'get my foot in the door,' they gave me confidence. I never thought I could secure an excellent position within a month!"

—B.G., Mountain View, California

"I read and used *Knock 'em Dead Resumes* as I searched for a job. I was called for an interview and was up against ten applicants. To make a long story short, I interviewed on Monday morning and by Monday afternoon knew I had the job."

—E.H. (no address given)

"I have averaged at least an interview per day for the last couple weeks, after two months of very sporadic interview activity. Some of this might be plain good luck, but I think revising my resume and cover letters several weeks ago had a positive effect."

—L.E. (no address given)

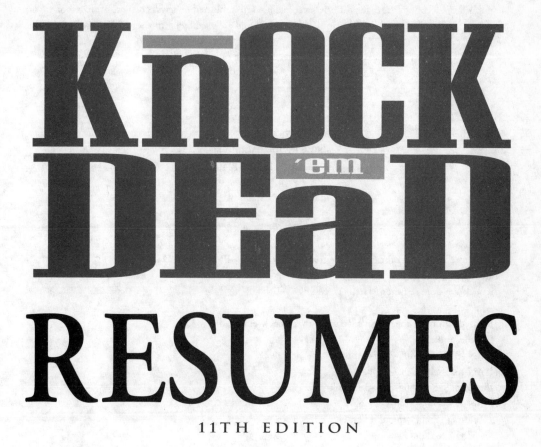

KNOCK 'em DEAD

RESUMES

11TH EDITION

A killer resume gets MORE job interviews!

MARTIN YATE, CPC

New York Times bestselling author

Avon, Massachusetts

Copyright © 2014, 2012, 2010, 2008, 2006, 2004, 2003, 2002, 2001, 1995, 1993 by Martin John Yate.
All rights reserved.
This book, or parts thereof, may not be reproduced in any form without permission from the
publisher; exceptions are made for brief excerpts used in published reviews. Portions of this book
have previously appeared in electronic form online and are used by permission of the author.

Published by Adams Media, a division of F+W Media, Inc.
57 Littlefield Street, Avon, MA 02322. U.S.A.
www.adamsmedia.com

ISBN 10: 1-4405-7907-5
ISBN 13: 978-1-4405-7907-3
eISBN 10: 1-4405-8140-1
eISBN 13: 978-1-4405-8140-3

Printed in the United States of America.

10   9   8   7   6   5   4   3   2

Library of Congress Cataloging-in-Publication Data
Yate, Martin John.
  Knock 'em dead resumes/Martin Yate, CPC. – 11th ed.
    p. cm.
  Revised edition of the author's Resumes that knock 'em dead.
  Includes index.
  ISBN-13: 978-1-4405-7907-3 (pb)
  ISBN-10: 1-4405-7907-5 (pb)
  ISBN-13: 978-1-4405-8140-3 (ebook)
  ISBN-10: 1-4405-8140-1 (ebook)
  1. Resumes (Employment) I. Title.
  HF5383.Y38 2014
  650.14'2--dc23

                        2014019106

This publication is designed to provide accurate and authoritative information with regard to the
subject matter covered. It is sold with the understanding that the publisher is not engaged in ren-
dering legal, accounting, or other professional advice. If legal advice or other expert assistance is
required, the services of a competent professional person should be sought.
        —From a *Declaration of Principles* jointly adopted by a Committee of the American
                        Bar Association and a Committee of Publishers and Associations

Many of the designations used by manufacturers and sellers to distinguish their product are claimed
as trademarks. Where those designations appear in this book and Adams Media was aware of a trademark claim, the designations have been printed with initial capital letters.

Cover design by Erin Dawson.

This book is available at quantity discounts for bulk purchases.
For information, please call 1-800-289-0963.

CONTENTS

Your resume is the most financially important document you will ever own. When it works, you work, and when it doesn't work, you don't.

How to create a template for the story your resume needs to tell in order to be successful.

Fifty percent of the success of any project depends on the preparation. Taking the time to gather the right information for your resume makes the difference between interviews and no interviews.

In any job search you are selling a product: You are a bundle of skills and capabilities suited to a particular set of challenges. Like any product you will do better when you give a distinct identity to what you are taking to market.

A resume's format can help emphasize or de-emphasize aspects of your professional background.

The most effective way to get a premium, powerful resume for a professional job in the shortest time with the least hassle.

First impressions are important. Editing polishes your content and helps it deliver a greater punch.

ACKNOWLEDGMENTS

Knock 'em Dead books have been in print here in America and in many languages around the world for thirty-plus years, and owe their success to constant updating and the millions of satisfied professionals whose careers are helped by them. This is only possible because *Knock 'em Dead* books work; they help you change the trajectory of your professional life.

There is a very small group who helps me write such books, and constantly update classics like *Knock 'em Dead Resumes*: Peter Archer, my managing editor of so many years he is now a grandfather; my editor Will Yate, who's consistent, conscientious, and persnickety in the best of ways; and Angela Yate, who takes care of our business and allows me the time to do good work; she also acts as the first soundingboard on the many issues that can make the difference between a good book and a perennial classic.

INTRODUCTION

The Facts of Life

On the list of things you want to do in life, fixing your resume is right up there with hitting yourself in the head with a hammer. Yet owning a killer resume is the foundation of every successful job search; show me a stalled job search and I'll show you a flawed resume. What you learn in these pages will give you the best resume you have ever owned, and if you pay close attention, you will learn how to change the trajectory of your career.

Your resume is the most financially important document you will ever own: when your resume works, you work; when it doesn't, you don't. It's the primary branding tool to introduce yourself to your professional world, and properly fashioned, it ensures that prospective employers and future colleagues see you as you want to be seen. Slack off on your resume and you can say goodbye to that new job and career success.

No one likes writing a resume, but it's an essential part of defining a commodity that your professional world is eager to embrace. When it comes to a job search, you are a commodity, and your resume is the styling and packaging that sells the product. This is critical in a world where your resume all too often disappears into resume databases with millions of others. When recruiters do find it, your resume will get a scan lasting five to forty-five seconds, and if a clearly defined and relevant brand doesn't jump out, they'll move on to the next one.

Knock 'em Dead Resumes will give you control over these issues, delivering a resume that will consistently get pulled from the resume databases and will resonate with recruiters on that first scan and also on deeper, more careful readings.

Remember: Managers hate to interview; they just want to find and hire someone who *gets* the job, so they can get back to work. *Knock 'em Dead Resumes* shows you how to convince hiring managers that you are a competent professional who *gets* the job. It will prepare you to talk about the job's big issues and answer the tough questions in ways you never thought possible . . . and it's all based on a commonsense approach you'll be able to grasp and apply to your future.

CHAPTER 1

YOUR RESUME—THE MOST FINANCIALLY IMPORTANT DOCUMENT YOU'LL EVER OWN

> *Read this book with a highlighter—*
> *it will save time as you refer back to important passages.*

YOUR RESUME IS the most financially important document you will ever own. When it works, the doors of opportunity open for you. When it doesn't work, they won't.

No one enjoys writing a resume, but it has such a major impact on the money you earn during your work life, and consequently on the quality of your life outside of work, that you know it needs to be done right.

You didn't come to this book for a good read. You came because you are facing serious challenges in your professional life. The way the professional world works has changed dramatically in the past few years, and nothing has changed as much as corporate recruitment. When hiring practices have changed beyond recognition, your approach to getting hired needs to be re-evaluated from top to bottom.

In these pages, you are going to learn very quickly how to build a resume that works. But you're going to learn something more. Since my approach to resumes is part of a larger strategy for achieving long-term career and personal success, everything I teach you about developing a kick-ass resume will apply to the broader challenges of the job search, interviewing, and career management.

In other words, not only will you leave this book with a killer resume, you'll leave it with critical job search and interview strategies, and even some amazing insights into winning raises and promotions.

Self-Awareness: The Key to Professional Survival and Success

Understanding what employers want and need from a specific job title, and how they express and prioritize those needs, will tell you what it takes to win and succeed in that job. It will also give you some hints about the story your resume needs to tell in order to get your foot in the door.

Employers Just Want to Make a Buck

Employees only get added to the payroll to help make a buck, to enhance profitability in some way. Think about this: If you owned a company, there just isn't any other reason you would add workers to your payroll. So it is implicit in any employment contract that *your job contributes to profitability in some way.*

Depending on your job, you can help an employer make a buck by:

- Making money for the company
- Saving money for the company
- Saving time/increasing productivity

No matter what your job, no matter how impressive your title, at its very core, your position exists to help an employer maintain and increase profitability by:

- The *identification* of problems within your area of responsibility
- The *prevention* of problems within your area of responsibility
- The *solution* to problems within your area of responsibility

No resume gets read, no one gets interviewed, and no one gets hired unless someone somewhere is trying to solve a problem. That problem may be finding a quicker way to manufacture silicon chips, speed up the accounts receivable process, leverage social networking for brand management, or any one of a million other profit challenges.

The only reason your job exists is because your employer needed someone to identify, prevent, and solve the problems that regularly occur in this area of professional expertise; it exists because not having someone like you is costing the company money.

Problem solving—the application of critical thinking to the challenges within your area of expertise—is what you are paid to do. It is why every job opening exists, and why every job gets filled with the person who seems to have the firmest grip on how to identify, prevent, and solve the problems that make up the everyday activities of that job.

Why No One Wants to Read Your Resume

You may think that resume writing is a tough job, but you've never had to *read* them. Go to the resume samples section at the end of the book and try to read and understand six resumes in a row. Your brain will first go numb, then start to melt, and by the sixth you'll understand why no one is really that anxious to read your resume.

No one reads resumes unless they have to, so when your resume does get read, it means that a job exists: a job that has been carefully defined, budgeted, and titled, with a salary range that has been authorized and for which funds have been released. *Whenever a recruiter searches a resume database or reads a resume, she is doing it with a specific job and the language and priorities of that job description in mind.*

Why a Hiring Manager May Never Get the Chance to Read Your Resume

The ongoing impact of technology on our world of work causes the nature of all jobs to change almost as rapidly as the pages on a calendar. Resumes today rarely go straight to a recruiter's or manager's desk (though I'll show you how to make this happen); more often they go to a resume database.

This means that before anyone actually looks at your resume, it must first have been pulled from that database *by a recruiter with a specific job and the language and priorities of that job description in mind.* Keep in mind that some of those databases contain more than 35 million resumes.

With this in mind, you can see that if your resume's just a jumble of everything you've ever done, or of everything that *you* happen to think is important (without reference to what your customers are actually buying), it is never going to work.

Understand Your Customer

"The customer is always right," "the customer comes first," and "understand your customer" are phrases that underlie all successful business stories. In the same way that corporations tailor products to be appealing to *their* customers, you need to create a resume tailored to *your* customers' needs.

Your resume works when it matches your skills and experiences to the responsibilities and deliverables of a specific target job. This requires that your resume focus on how employers— your customers—think about, prioritize, and describe the job's deliverables: those things you are expected to deliver as you execute your assigned responsibilities.

A resume focused on a specific target job and built from the ground up with the customers' needs in mind will perform better in the recruiters' resume database searches, and it will resonate far more with human eyes already glazed from the tedium of resume reading.

This Is Not Your Last Job Change

In a world without job security, when job and even career changes are happening ever more frequently, being able to write a productive resume is one of life's critical survival skills.

This is probably not your first, and almost certainly won't be your last, job change. You are somewhere in the middle of a half-century work-life, a span during which you are likely to have three or more distinct careers and are statistically likely to change jobs about every four years; where economic recessions come around every seven to ten years and age discrimination can begin to kick in around age fifty.

Enlightened Self-Interest

When I started to talk about these issues of professional survival twenty-five years ago, I was called a communist and asked how I could suggest that Americans be disloyal to their employers. History has shown that it is the corporations that broke the employment contract, yet today we still hear of companies demanding unblinking loyalty from their employees. If you accept this double standard, your life and the lives of your loved ones will suffer.

Wake up! Times have changed. You need a tougher, more pragmatic approach to your professional life. You still need to do your best for your employer and your team, but you also need to put yourself first, because you need to survive and, hopefully, prosper in life. To do that, you need to find a more sophisticated approach to managing your professional life and guiding your destiny.

Start to think of yourself as a corporation: MeInc, a financial entity that must always plan and act to ensure its economic survival. Like any corporation, MeInc constantly has new products and services in development. These are the ever-evolving skill bundles that define the professional you. Again, just like any corporation, these products and services are branded and sold to your targeted customer base: employers who hire people like you.

The success of MeInc depends on how well you run your company, and like every successful company, you'll need initiatives for Research and Development, Strategic Planning, Marketing, Public Relations, and Sales.

- *Research and Development*: Every company is continually involved in the identification and development of products and services that will appeal to their customers. You must have similar ongoing initiatives. This translates into skill building in response to market trends, which you do by connecting to your profession and by monitoring the changing market demands for your job on an ongoing basis.
- *Strategic Planning*: The development of career management strategies. You'll begin to think of your career over the long term, of where you want to be and how you are going to get there. How you will stay on top of skill development, and how you will develop and maintain a desirable professional brand.
- *Marketing and PR*: The effective branding of MeInc as a desirable product requires establishing credibility for the services you deliver and positioning these services so that the professional you becomes visible to an ever-widening circle. You want to make yourself known within a company, to encourage professional growth, and within your profession, to encourage your employability elsewhere.
- *Sales*: MeInc needs a state-of-the-art sales program to market your products and services.

Your new resume is the primary sales tool for MeInc, the company you embody. It is the most financially important document you will ever own, and you can learn how to do it right, starting right now.

CHAPTER 2

Your Customer Knows What He Wants—How to Get Inside His Head

"THE CUSTOMER IS always right" is probably the first business lesson we ever learn. The customer has the money to buy the product you want to sell and that customer knows exactly what he wants; when you accurately tailor your product to your customer's needs, you'll experience a much shorter and more successful sales cycle. This chapter is about how to effectively customize your resume to your customers' needs.

Your resume is the primary marketing device for every job and career change (probably between twelve and twenty changes) throughout your career. In addition, it plays a role in subsequent internal promotions. In short, it is absolutely vital in determining your professional success. Yet when it comes to creating a resume, the most financially valuable document any of us will ever own, no one ever seems to think about what the customer wants to buy! Instead, we just want to get it done as quickly as possible and with as little thought and effort as possible.

Your current resume is probably a simple recitation of all you have done: It lists everything that you *think* is important. I bet this resume just isn't working. That's because a simple recitation of all your accomplishments and activities results in a hodgepodge of what you think is important, *not what your customers **know** is important.* When you build a resume that tries to be all things to all people, you are creating the equivalent of a Swiss Army knife. Have you ever looked at a Swiss Army knife? It's got knife blades, bottle openers, screwdrivers . . . it does practically everything. But companies aren't hiring human Swiss Army knives; they are hiring human lasers, with exceptional skills focused in a specific area. *You need a resume that speaks to the priorities of your customers,* because they won't make the time to struggle through an unfocused resume to see if you might have what they want. Why should they, when enough people have taken the time to learn what's needed?

Settle on a Target Job Title

With just a few years' experience in the professional world, most people reach a point where they have experience that qualifies them for more than one job; still, this is not an argument for having a general resume as your primary marketing document. Right now, there are probably two or more jobs you can do, but with the way recruitment works today, you have no choice but to go with a resume that focuses on a single target job. So your first task is to look at all the jobs you can do (they are probably all closely related in some way) and choose which one will represent the prime thrust of your job search.

After your primary resume is completed, it is fairly easy to create a resume for any additional job you want to pursue. I'll explain exactly how you do this later in the book, but to set your mind at ease, that second job-targeted resume will have a number of things in common with the job you described in your primary resume. This means that you'll already have a template to start with, plus the dates, layout, chronology, contact information, and possibly even the list of employers you're going to contact. I'll show you a methodology that helps you quickly refashion and edit your primary resume into a resume for that second or third target job.

But you don't get any of those good things until you build a primary resume, so before going further, you need to think through your options and decide on the job title that your *primary resume* will target.

You can make this decision on many unique criteria, but assuming your main goal is to get back to work, or out of the hellhole you work in today, your best bet is to go with the job you can nail. This is the job that you can make the most convincing case for on paper, the strongest argument for in person, and the job where, when you hit the ground running, you won't trip over your shoelaces. Once you've decided, you build a primary resume around this target job.

To Really Understand Your Target Job, Deconstruct It

The most productive resumes start with a clear focus on the target job and its responsibilities from the point of view of the recruitment process and the selection committee. In other words, the customer comes first, so let's get inside the customer's head.

There's a practical and easy way to get inside the employer's head. It's called a Target Job Deconstruction (TJD). It's a way to get a tight focus on what your customers are buying and what will sell before you even start writing your resume. Take half a day to do a TJD and your investment will yield:

- A template for the story your resume *must* tell to be successful
- An objective standard against which you can measure your resume's likely performance
- A complete understanding of where the focus will be during interviews
- A very good idea of the interview questions that will be heading your way and why
- Relevant examples with which to illustrate your answers
- A behavioral profile for getting hired and promoted, and therefore . . . greater professional success throughout your career
- A behavioral profile for *not* getting hired and for ongoing professional failure

Target Job Deconstruction: The Way Into Your Customer's Head

Step One: Collect Postings

Collect 6–10 job postings of *a single job* you can do and would enjoy. Save the postings in a folder and also print them out. If you are interested in more than one job, you must prioritize them. The most productive resumes focus on a single job. I'll show you a very fast and effective editing technique a little later in the chapter to develop a custom resume for each job (and also a place to use that Swiss Army knife resume that currently isn't working).

Not sure where to start? Try these job aggregators (or spiders, robots, or bots) that run around thousands of job sites looking for jobs with your chosen keywords:

www.indeed.com
www.simplyhired.com
www.WorkTree.com
www.JobBankUSA.com
www.Job-Search-Engine.com
www.JobSniper.com
www.SourceTool.com
www.jobster.com

Step Two: Create a Document

Create a new document and title it "TJD for [your chosen target job title]."

Step Three: Identify Target Job Titles

Start by inserting in your document the subhead: "Target job titles." Then copy and paste in all the variations from your collection of job descriptions. Looking at the result, you can say, "When employers are hiring people like this, they tend to describe the job title with these words." From this, you can come up with a suitably generic target job title for your resume, which you will type after your name and contact information. This will help your resume's database performance and also act as a headline, giving the reader's eyes an immediate focus.

Step Four: Identify Skills and Responsibilities

Add a second subhead titled "Skills/Responsibilities/Requirements/Deliverables/etc." Look through the job postings—it might be easier to spread the printouts across your desk. You are looking for a requirement that is common to all of your job postings. Take the most complete description and copy and paste it (with a "6" beside it, signifying it is common to all six of your samples) into your document. Underneath this, add additional words and phrases from the other job postings used to describe this same requirement. Repeat this exercise for any other requirements common to all six of your job postings.

The greater the number of keywords in your resume that are directly relevant to your target job, the higher the ranking your resume will achieve in recruiters' database searches. *And the higher your ranking, the greater the likelihood that your resume will be rescued from the avalanche and passed along to human eyes for further screening.* This database search has led directly to the denser resumes that are more common today and the increasing prevalence of Core Competencies sections that capture all relevant keywords in one place. (More about Core Competencies sections later.)

Repeat the exercise for requirements common to five of the jobs, then four, and so on, all the way down to those requirements mentioned in only one job posting.

Step Five: Identify Problems to Solve

At their most elemental level, all jobs are the same—all jobs focus on problem identification, prevention, and solution in that particular area of expertise; this is what we all get paid for, no matter what we do for a living.

Go back to your TJD and start with the first requirement. Think about the problems you will typically need to identify, solve, and/or prevent in the course of a normal workday as you deliver on this requirement of the job. List specific examples, big and small, of your successful identification, prevention, and/or solution to the problems. Quantify your results when possible.

Repeat this with each of the TJD's other requirements by identifying the problems inherent in that particular responsibility. Some examples may appear in your resume as significant professional achievements, while others will provide you with the ammunition to answer all those interview questions. Interviewers are concerned with your practical problem identification and solution abilities, and they want to see them in action. That's why some questions at job interviews begin, "Tell me about a time when . . ." So at the same time that you're working on your resume, you're also beginning to collect the illustrations you will use in response to those interview questions.

Step Six: Identify the Behavioral Profile of Success

Think of the *best* person you have ever known doing this job and what made her stand out. Describe her performance, professional behavior, interaction with others, and appearance: "That would be Carole Jenkins, superior communication skills, a fine analytical mind, great professional appearance, and a nice person to work with." Do this for each and every requirement listed on your TJD, and you are describing the person all employers want to hire. *This is your behavioral profile for professional success.* Apply what you learn from this exercise to your professional life. It will increase your job security by opening doors to the inner circles that exist in every department and company, and by leading to the plum assignments, raises, and promotions that over time add up to professional success.

Step Seven: Identify the Behavioral Profile of Failure

Now think of the *worst* person you have ever known doing this job and what made that person stand out in such a negative way. Describe his performance, professional behaviors, interaction with others, and appearance: "That would be Jack Hartzenberger, morose, critical, passive aggressive, always looked like he slept in his suit, and smelled like it too." You are describing the person that all employers want to avoid and, incidentally, a behavioral profile for professional suicide.

Now You Know Your Customers' Needs

Once you complete and review your TJD, you will have a clear idea of exactly the way employers think about, prioritize, and express their needs when they hire someone for the job you want.

Now you know the story your resume needs to tell to be maximally productive in the resume databases, which means getting retrieved for human review. You now have the proper focus for a killer resume.

When doing the TJD, you'll come across some skills that you possess or even excel at: "Wow, all six of these job postings require competency in Microsoft Excel, and I'm the office Excel guru!" But there will be other skills that you don't have, or that need polishing: "Wow, everyone's looking for Six Sigma and lean management skills and I don't even know what those words mean." As a rule of thumb (the separate issues of changing careers aside), you need about 70 percent of a job's requirements to pursue that job with reasonable hope of landing interviews, especially in a down economy, when competition is more fierce. If you complete the TJD process and realize you don't make the grade, you have probably saved yourself a good deal of frustration pursuing a job you had no real chance of landing. What you need to do in this instance is pull your title goals back one level. Use this TJD and the missing skills it identifies as a professional development tool: To warrant that next promotion, you'll need to develop these abilities.

Here is a simple before-and-after example that will illustrate how powerful this process can be. The resume is for a young graduate with a computer science degree looking for her first position in the professional world. When we first spoke, she had been out of school for nearly three months and had had a couple of telephone interviews and one face-to-face interview. Her search was complicated by the fact that she is a foreign national and needed to find a company that would sponsor her. This is not easy at the best of times, but in today's tough job environment, it is a significant additional challenge. The first resume is the one she was using; the second she created after completing the Target Job Deconstruction process.

KATHARINE HEPBURN

123 ABERCORN STREET, APT 12
SAVANNAH, GA 31419
EXAMPLE@EMAIL.COM
(401) 555-3412

Education

- Armstrong Atlantic State University, Savannah, GA
- MSc. Computer Science (3.5 GPA), December 2007
- University of Technology, Kingston, Jamaica
- BSc. Computing & Information Technology, November 2005
- Graduated Magna Cum Laude (3.7 GPA)

Key Skills

- Programming
- Programming Languages: C, C++, Java, VB.Net
- Database Programming: SQL
- Website Design
- Design Languages/Tools: HTML, CSS, JavaScript, Dreamweaver
- Problem Solving and Leadership
- Honed an analytical, logical, and determined approach to problem solving and applied this as group leader for my final year (undergraduate) research project.
- Team Player
- Demonstrated the ability to work effectively within a team while developing a Point-of-Sale system over the course of three semesters.
- Communication
- Demonstrated excellent written and oral communication skills through reports and presentations while pursuing my degrees, and as Public Relations Officer for the University of Technology's Association of Student Computer Engineers (UTASCE).

Work Experience

January 2006–December 2007
- Armstrong Atlantic State University, Savannah, GA
- Graduate Research Assistant, School of Computing
- Developed a haptic application to demonstrate human-computer interaction using Python and H3D API.
- Developed an application to organize text documents using the Self-Organizing Map algorithm and MATLAB.

July–November 2005
- Cable & Wireless Jamaica Ltd, Kingston, Jamaica
- Internet Helpdesk Analyst
- Assisted customers with installing and troubleshooting modems and Internet service-related issues via telephone.

July–August 2003
- National Commercial Bank Ja. Ltd, Kingston, Jamaica
- Change Management Team Member
- Generated process diagrams and documentation for systems under development using MS Visio, MS Word, and MS Excel.

Awards/Honors

- President's Pin for graduating with a GPA above 3.75   November 2005
- Latchman Foundation Award for Academic Excellence & Outstanding Character   March 2005
- Nominated School of Computing student of the year   March 2005
- Recognized by Jamaica Gleaner as top student in School of Computing & IT   February 2005
- Nominated for Derrick Dunn (community service) Award   March 2004
- Honor roll/Dean's List   2002–2005

Languages

- French (fluent), Italian (basic)

Extracurricular Activities

- Singing, acting, chess, reading
- Member of Association for Computing Machinery, AASU student chapter

References

- Available upon request.

KATHARINE HEPBURN

123 Abercorn Street, Apt 12
Savannah, GA 31419
example@email.com
(401) 555-3412

Talented, analytical, and dedicated Software Engineer with strong academic background in object-oriented analysis and design, comfort with a variety of technologies, and interest in learning new ones.

SUMMARY OF QUALIFICATIONS

- Excellent academic record. Achieved 3.55 GPA (Master's) and 3.77 GPA (Bachelor's, Dean's List for all eight semesters).
- Familiarity with the software development lifecycle, from identifying requirements to design, implementation, integration, and testing.
- Familiarity with agile software development processes.
- Strong technical skills in Java development and Object-Oriented Analysis and Design (OOA/D).
- Strong understanding of multiple programming languages, including C, C++, JavaScript, Visual Basic, and HTML.
- Familiar with CVS version control software.
- Excellent communication skills with an aptitude for building strong working relationships with teammates.
- Proven background leading teams in stressful, deadline-oriented environments.

TECHNICAL SKILLS

Languages:	Java, JavaScript, C, C++, Visual Basic, HTML, SQL, VB.Net, ASP.Net, CSS
Software:	Eclipse, NetBeans, JBuilder, Microsoft Visual Studio, Microsoft Office Suite (Word, PowerPoint, Excel, Access), MATLAB
Databases:	MySQL, Oracle
Operating Systems:	Windows (NT/2000/XP Professional)
Servers:	Apache Server

EDUCATION

MS in Computer Science, Armstrong Atlantic State University, Savannah GA, December 2007
- Completed a thesis in the area of Computer Security (Digital Forensics: Forensic Analysis of an iPod Shuffle)

BS in Computing & IT, University of Technology, Kingston, Jamaica, November 2005

LANGUAGES

Fluent in English, French, and Italian

PROFESSIONAL EXPERIENCE

Armstrong Atlantic State University, Savannah, GA 01/2006–12/2007

Graduate Research Assistant, School of Computing
- Developed a haptic application to demonstrate human-computer interaction using Python and H3D API.
- Developed an application to organize text documents using the Self-Organizing Map algorithm and MATLAB.

Cable & Wireless Jamaica Ltd, Kingston, Jamaica   07/2005–11/2005
Internet Helpdesk Analyst
- Assisted customers with installing and troubleshooting modems and Internet service-related issues via telephone.

National Commercial Bank Ja. Ltd, Kingston, Jamaica   07/2003–08/2003
Change Management Team Member
- Generated process diagrams and documentation for systems under development using MS Visio, MS Word, and MS Excel.

AWARDS/HONORS
- President's Pin for graduating with a GPA above 3.75 11/2005
- Latchman Foundation Award for Academic Excellence & Outstanding Character 03/2005
- Nominated School of Computing student of the year 03/2005
- Recognized by Jamaica Gleaner as top student in School of Computing & IT 02/2005
- Nominated for Derrick Dunn (community service) Award 03/2004

PROFESSIONAL AFFILIATIONS

Association for Computing Machinery (ACM)

REFERENCES

Available upon request.

I have taken professionals from entry level through C-suite executives in *Fortune* 25 companies through this process. They all say a couple of things: It was a pain but it was a logical, sensible thing to do and worth it. They almost all get job offers surprisingly quickly. I can't guarantee that, of course, but unless you have rocks for brains you have to see the logic in this approach.

Now, what was the result of this resume revamping? She started using the new resume at the beginning of March 2008 and almost immediately got an invitation to interview. She subsequently relocated out of state and started work for that company on April 14; she has been promoted and is still with the company today.

The target job–focused resume opened doors, positioned her professionally, told her what the employer would want to talk about, and was a powerful spokesperson after she left the interview. The end result was a great start to a new career. It all came about because she took the time to understand how her customer—the employer—was thinking about, and expressing the responsibilities of, the job she wanted to do!

Here is another example, starting with the "before" resume. After writing this initial resume, the job hunter did a Target Job Deconstruction. You'll see two post-TJD drafts: her third and her eighth—and final—draft. The final version generated eight interviews in the second quarter of 2010, and in August I got an e-mail that said in part, "*Two offers, twice what I was expecting, and that is without the signing bonus or the stock options. Amazing!!*" This is a senior PR professional with a substantial track record, coming back to the workplace after four years largely spent raising children and doing a little PR work when time allowed. The resume process took about three weeks parallel with organizing a job search plan of attack.

Look at each of these three versions of an evolving resume to see how a really stellar resume comes together. The first resume is a best effort without having done a Target Job Deconstruction. The second document is the third version of her resume and begins to reflect the focus that the TJD made possible. Finally, you will see the eighth and final version of the resume, and you already know what that achieved after being coupled with a good job search plan of attack.

Nancy Wright

123 Main Street
Anywhere, VA 22652

(555) 555-5555
example@yahoo.com

Public Relations Experience

Nancy Wright has more than thirteen years of public relations experience, primarily focused on high-tech and start-up companies. An Olympic gold medalist in swimming, Wright also spent twelve years serving as a free-lance color commentator for sports/news outlets including NBC and ESPN.

Wright & Company Public Relations, *Founder and Principal*   2003 – present
Provide the professional work of a large public relations agency along with the personal service available from a smaller company. Develop and execute PR campaigns that meet the specialized needs of each client. Programs and services include corporate and product positioning, ongoing PR strategy and tactics, leadership branding, media training, speaker placement, and ongoing media contact. Clients have included: *AirPlay Networks, ReligiousSite.com, PanJet Aviation.*

Three Boys Public Relations, *Co-Founder and Principal*   2001 – 2003
Established a Silicon Valley PR firm that helped high-tech companies accomplish objectives by managing leadership positioning, strategic branding, and publicity. Clients included:
- *ABC Systems* – Project work included managing all annual Sales Conference communications for Charles Smith, Group Vice President, U.S. Service Provider group. Helped launch Smith's new fiscal year strategy, objectives, and goals to his 1,000+ employees.
- *NextLink Technologies* – Successfully positioned the start-up as an industry leader by leveraging the market's widespread use of NextLink's industry-standard GreatD networking software. Rapidly expanded the company's leadership position by garnering positive coverage in all targeted publications.

ABC Systems, *Marketing Manager*   2000 – 2001
Directed internal marketing activities for the iProduct after ABC acquired InfoGame and its technology. Shortly after the acquisition, ABC reorganized InfoGame and later licensed the iProduct trademark to Apple.

InfoGame Technology Corporation, *Public Relations Manager*   1998 – 2000
Designed and executed all company and product strategy. Placed hundreds of stories with news and feature media including the Today Show, Regis & Kathie Lee, ABC's Y2K special hosted by Peter Jennings, The Wall Street Journal, The New York Times and Fast Company. Within eighteen months of launching InfoGame's PR, the company was acquired by ABC Systems.

XYZ Public Relations, *Account Manager; Senior Account Executive; Account Executive*   1996 – 1998
Designed and managed all PR strategy and activities for start-up and unknown software, Internet, and networking companies. Managed teams of up to 10 PR professionals. Promoted annually for delivering results for the following clients:
- *InfoGame Technology Corporation* – Repositioned InfoGame from fledgling company to a leader in the Internet appliance space. Introduced the new management team, the iProduct and the back-end software. Garnered positive coverage in hundreds of media outlets including The Wall Street Journal, The New York Times, and USA Today. InfoGame was acquired by ABC Systems within 18 months of PR campaign.
- *Triiliux Digital Systems* – Accelerated Triiliux and its CEO out of obscurity and into a position of undisputed leadership. Successfully positioned CEO as an industry expert with ongoing speaker placement and quotes in all of Triiliux's top publications. Placed CEO on the magazine cover of the company's topmost publication. Triiliux was acquired by Intel after the two year PR campaign.
- *LinkExchange* – Transformed unknown company into a "player" in the Internet advertising arena. Placed hundreds of stories in both business and industry media including the The Wall Street Journal, CNNfn, and AdWeek. LinkExchange was acquired by Microsoft after an eighteen month PR campaign.

- *The Internet Mall* – Launched this obscure company to the press, landing continual coverage in all top Internet and business publications including The New York Times and Internet World. Within a year of the campaign, the company was acquired by TechWave, now Network commerce.

Other Relevant Experience

Motivational Speaker/Guest Celebrity   **1989 – present**
Coach audiences at corporations, business forums, schools, and functions how to effectively set and achieve goals, using the road to the Olympics as a model. Travel the country making guest appearances at events, functions, and parades. Past or present clients include: IBM, Hardees, Speedo America, Busch Gardens, Alamo Rent-A-Car, and others.

Television Color Commentator   **1988 – 2000**
- Provided expert commentary for swimming events, including the Olympics for NBC.
- Provided half-time interviews and feature packages for the Miami Heat.
- Work included NBC, ESPN, FoxSports, SportsChannel, Turner Sports, SportSouth, and others.

The College Conference, Associate Commissioner   **1991 – 1993**
- Managed all aspects of Conference television and marketing packages.
- Increased marketing revenue by 33% in the first year.

International Swimming Hall of Fame, Assistant Director   **1989 – 1991**
- Helped drive fundraising efforts for new building.
- Served as one of three spokespeople for the Hall of Fame, delivering speeches at community events.
- Successfully managed and completed all fundraising aspects for the NCAA Wall of Fame.
- Developed community affairs programs.

Awards and Honors
- Two Olympic gold medals (1984 Los Angeles, USA), and a silver and bronze (1988 Seoul, Korea).
- Two-time NCAA Champion.
- 26-time NCAA All-American.
- Hall of Fame Inductee: International Swimming Hall of Fame, University of Florida Athletic HOF, Region Swimming HOF, Anywhere High School HOF.

Education
University of Florida, Bachelor of Science, Journalism   **1989**

Third resume:

N_____pervisor

123 Spring Mountain W_____el: 540.555.1234 Cell: 540.555.2345

Performance Profile/Pe_____

High tech public relations _____ _____ding seven in Silicon Valley – in a variety of sectors including software, Internet, networking, and consumer electronics. Substantial experience in PR campaigns that lead to company acquisitions. Expertise in all aspects of strategic and tactical communications, from developing and managing PR campaigns, multiple accounts, and results-oriented teams, to writing materials and placing stories. Twenty years' experience as a motivational speaker and twelve as a free-lance TV color commentator. Two-time Olympic gold medalist.

Core Competencies

High Tech Public Relations • Strategic Communications • Counsel Executives • Manage Teams • Manage Budgets • Multiple Accounts • Multiple Projects • Leadership Positioning • PR Messaging • Client Satisfaction • Media Training • Media Relations • Pitch Media • Craft Stories • Place Stories • PR Tactics • Press Releases • Collateral Materials • Research • Edit • Manage Budgets • Manage Teams • Mentor • Strong Writing Skills • Detail Oriented • Organizational Skills • Motivated • Team Player • New Business

Strategic Public Relations Leadership

Position companies as both industry leaders and sound investments. The following four companies were acquired within two years of commencing the PR campaigns: InfoGear Technologies (acquired by Cisco), Trillium Digital Systems (acquired by Intel), LinkExchange (acquired by Microsoft), and The Internet Mall (acquired by TechWave, now Network Commerce).

Executive Communications Manager

Develop executive communications. Created positioning for ****, Group VP, and launched it to his 1,000+ employees at the ABC Sales Conference. Refined ****'s public speaking delivery and style.

Media Coverage

Proactively place stories. Samplings of past placements include: ABC World News Tonight, CNN, The Today Show, Associated Press, Baltimore Sun, Boston Globe, Business Week, Fast Company, Financial Times, Forbes, Fortune Magazine, Inc., MSNBC.com, New York Times, Parade, San Jose Mercury News, SJ Business Journal, SF Chronicle, USA Today, Wired, Wall Street Journal, AdWeek, CommsDesign, Computer Reseller News, Computer Retail Week, Computer Shopper, Computer World, CRN, CNET, EE Times, Embedded.com, Internet.com, InformationWeek, Internet.com, Internet Telephony Magazine, Light Reading, Network World, Phone+, PC Magazine, Red Herring, TMCnet, VoIP News, VON and ZDNet, Dataquest, Forrester Research, Frost and Sullivan, Jupiter Communications and Yankee Group.

PROFESSIONAL EXPERIENCE

Wright & Associates Public Relations, Anywhere, VA   **2006-present**

Develop and deliver strategic communications that meet the specific needs of each client. Drive all PR strategy and tactics, messaging, media training, media relations, budget management, story creation and placement. Sampling of past or present clients include AirTight Networks (also a former InfoGear, Cisco, NextHop client), JesusCentral. com (eHealthInsurance.com founder), and ProJet Aviation.

Co-Founder and Principal, **Three Boys Public Relations**, Redwood City, CA   **2001-2003**

Silicon Valley PR firm that partnered with high tech clients to meet their corporate objectives. In charge of developing and managing all strategic and tactical aspects of public relations including thought leadership, leadership branding, press materials, stories, media relations, and publicity.

- Cisco Systems – Acting Executive Communications Manager to Carlos Dominguez, VP.
- NextHop Technologies – Company's first PR counsel. Repositioned obscure company, impaired by trademark dilution, into an industry leader. (Acquired by U4EA Technologies in 2008.)

Marketing Manager, ABC Network Systems, San Jose, CA   **2000-2001**

Directed internal, cross-functional marketing activities for the iProduct® after Cisco acquired InfoGear and its technology. Shortly after the acquisition, Cisco dissolved the InfoGear/Managed Appliances Business Unit (MASBU) and later licensed the iProduct trademark to Apple.

Public Relations Manager, InfoGame Technology Corporation, Redwood City, CA   **1998-2000**

Company's first PR counsel. Advised CEO and VP of marketing on all aspects of PR. Developed and implemented ongoing PR campaign, strategies, and tactics.
- Established "iProduct Reviews" program, garnering hundreds of additional positive stories.
- Managed and inspired cross-functional teams of marketing, operations, and customer service.

Account Supervisor, Senior Account Executive, Account Executive, XYZ Advertising & Public Relations (Acquired by FLEISHMAN-HILLARD in 2000), Mountain View, CA   **1996-1998**

Promoted annually for successful track record of positioning unknown start-up companies into industry leaders. Designed and managed all PR strategy and activities for start-up, software, Internet, and networking companies. Managed teams of up to ten PR professionals.
- Accelerated Trillium and its CEO out of obscurity and into undisputed leadership. Continually landed top speaking placements and media coverage.
- Transformed the unknown LinkExchange into a highly publicized leader in the Internet advertising arena. Placed hundreds of stories in both business and industry media.
- Designed and managed InfoGear Technology's repositioning from fledgling company to a leader in the Internet appliance space.
- Launched newcomer The Internet Mall, landing continual coverage in all top Internet and business publications.

OTHER RELEVANT EXPERIENCE

Motivational Speaker/Guest Celebrity

Representative clients: IBM, Hardees, Speedo America, Busch Gardens, Alamo Rent-A-Car   **1989-present**
- Coach audiences on how to use the Olympic model to set and achieve goals, and succeed in business and life.

Television Sports Commentator

Swimming analyst for NBC, ESPN, FoxSports, SportsChannel, Turner Sports, and others   **1988-2000**
- Covered the Barcelona Olympics. Half-time reporter for Miami Heat and Southern Conference games.

AWARDS & ACHIEVEMENTS

Four Olympic swimming medals: two gold, one silver, one bronze
- Southland Corporation's Olympia Award for academic and athletic leadership.
- Southeastern Conference, NCAA, and USA Swimming Champion.
- Hall of Fame Inductee: International Swimming Hall of Fame, University of Florida, Pacific Northwest Swimming, Washington State Swimming Coaches Assoc., Mercer Island H.S.

EDUCATION

University of Florida, Gainesville, FL
- Bachelor of Science in Journalism.
- Minor in Speech.

Eighth resume:

123 Main Street
Anywhere, VA 22222

Nancy Wright

Home (555) 555-5555
Mobile (555) 333-5555
example@yahoo.com

Group Manager • Account Director • PR Manager

Performance Profile/Performance Summary

High tech public relations professional with 13 years' experience, including nine in Silicon Valley, in the software, Internet, networking, consumer electronics, and wireless industries. Substantial experience in PR and strategic communications campaigns that lead to company acquisitions. Experienced in all aspects of strategic and tactical communications from developing and managing multiple campaigns, accounts, and results-oriented teams to developing and placing stories. Seasoned motivational speaker and freelance TV color commentator. Two-time Olympic gold medalist.

Core Competencies

High Tech Public Relations	Craft & Place Stories	Budget Management	Client Satisfaction
Strategic Communications	Strong Writing Skills	Account Management	Organizational Skills
Executive Communications	Media Training	Project Management	Thought Leadership
PR Messaging & Tactics	Multiple Projects	Detail Oriented	PR Counsel
Story Telling	Story Placement	Acquisition Positioning	Social Media
Collateral Materials	Counsel Executives	Pitch Media	
Leadership Branding	Strong Editing Skills	Market Research	
Analyst Relations	New Business Development	Build & Lead Teams	
Media Relations	Team Management	Mentor	

Strategic Public Relations Leadership

Orchestrated PR campaigns that positioned companies as both industry leaders and sound investments. Developed and directed PR campaigns for four companies that were subsequently acquired within two years of the campaigns: *InfoGame Technologies* (creator of the first iProduct®, acquired by *ABC Network*), *Triiliux Digital Systems* (acquired by *Intel*), *LinkExchange* (acquired by *Microsoft*), and *The Internet Mall* (acquired by *TechWave*). Proven client satisfaction demonstrated in repeat business and account growth: over a span of ten years, contracted by former *InfoGame* execs to serve as communications counsel for *NextLink Technologies*, *ABC Network Systems*, and *AirPlay Networks*.

Executive Communications Management

Executive Communications Manager for iconic executive and public speaker, ******, *Group VP, Service Provider Sales, ABC Network Systems* (currently *senior VP* and *technology evangelist* for *ABC Network*). Developed communication messaging, strategy and platform skills for VP, Group VP, and C-level executives.

Media Coverage

ABC World News Tonight, CNN, The Today Show, Associated Press, Baltimore Sun, Boston Globe, Business Times, Business Week, CNN.com, Fast Company, Financial Times, Forbes, Fortune Magazine, Inc., MSNBC.com, New York Times, Parade, San Jose Mercury News, SF Chronicle, USA Today, Wired, Wall Street Journal, AdWeek, CommsDesign, Computer Reseller News, Computer Retail Week, Computer Shopper, Computer World, CRN, CNET, EE Times, Embedded Systems Design, Internet.com, InfoWorld, InformationWeek, Internet.com, Internet Telephony, LightReading, Network World, Phone+, PC Magazine, Red Herring, TMCnet, VoIP News, VON and ZDNet, Dataquest, Forrester Research, Frost and Sullivan, Jupiter Communications, Yankee Group.

—— **Professional Experience** ——

Principal   **2003 to Present**

Wright & Associates Public Relations, Anywhere, VA

Develop and deliver strategic communications. Drive all PR strategy and tactics, messaging, media training, media relations, budget management, story creation and placement for technology clients.
  • Representative clients include *AirPlay Networks* (former *InfoGame* and *NextLink client*), *ReligiousSite.com* (founded by *eCompany.com* founder), and *PanJet Aviation*.

Principal   **2001 to 2003**
Three Boys Public Relations, Redwood City, CA
Developed and implemented all strategic and tactical aspects of public relations for Silicon Valley clients, including thought leadership, leadership branding, story creation and telling, media materials, stories, media relations, and publicity.
- *ABC Network Systems*—Executive Communications Manager to ****, Group VP at *ABC Network*, a highly pursued public speaker.
- *NextLink Technologies*—Company's first PR counsel. Repositioned obscure company, impaired by trademark dilution, into an industry leader by leveraging market's widespread knowledge and use of *NextLink's* industry-standard *GreatD* networking software.

Marketing Manager   **2000 to 2001**
ABC Network Systems, San Jose, CA
Directed internal, cross-functional marketing for iProduct, following ABC Network acquisition of *InfoGame* and its technology.
- Shortly after acquisition, ABC Network dissolved *InfoGame/Managed Appliances Business Unit (MASBU)*.

Public Relations Manager   **1998 to 2000**
InfoGame Technology Corporation, Redwood City, CA
Advised CEO and VP of marketing on all aspects of PR. Developed and implemented all strategies, tactics, and stories.
- Revamped the start-up's teetering image, which was ruining *iProduct* sales. After two press tours, garnered hundreds of additional stories in all top trade and consumer media with the *iProduct Reviews* program. Catapulted company into a leadership position in the Internet appliance industry, setting it up for acquisition. *iProduct* is now a household name.
- Managed and inspired cross-functional teams of marketing, operations and customer service to work outside their job responsibilities to deliver excellent service to hundreds of editors beta testing the *iProduct 2.0*.

Account Supervisor; Senior Account Executive; Account Executive   **1996 to 1998**
XYZ Advertising & Public Relations (Acquired by FLEISHMAN-HILLARD in 2000), Mountain View, CA
Promoted annually for successful track record of positioning unknown companies as both industry leaders and solid investments/acquisitions. Designed and managed all PR strategy and activities for start-up, software, Internet, and networking companies. Managed teams of up to ten PR professionals.
- Repositioned, rebranded, relaunched, and reintroduced *InfoGame*, the *iProduct 1.0* and *2.0*, positioning them collectively as leading the nascent Internet appliance space.
- Accelerated *Triiliux* and its CEO out of obscurity and into undisputed leadership through media placement and top speaking engagements.
- Transformed unknown *LinkExchange* into a highly publicized leader in the Internet advertising arena. Placed hundreds of stories in both business and industry media.
- Launched *The Internet Mall,* landing continual coverage in all top Internet and business publications.

—— **Complementary Experience** ——

Motivational Speaker/Guest Celebrity   **1989 to Present**
Coach audiences on how to use the Olympic model to set and achieve goals and succeed in business and life. Representative clients: IBM, Hardees, Speedo America, Busch Gardens, Alamo Rent-A-Car.

Television Sports Commentator   **1987 to 2000**
Swimming analyst for NBC, ESPN, FoxSports, SportsChannel, Turner Sports, and others. Covered the Olympics. Half-time reporter for Miami Heat and The College Conference.

Awards & Achievements
Winner—Two Olympic swimming gold medals plus one silver and one bronze.
Recipient Southland Corporation's Olympia Award for academic and athletic leadership.
NCAA, USA, Southeastern Conference swimming champion, and 26-time NCAA All American.
Hall of Fame Inductee: International Swimming Hall of Fame, University of Florida, Pacific Northwest Swimming, Washington State Swimming Coaches Association, Mercer Island High School.

EDUCATION—University of Florida, Gainesville, FL; B.S. in Journalism, Minor in Speech.

CHAPTER 3

Your Resume Is a Garbage In/ Garbage Out Proposition

HOW WELL THE most financially important document you are ever going to own comes out depends on what goes in. So if you don't want a garbage resume, you need a logical way to gather the right information to tell that story.

When you got inside your customer's head in the previous chapter, you gained a clear understanding of the story your resume needs to tell. Now, with the requirements and deliverables of your Target Job Deconstruction (TJD) document in front of you for focus, it's time to work through your professional life, methodically pulling out the skills and experiences that will help your resume tell the most effective story of someone who can nail this target job.

The Right Way to Look Into Your Work History

Your resume is a document that tells a story about your collective professional work experiences. For the most powerful resume, you should examine your work history through the lens of your TJD, because it succinctly defines exactly what your customer—the employer—wants to find. This gives you guidelines for the most effective ways to define the professional you. The information you gather will be customized to your customers' needs, giving you the raw materials for a killer resume. The more information you gather, the better. Even if some of it doesn't make it into your resume, it will still have immense value preparing you for the interviews, because this information-gathering exercise will continue to increase the insights you gain into the real professional you as a commodity and a brand. (More on this later.)

Fifty Percent of the Success of Any Project Is in the Preparation

Here's the link *www.knockemdead.com/downloads* for the information-gathering questionnaire I use for my professional resume-writing service clients. It will help you gather all the resume-relevant information about your professional life in one place. To help you get the most out of this not-very-exciting task, you'll find a lot of "how to and why to" advice as you work through it.

It's obviously best to do this kind of work on your computer: you never run out of space and all the information will be collected and saved in a Microsoft Word document, ready to be molded into a finished resume. Go to *www.knockemdead.com* and click on the "Downloads" page to find and download your Microsoft Word copy of the following "Resume Questionnaire." Remember: Half the success of any project depends on the preparation. The work you do here is also going to have a real impact on your career and the quality of your life outside of work for years to come. So bite the bullet and do it right.

Resume Questionnaire

Please Note: An electronic document is expandable, so if you need additional space, don't limit yourself to the lines/pages provided.

Your first step is to complete the critical Target Job Deconstruction exercise. This will create a composite job description and bring focus to the story your resume needs to tell.

Name (exactly as wanted on resume): _____

Address: _____

City: _____ State: _____ Zip: _____

Home Phone: _____ Mobile Phone: _____

E-mail: _____

Are you willing to relocate?   Yes ( ) No ( )

Are you willing to travel?   Yes ( ) No ( )

Please answer the following questions as completely and accurately as possible. Not all questions may apply to you. If they do not apply, mark them "N/A."

Position/Career Objective: List top three job title choices in order of preference.

If the titles are for related positions (*e.g. 1–Sales; 2–Marketing; 3–Business Development*) your resume will be developed to reflect the cross-functional target(s). If the goals are not related (*e.g. 1–Rocket Scientist; 2–Pastry Chef; 3–Landscape Designer*), the resume will be written to fit your first selection. (We will discuss creating additional versions of your resume later.)

1. _____

2. _____

3. _____

Desired Industry Segment _____

Is this a career change for you? Yes ( ) No ( )

Purpose of Resume (e.g. job change, career change, promotion, business development/marketing tool) _____

Summarize your experience in this field in a couple of sentences. Do not provide details of positions here: we only want to get the big picture; just a sentence or two about your background. *For example: I have been in the accounting field for twelve years and received three promotions to my current position, which I've held for two years.*

_____

_____

_____

_____

_____

What are some terms (keywords) specific to your line of work? *(You found these during the TJD process.)*

_____

_____

_____

_____

What are the key strengths that you want to highlight on your resume? What makes you stand out from your competitors? Drill down to the essence of what differentiates your candidacy.

_____

_____

_____

_____

Current Salary: _____   **Expected Salary:** _____

Education

List all degrees, certificates, diplomas received, dates received, school or college, and location of school or college. Begin with the most recent and work backward.

Name of College/Univ: _____

City/State: _____

Degree Obtained (i.e., BS, BA, MBA, AA): _____   Year Completed: _____

Major: _____   Minor: _____

Overall GPA: _____   GPA in Major: _____

Honors (include scholarships):

_____

_____

_____

Extracurricular Activities (include leadership, sports, study abroad, etc.):

_____

_____

_____

Name of College/Univ: _____

City/State: _____

Degree Obtained (i.e., BS, BA, MBA, AA): _____ Year Completed: _____

Major:_____ Minor:_____

Overall GPA:_____ GPA in Major: _____

Honors (include scholarships):

_____

_____

_____

Extracurricular Activities (include leadership, sports, study abroad, etc.):

_____

_____

_____

_____

_____

High School (only if no college)

Name:_____ City/State: _____ Year: _____

Professional Development (training courses/seminars/workshops, etc.)

Ongoing professional education signals commitment to success. If you attended numerous courses, list the most recent and/or relevant to your career and indicate that additional course information is available. Ignore those courses that have been rendered obsolete by technology and the passage of time.

Course Name: _____

Completion Date:_____ Duration: _____

Certification Obtained: _____ Location of Training: _____

Sponsoring Organization: _____

Course Name: _____

Completion Date: _____ Duration: _____

Certification Obtained: _____ Location of Training: _____

Sponsoring Organization: _____

Course Name: _____

Completion Date: _____ Duration: _____

Certification Obtained: _____ Location of Training: _____

Sponsoring Organization: _____

Professional Certifications

_____

_____

Professional Licenses

_____

_____

Military (include branch of service, locations, position, rank achieved, years of service, honorable discharge, key accomplishments, special recognition, awards, etc.)

_____

_____

_____

Professional Organizations/Affiliations

Active membership in a professional association is a key tool for career resiliency and success.

Name of Organization (include city/state or chapter): _____

_____

Leadership Roles Held: _____

Name of Organization (include city/state or chapter): _____

_____

Leadership Roles Held: _____

Name of Organization (include city/state or chapter): _____

_____

Leadership Roles Held: _____

Name of Organization (include city/state or chapter): _____

_____

Leadership Roles Held: _____

Name of Organization (include city/state or chapter): _____

_____

Leadership Roles Held: _____

Name of Organization (include city/state or chapter): _____

_____

Leadership Roles Held: _____

Publications/Presentations

_____

_____

_____

_____

_____

_____

Patents and Copyrights

You can also include here your work on projects that resulted in copyrights and patents, so long as you make clear your real contribution.

_____

_____

_____

_____

_____

_____

Computer Skills (include hardware, operating systems, software, Internet, e-mail, etc.)

Maybe it's just Microsoft Word and Excel or maybe it runs to languages and protocols. Nobody today gets ahead without technological adeptness. Capture your fluency here and update regularly; that alphabet soup of technology just might help your resume in database searches.

Hardware:

_____

_____

_____

_____

Operating Systems:

_____

_____

_____

_____

Software Applications:

_____

_____

_____

_____

Other if relevant:

_____

_____

_____

_____

Foreign Languages (indicate level of fluency and if verbal/written)

_____

_____

_____

_____

Global Experience/Cultural Diversity Awareness

In our global economy any exposure here is relevant, and it doesn't have to be professional in nature. If you've traveled extensively or you were an Army brat and grew up in ten different countries, that can be a big plus. Just name the countries, not the circumstances.

Corporate Awards/Recognition (indicate where and when received):

_____

_____

_____

_____

Community/Volunteer Activities (name of organization, years involved, positions held):

_____

_____

_____

_____

Hobbies/Interests/Avocations

Include activities with which you fill your out-of-work hours. Your resume may include those activities that say something positive about the professional you. For example, in sales and marketing just about all group activities show a desirable mindset. Bridge might argue strong analytical skills, and the senior exec who still plays competitive lacrosse and runs marathons is crazy not to let the world know.

_____

_____

_____

_____

Action Verbs

In describing your work experience at each position you have held, it might be helpful to select from the following list the action verbs that best characterize your daily work, duties, responsibilities, and level of authority. Select from the following list or use other "action verbs" when completing the sections stating: Briefly describe your routine duties, responsibilities, and level of authority.

Do not provide the information here; instead, use it as a guide in completing the information for each position you've held.

These are just suggestions. Please don't limit yourself to the use of these verbs only.

accepted	conceptualized	evaluated	interviewed
accomplished	conducted	examined	introduced
achieved	consolidated	executed	invented
acted	contained	expanded	launched
adapted	contracted	expedited	lectured
addressed	contributed	explained	led
administered	controlled	extracted	maintained
advanced	coordinated	fabricated	managed
advised	corresponded	facilitated	marketed
allocated	counseled	familiarized	mediated
analyzed	created	fashioned	moderated
appraised	critiqued	focused	monitored
approved	cut	forecast	motivated
arranged	decreased	formulated	negotiated
assembled	defined	founded	operated
assigned	delegated	generated	organized
assisted	demonstrated	guided	originated
attained	designed	headed up	overhauled
audited	developed	identified	oversaw
authored	devised	illustrated	performed
automated	diagnosed	implemented	persuaded
balanced	directed	improved	planned
budgeted	dispatched	increased	prepared
built	distinguished	indoctrinated	presented
calculated	diversified	influenced	prioritized
cataloged	drafted	informed	processed
chaired	edited	initiated	produced
clarified	educated	innovated	programmed
classified	eliminated	inspected	projected
coached	emended	installed	promoted
collected	enabled	instigated	proposed
compiled	encouraged	instituted	provided
completed	engineered	instructed	publicized
composed	enlisted	integrated	published
computed	established	interpreted	purchased

recommended	researched	set	systemized
reconciled	resolved	shaped	tabulated
recorded	restored	solidified	taught
recruited	restructured	solved	trained
reduced	retrieved	specified	translated
referred	revamped	stimulated	traveled
regulated	revitalized	streamlined	trimmed
rehabilitated	saved	strengthened	upgraded
remodeled	scheduled	summarized	validated
repaired	schooled	supervised	worked
represented	screened	surveyed	wrote

Accomplishments/Achievements/Successes

When completing the next few pages of the questionnaire, refer to the following questions to refresh your memory regarding accomplishments and achievements (professional experience) for each position. Remember: People hire results (accomplishments and achievements) and look to past performance as an indication of the value you offer.

You don't need to provide answers to all these questions here. Rather, consider the various positions you've held and come up with 4–6 of the strongest contributions you made in each position. As you think about this, read through the questions to help stimulate your thinking. Above all, ask yourself how your current employer is better off now than when the company hired you.

1. Did you increase sales/productivity/volume? Provide percentage or amount.
2. Did you generate new business or increase client base? How? What were the circumstances?
3. Did you forge affiliations, partnerships, or strategic alliances that increased company success? With whom, and what were the results?
4. Did you save your company money? If so, how and by how much?
5. Did you design and/or institute any new systems and procedures? If so, what were the results?
6. Did you meet an impossible deadline through extra effort? If so, what difference did this make to your company?
7. Did you bring a major project in under budget? If so, how did you make this happen? What was the budget? What were you responsible for saving in terms of time and/or money?
8. Did you suggest and/or help launch a new product or program? If so, did you take the lead or provide support? How successful was the effort? What were the results?
9. Did you assume new responsibilities that weren't part of your job? Were they assigned or did you do so proactively? Why were you selected?

10. Did you improve communication in your firm? If so, with whom, and what was the outcome?

11. How did your company benefit from your performance?

12. Did you complete any special projects? What were they and what was the result?

When describing your accomplishments/achievements, use the following three-step CAR format:

C = Challenge (What challenge did you face or what problem did you resolve?)

A = Action (What action did you take?)

R = Results (What was the result of the action you took? What was the value to the company?)

Professional Experience

All right, now you're ready to assemble information about your work history and experience. Begin with your present employer/project. Include self-employment, contract, and volunteer or unpaid work if it applies to your career target.

Be sure to list different positions at the same company as separate jobs. Repeat the section below as many times as you need to in order to encompass all the professional positions you've held.

Name of company: _____

City/State: _____ Dates of employment: _____

Your actual job title: _____

Your functional/working job title if different from actual title: _____

Title of person you report to: _____

Number of people you supervise: _____

Their titles or functions: _____

Briefly describe the size of the organization (volume produced; revenues; number of employees; local, national, or international, etc.): _____

_____

_____

What do they do, make, or sell? _____

_____

_____

Where do they rank in their industry in terms of their competitors? _____

_____

_____

_____

What were you hired to do?

Briefly describe your routine duties, responsibilities, and level of authority. Use numbers (size) and percentages, quantify budgets, state with whom you interacted, etc. Provide two to three brief sentences about your major overall area of responsibility and list them in order of importance. Refer back to the list of action verbs to help you brainstorm.

Example

Selected to re-engineer and revitalize this $65 million business unit with accountability for thirty-two direct reports in four cities across the United States. Established strategic vision and developed operational infrastructure. Managed Supply Chain, Logistics/Distribution, Forecasting, System Integration, Project Management, Contracts Administration, and Third-Party Site Operations.

Or more simply: Drove production for world's largest wallboard plant, with 258 employees working in multiple shifts.

1. _____
_____
_____
_____

2. _____
_____
_____
_____

3. _____
_____
_____
_____

Briefly describe 3–5 of your accomplishments in this position. Use the most significant achievements or contributions that best support your career target and describe them in a brief statement, referring to the accomplishments guidelines. Use numbers wherever possible. Give facts and figures. Please note: Distill the accomplishments into their essence. How did your accomplishment contribute to bottom line performance/ROI?

1. _____
_____
_____
_____

2. _____

_____

_____

_____

3. _____

_____

_____

_____

4. _____

_____

_____

_____

5. _____

_____

_____

_____

Take Your Time: You're Laying the Foundation for Career Success

Be sure to take the time to do this exercise right. It may be tempting to rush through it or look for shortcuts, but remember that you're assembling the information that's going to be the brick and mortar of your resume, the most financially important document you are ever going to own. You need it to be as complete and well thought out as possible.

CHAPTER 4

How to Define and Build a Desirable Professional Brand

A RESUME IS the primary tool that all professionals use to define and disseminate their professional brand to an ever-expanding world of contacts. Long-term success— rewarding work without layoffs, and professional growth that fits your goals—is much easier to achieve when you are credible and visible within your profession. Creating and nurturing a professional brand as part of your overall career management strategy will help you achieve credibility and visibility throughout your profession, because an identifiable brand gives *you* focus and motivation, and *others* a way to differentiate you.

Establishing a desirable professional brand takes time; after all, you have to brand something that is worth branding, something your customers want to buy. A worthwhile brand doesn't spring into being overnight, it evolves over years; but you need to start somewhere, and you need to start now.

The greater the effort you put into working toward credibility and visibility—which over time translates into a steadily widening professional reputation in your area of expertise—the quicker you enter the inner circles in your department, your company, and ultimately your profession. And it is in these inner circles that job security, plum assignments, raises, promotions, and professional marketability all dwell.

Think of your brand as the formal announcement to the professional community of how you want to be seen in your professional world, and recognize that your resume, and the social networking profiles that grow from it, are the primary tools you will use to introduce and maintain a consistent message of your brand: how you want to be seen as a professional in your field. It's the narrative of your resume that tells this story in a very particular way: It captures your experience, skills, capabilities, and professional behavioral profile *as they relate to what your customers want to buy.*

Components of a Desirable Professional Brand

A viable professional brand must be built on firm foundations. This means you must understand what employers look for when they hire (and subsequently promote) someone in your profession, at your level, and with your job title. Understanding how your employers think is critical for the success of this job search and for your career going forward; it's why you spent Chapter 2 learning how employers deconstruct your job into its component parts, and how they then order and prioritize those parts and, most important, the words they use to express these judgments . . . and by extension how they will reward those who give them what they want.

In this chapter, we'll examine a couple of additional and equally important dimensions of the professional you, ones that will play into your resume, your interviews, and your success in that next job on your career path. Specifically, we'll look at a sequence of transferable skills and professional values that underlie all professional success, no matter what you do. I'll also explain a process to help you identify and give voice to the unique combination of attributes that make up the professional you.

Over the years, I've read a lot of books about finding jobs, winning promotions, and managing your career. A few were insightful and many were innocuous, but one theme that runs through them all is the absurd and harmful advice to "Just be yourself."

"Who you are is just fine. Be yourself and you'll do fine." Wrong. Remember that first day on your first job, when you went to get your first cup of coffee? You found the coffee machine, and there, stuck on the wall behind it, was a handwritten sign reading:

YOUR MOTHER DOESN'T WORK HERE
PICK UP AFTER YOURSELF

You thought, "Pick up after myself? Gee, that means I can't behave like I do at home and get away with it." And so you started to observe and emulate the more successful professionals around you. You behaved in a way that was appropriate to the environment, and in doing so demonstrated *emotional intelligence.* Over time you developed many new ways of conducting yourself at work in order to be accepted as a professional in your field. You weren't born this way. You developed a behavioral profile, a *professional persona* that enabled you to survive in the professional world.

Some people are just better than the average bear at everything they do, and they become more successful as a result. It doesn't happen by accident; there is a specific set of *transferable skills* and *professional values* that underlies professional success: skills and values that employers all over the world in every industry and profession are anxious to find in candidates from the entry-level to the boardroom. Why this isn't taught in schools and in the university programs that cost a small fortune is unfathomable, because these skills and values are the foundation of every successful career. They break down into these groups:

1. *The Technical Skills of Your Current Profession.* These are the technical competencies that give you the *ability* to do your job. The skills needed to complete a task and the know-how to use them productively and efficiently. These *technical skills* are mandatory if you want to land a job within your profession. *Technical skills,* while transferable, vary from profession to profession, so many of your current *technical skills* will only be transferable within your current profession.
2. *Transferable Skills That Apply in All Professions.* The set of skills that underlies your ability to execute the *technical skills* of your job effectively, whatever your job might be. They are the foundation of all the professional success you will experience in this and any other career (including dream and entrepreneurial careers) that you may pursue over the years.
3. *Professional Values.* This set of skills is complemented by an equally important set of *professional values* that are highly prized by employers. *Professional values* are an interconnected set of core beliefs that enable professionals to determine the right judgment call for any given situation.

The importance of the whole series of *transferable skills* and *professional values* led to an entirely new approach to interviewing and the science of employee selection: behavioral interviewing.

These behavioral interviewing techniques (discussed in detail in *Knock 'em Dead 2014* and *Knock 'em Dead: Secrets & Strategies for Success in an Uncertain World*) now predominate in the selection process because of their ability to determine whether you possess those *transferable skills* and *professional values*.

A Review of Transferable Skills and Professional Values

As you read through the following breakdown of each *transferable skill* and *professional value* you may, for example, read about *communication*, and think, "Yes, I can see how communication skills are important in all jobs and at all levels of the promotional ladder, and, hallelujah, I have good communication skills." Take time to recall examples of your *communication skills* and the role they play in the success of your work.

You might also read about *multitasking skills* and realize that you need to improve in that area. Whenever you identify a *transferable skill* that needs work, you have found a *professional development project:* improving that skill. Your attention to those areas will repay you for the rest of your working life, no matter how you make a living.

Here are the *transferable skills* and *professional values* that will speed the conclusion of this job search and your long-term professional success. You'll find that you already have some of them to a greater or lesser degree, and if you are committed to making a success of your life, you'll commit to further development of all of them.

Transferable Skills	**Professional Values**
Technical	*Motivation and Energy*
Critical Thinking	*Commitment and Reliability*
Communication	*Determination*
Multitasking	*Pride and Integrity*
Teamwork	*Productivity*
Leadership	*Systems and Procedures*
Creativity	

Transferable Skills

Technical Skills

The *technical skills* of your job are the foundation of success within your current profession; without them you won't even land a job, much less keep it for long or win a promotion. They speak to your *ability* to do the job, those skills necessary for the day-to-day execution of your duties. These *technical skills* vary from job to job and profession to profession.

A recruitment metrics company said in a recent study that by 2015, 60 percent of the jobs available will require skills held by 20 percent of the population. Technology constantly changes the nature of our jobs and the ways in which they are executed. As a result, if you want to stay employable, you need to stay current with the skills most prized in your professional world.

In addition to the technical skills that are specific to your job alone, and which you take from position to position within your current profession, there is also a body of skills that are as desirable in other jobs and other professions, just as much as they are in yours. Possession of these transferable skills will not only enhance your employability in your current profession, it is also likely to ease your transition should you ever change your career; something that the statistics say you will do three or more times over the span of your work life.

Any employer would welcome an employee who, as well as the must-haves of the job, possesses the written communication skills to create a PR piece or a training manual; who knows how to structure and format a proposal; who is able to stand up and make presentations; or who knows how to research, analyze, and assimilate hard-to-access data.

Some of the transferable technical skills sought across a wide spectrum of jobs include:

- Selling skills—even in nonsales jobs, the art of persuasive communication is always appreciated, because no matter what the job . . . you are always selling something to someone.
- Project management skills
- Six Sigma skills
- Lean management skills
- Quantitative analysis skills
- Theory development and conceptual thinking skills
- Counseling and mentoring skills
- Writing skills for PR, technical, or training needs
- Customer Resource Management (CRM) skills
- Research skills
- Social networking skills

While the technical skills of your job are not necessarily technological in nature, it is a given that one of the *technical skills* essential to almost every job is technological competence. You must be proficient in all the technology and Internet-based applications relevant to your work.

Even when you are not working in a technology field, strong *technology skills* will enhance your stability and help you leverage professional growth.

Some of your technology skills will only be relevant within your current profession, while others (Word, Excel, PowerPoint, to name the obvious) will be transferable across all industry and professional lines. Staying current with the essential *technical* and *technology skills* of your chosen career path is the keystone of your professional stability and growth.

There are also technology skills that have application within all professions in our technology-driven world. It is pretty much a given that you need to be computer literate to hold down any job today. Just about every job expects competence with Microsoft Word and e-mail; similarly Excel or PowerPoint are becoming skills it is risky not to possess.

Any employer is going to welcome a staff member who knows her way around spreadsheets and databases, who can update a webpage, or who is knowledgeable in CRM.

Some of the technology skills that enhance employability on non-technology jobs include:

- Database management
- Spreadsheet creation
- Word processing
- Building and designing of presentations
- E-mail and social media communication

Eventually, more and more of these skills will become specific requirements of the jobs of the future, but the fact that you possess these transferable technical skills now adds a special sauce to your candidacy for any job.

Critical Thinking Skills

As I noted earlier, your job, whatever it is, exists to solve problems and to prevent problems from arising within your area of expertise. *Critical thinking, analytical*, or *problem-solving skills* represent a systematic approach to dealing with the challenges presented by your work. *Critical thinking skills* allow you to think through a problem, define the challenge and its possible solutions, and then evaluate and implement the best solution from all available options.

Fifty percent of the success of any project is in the preparation; *critical thinking* is at the heart of that preparation. In addition, using *critical thinking* to properly define a problem always leads to a better solution.

Communication Skills

As George Bernard Shaw said: "The greatest problem in communication is the illusion that it has been accomplished." Every professional job today demands good *communication skills*, but what are they?

When the professional world talks about *communication skills*, it is referring not just to listening and speaking but to four primary skills and four supportive skills.

The primary *communication skills* are:

- Verbal skills—what you say and how you say it.
- Listening skills—listening to understand, rather than just waiting your turn to talk.
- Writing skills—clear written communication creates a lasting impression of who you are and is essential for success in any professional career.
- Technological communication skills—your ability to evaluate the protocols, strengths, and weaknesses of alternative communication media, and then to choose the medium appropriate to your audience and message.

The four supportive *communication skills* are:

- Grooming and dress—these tell others who you are and how you feel about yourself.
- Social graces—how you behave toward others in all situations; this defines your professionalism.
- Body language—this displays how you're feeling deep inside, a form of communication that precedes speech. For truly effective communication, what your mouth says must be in harmony with what your body says.
- Emotional IQ—your emotional self-awareness, your maturity in dealing with others in the full range of human interaction.

All the transferable skills are interconnected—for example, good *verbal skills* require both *listening* and *critical thinking skills* to accurately process incoming information and enable you to present your outgoing verbal messaging persuasively in light of the interests and sophistication of your audience so that it is understood and accepted. Develop effective skills in all eight of the subsets that together comprise *communication skills* and you'll gain enormous control over what you can achieve, how you are perceived, and what happens in your life.

Multitasking

This is one of the most desirable skills of the new era. According to numerous studies, however, the *multitasking* demands of modern professional life are causing massive frustration and meltdowns for professionals everywhere. The problem is *not multitasking*, the problem is the assumption that *multitasking* means being reactive to *all* incoming stimuli and therefore jumping around from one task to another as the emergency of the moment dictates. Such a definition of *multitasking* would of course leave you feeling that wild horses are attached to your extremities and tearing you limb from limb.

Few people understand what *multitasking* abilities are really built on: sound *time management* and *organizational* skills. Here are the basics:

ESTABLISH PRIORITIES

Multitasking is based on three things:

1. Being organized
2. Establishing priorities
3. Managing your time

THE PLAN, DO, REVIEW CYCLE

At the end of every day, review your day:

- What happened: A.M. and P.M.?
- What went well? Do more of it.
- What went wrong? How do I fix it?
- What projects do I need to move forward tomorrow?
- Rank each project. A= Must be completed tomorrow. B= Good to be completed tomorrow. C= If there is spare time from A and B priorities.
- Make a prioritized To Do list.
- Stick to it.

Doing this at the end of the day keeps you informed about what you have achieved, and lets you know that you have invested your time in the most important activities today and will do so again tomorrow. That peace of mind helps you feel better, sleep better, and come in tomorrow focused and ready to rock.

Teamwork

Companies depend on teams because the professional world revolves around the complex challenges of making money, and such complexities require teams of people to provide ongoing solutions. This means that you must work efficiently and respectfully with other people who have totally different responsibilities, backgrounds, objectives, and areas of expertise. It's true that individual initiative is important, but as a professional, much of the really important work you do is done as a member of a group. Your long-term stability and success require that you learn the arts of cooperation, team-based decision-making, and team communication.

Teamwork demands that a commitment to the team and its success comes first. This means you take on a task because it needs to be done, not because it makes you look good.

As a team player you:

- Always cooperate.
- Always make decisions based on team goals.
- Always keep team members informed.
- Always keep commitments.
- Always share credit, never blame.

If you become a successful leader in your professional life, it's a given that you were first a reliable team player, because a leader must understand the dynamics of teamwork before she can leverage them. When teamwork is coupled with the other *transferable skills* and *professional values, it results in greater responsibility and promotions.*

Leadership Skills

Leadership is the most complex of all the *transferable skills* and combines all the others. As you develop *teamwork skills*, notice how you are willing to follow true leaders, but don't like falling in line with people who don't respect you and who don't have your best interests at heart. When others believe in your competence, and believe you have everyone's success as your goal, they will follow you. When your actions inspire others to think more, learn more, do more, and become more, you are becoming a leader. This will ultimately be recognized and rewarded with promotion into and up the ranks of management.

- Your job as a leader is to help your team succeed, and your *teamwork skills* give you the smarts to pull a team together as a cohesive unit.
- Your *technical* expertise, *critical thinking*, and *creativity skills* help you correctly define the challenges your team faces and give you the wisdom to guide them toward solutions.
- Your *communication skills* enable your team to *buy into* your directives and goals. There's nothing more demoralizing than a leader who can't clearly articulate why you're doing what you're doing.
- Your *creativity* (discussed next) comes from the wide frame of reference you have for your work and the profession and industry in which you work, enabling you to come up with solutions that others might not have seen.
- Your *multitasking skills*, based on sound *time management* and *organizational* abilities, enable you to create a practical blueprint for success. They also allow your team to take ownership of the task and deliver the expected results on time.

Leadership is a combination and outgrowth of all the *transferable skills* plus the clear presence of all the *professional values* we are about to discuss. Leaders aren't born; they are self-made. And just like anything else, it takes hard work.

Creativity

Your creativity comes from the frame of reference you have for your work, profession, and industry. This wide frame of reference enables you to see the *patterns* that lie behind challenges, and so connect the dots and come up with solutions that others might not have seen. Others might be too closely focused on the specifics of the issue—thus, they don't have that holistic frame of reference that enables them to step back and view the issue in its larger context.

There's a big difference between *creativity* and just having ideas. Ideas are like headaches: We all get them once in a while, and like headaches, they disappear as mysteriously as they arrived. *Creativity*, on the other hand, is the ability to develop those ideas with the strategic and tactical know-how that brings them to life. Someone is seen as creative when his ideas produce tangible results. *Creativity* also demands that you harness other transferable skills to bring those ideas to life. *Creativity* springs from:

- Your *critical thinking skills*, applied within an area of *technical expertise* (the area where your *technical skills* give you a frame of reference for what works and what doesn't).
- Your *multitasking skills*, which in combination with your *critical thinking* and *technical skills* allow you to break your challenge down into specific steps and determine which approach is best.
- Your *communication skills*, which allow you to explain your approach and its building blocks persuasively to your target audience.
- Your *teamwork* and *leadership skills*, which enable you to enlist others and bring the idea to fruition.

Creative approaches to challenges can take time or can come fully formed in a flash, but the longer you work on developing the supporting skills that bring *creativity* to life, the more often they *will* come fully formed and in a flash. Here are five rules for building creativity skills in your professional life:

1. **Whatever you do in life, engage in it fully.** Commit to developing competence in everything you do, because the wider your frame of reference for the world around you, the more you will see the patterns and connectivity in your professional world, delivering the higher-octane fuel you need to propel your ideas to acceptance and reality.
2. **Learn something new every day.** Treat the pursuit of knowledge as a way of life. Absorb as much as you can about everything. Information exercises your brain, filling your mind with information and contributing to that ever-widening frame of reference that allows you to see those patterns behind a specific challenge. The result is that you will make connections others won't and develop solutions that are seen as magically creative.
3. **Catch ideas as they occur.** Note them in your smartphone or on a scrap of paper. Anything will do, so long as you capture the idea.

4. **Welcome restrictions in your world.** They make you think, they test the limits of your skills and the depth of your frame of reference; they truly encourage *creativity*. Ask any successful business leader, entrepreneur, writer, artist, or musician.
5. **Don't spend your life glued to YouTube or the TV.** You need to live life, not watch it go by out of the corner of your eye. If you do watch television, try to learn something or motivate yourself with science, history, or biography programming. If you surf the Internet, do it with purpose.

Building *creativity skills* enables you to bring your ideas to life; and the development of each of these seven interconnected *transferable skills* will help you bring your dreams to life.

Professional Values

Professional values are an interconnected set of core beliefs that enable professionals to determine the right judgment call for any given situation. Highly prized by employers, this value system also complements and is integral to the *transferable skills*.

Motivation and Energy

Motivation and *energy* express themselves in your engagement with and enthusiasm for your work and profession. They involve an eagerness to learn and grow professionally, and a willingness to take the rough with the smooth in pursuit of meaningful goals. *Motivation* is invariably expressed by the *energy* you demonstrate in your work. You always give that extra effort to get the job done right.

Commitment and Reliability

This means dedication to your profession, and the empowerment that comes from knowing how your part contributes to the whole. Your *commitment* expresses itself in your *reliability*. The *committed* professional is willing to do whatever it takes to get a job done, whenever and for however long it takes to get the job done. Doing so might include duties that don't appear in a job description and that might be perceived by less enlightened colleagues as "beneath them."

Determination

The *determination* you display with the travails of your work speaks of a resilient professional who does not back off when a problem or situation gets tough. It's a *professional value* that marks you as someone who chooses to be part of the solution.

The *determined* professional has decided to make a difference with her presence every day, because it is the *right* thing to do.

She is willing to do whatever it takes to get a job done, and she will demonstrate that determination on behalf of colleagues who share the same values.

Pride and Integrity

If a job's worth doing, it's worth doing right. That's what *pride* in your work really means: attention to detail and a *commitment* to doing your very best. *Integrity* applies to all your dealings, whether with coworkers, management, customers, or vendors. Honesty really *is* the best policy.

Productivity

Always working toward *productivity* in your areas of responsibility, through efficiencies of time, resources, money, and effort.

Economy

Remember the word "frugal"? It doesn't mean poverty or shortages. It means making the most of what you've got, using everything with the greatest efficiency. Companies that know how to be frugal with their resources will prosper in good times and in bad, and if you know how to be frugal, you'll do the same.

Systems and Procedures

This is a natural outgrowth of all the other *transferable skills* and *professional values*. Your *commitment* to your profession in all these ways gives you an appreciation of the need for *systems and procedures* and their implementation only after careful thought. You understand and always follow the chain of command. You don't implement your own "improved" procedures or encourage others to do so. If ways of doing things don't make sense or are interfering with efficiency and profitability, you work through the system to get them changed.

Development of *transferable skills* and *professional values* supports your enlightened self-interest, because it will be repaid with better job security and improved professional horizons. The more you are engaged in your career, the more likely you are to join the inner circles that exist in every department and company, and that's where the plum assignments, raises, and promotions live.

Transferable Skills, Professional Values, and the Secret Language of Job Postings

There are six keywords and phrases that you see in almost every job posting: *communication skills, multitasking, teamwork, creativity, problem solving*, and *leadership*. They are so commonly used that they are often dismissed as meaningless.

Far from being meaningless, you know they represent a secret language that few job hunters understand. The ones who do "get it" are also the ones who get the job offers. Understanding the secret language of job postings can supercharge your resume and your cover letters and will help you turn job interviews into job offers. That is because these six key phrases represent the very skills that power success; they represent the specific *transferable skills* that enable you to do your job well, whatever your job may be. You know them as *transferable skills* because no matter what the job, the profession, or the elevation of that job, your possession of these skills can make the difference between success and failure.

Decoding Made Easy

For example, when problem-solving skills are mentioned in a job posting, it means the employer is looking for someone who knows his area of responsibility well enough to identify, prevent where possible, and solve the problems that the job generates on a daily basis. The employer wants someone who has thought through and can discuss the challenges that lie at the heart of that job and who has developed intelligent strategies and tactics in response.

Think about how a job-posting requirement for "teamwork" applies to your job. Consider which deliverables of your work require you to interact with other people and other departments to get your work done. For example, an accountant working in Accounts Receivable will think about problem accounts and how such accounts can require working with sales and the nonpaying customer, as well as working laterally and upward within the Accounting Department.

Teamwork also embraces other *transferable skills*—for instance, the communication skills you need to work effectively with others. You understand that talk of communication always refers to verbal, written, and listening skills, and you also know that, to an employer, it also refers to the supporting communication skills of:

1. Digital communication literacy
2. Dress
3. Body language
4. Social graces
5. Emotional maturity

Together, these five components of effective communication impact the power and persuasiveness of all your interactions with others.

When you relate each of the *transferable skills* to each of your professional responsibilities, you'll discover the secrets to success in your profession. When you express your possession of them in your resume and cover letters, you can dramatically increase interviews. When you understand how these skills impact every action you take with every responsibility you hold, and you can explain to interviewers how you integrate these skills into all you do, you become a more desirable employee and colleague.

In Your Resume

You might decide to highlight special achievements with a *Performance Highlights* or a *Career Highlights* section. This is usually a short sequence of bulleted statements, each addressing one of the company's stated requirements and thereby emphasizing the fit between employer needs and your capabilities. Illustrate with an example if you can do so succinctly:

Performance Highlights

35% increase in on-time delivery + 20% reduction in client complaints

Effective Operations Management demands understanding every department's unique problems and timelines. Building these considerations into daily activities helped:

• Finance & Supply Chain, saved $55,000 in last three quarters
• Increased productivity, with a 35% increase in on-time delivery

These on-time delivery increases were achieved with improved communications, connecting Purchasing, Supply Chain, Customers, and Customer Service:

• Delivered 20% reduction in client complaints

In a Cover Letter

Where there is more space, these same achievements might appear with the company's requirement above:

"Problem-solving skills"
• Thorough knowledge of the problems that impact productivity in Operations enabled a 35% increase in on-time delivery.

"Work closely with others"
• Improvements in on-time delivery made possible by improved communications with Purchasing, Supply Chain, Customers, and Customer Service. This delivered a 20% reduction in client complaints.

"Multitasking"
• Effective Operations Management demands understanding of every department's critical functions and timelines. Building these considerations into daily activities helped Finance & Supply Chain save $55,000 in last three quarters.

In Your Life

Every time you see a job posting that mentions any of the *transferable skills* or *professional values*, think how *that skill or value is applied in each aspect of your work*. Then recall examples that illustrate how you used that skill in the identification, prevention, and solution of the daily problems that get in the way of the smooth functioning of your job.

Understanding the secret language of job postings will do more than help you land that next job; it can change your destiny. When you apply that understanding to your professional life, you will be known and respected as a consummate professional, the kind of man or woman that everyone wants to work with.

Understanding the *transferable skills* and *professional values* you possess and how they differentiate you from others is an important step in defining your professional brand. The examples of your application of these skills or the impact of these values on your work can be used in your resume, in your cover letters, and as illustrative answers to questions in interviews. But most important, if you want to be successful, these skills need to become a part of your life.

Now I'm going to take you through a process—Identifying Your Competitive Difference—that helps you identify your professional strengths and, ultimately, your competitive difference. Having a firm grip on the unique blend of competencies that set you apart from others can help strengthen your resume with brand statements and empower your interview performance.

Identifying Your Competitive Difference

The people who will hire you first need to differentiate you from other candidates. The following questionnaire will help you identify all the factors that help make you unique. Each of these is a component of your professional brand.

You aren't going to discover anything earth-shattering here, just a continuum of behaviors and beliefs you've always had, but the value of which you've perhaps never understood. It'll be a series of those "Of course, I knew that" moments.

An expandable version of this questionnaire is available in Microsoft Word at *www.knockemdead.com/downloads* under the title: The Competitive Difference Questionnaire.

The Competitive Difference Questionnaire

List and prioritize the transferable skills, behaviors, and values that best capture the essence of the professional you.

_____

_____

_____

_____

Which of the transferable skills, behaviors, and values have you identified for further professional development? What are you going to do about it?

_____

_____

_____

_____

What skills/behaviors/values or other characteristics do you share with top performers in your department/profession?

_____

_____

_____

_____

What have you achieved with these qualities?

_____

_____

_____

_____

What makes you different from others with whom you have worked?

_____

_____

_____

_____

What do you see as your four most defining transferable skills and professional values and how does each help your performance?

_____

_____

How do your most defining professional traits help you contribute to the team?

     1. _____
     2. _____
     3. _____
     4. _____

How do your most defining professional traits help you contribute your departmental goals and/or help you support your boss?

     1. _____
     2. _____
     3. _____
     4. _____

Why do you stand out in your job/profession?

_____

_____

_____

If you realize you don't stand out and you want to, explain in a few sentences why the people you admire stand out. What plans do you have for change?

_____

_____

_____

In what ways are you better than others at your workplace who hold the same title?

_____

_____

What excites you most about your professional responsibilities?

_____

_____

What are your biggest achievements in these areas?

_____

_____

What do your peers say about you?

_____

_____

What does management say about you?

_____

_____

_____

What do your reports say about you?

_____

_____

What are your top four professional skills?

Skill #1: _____

Quantifiable achievements with this skill: _____

Skill #2: _____

Quantifiable achievements with this skill: _____

Skill #3: _____

Quantifiable achievements with this skill: _____

Skill #4: _____

Quantifiable achievements with this skill: _____

What are your top four leadership skills?

Skill #1: _____
Quantifiable achievements with this skill: _____

Skill #2: _____
Quantifiable achievements with this skill: _____

Skill #3: _____
Quantifiable achievements with this skill: _____

Skill #4: _____
Quantifiable achievements with this skill: _____

What do you believe are the three key deliverables of your job?

_____
_____
_____

What gives you greatest satisfaction in the work you do?

_____
_____

What **value** does this combination of transferable skills, professional values, and achievements enable you to bring to your targeted employers?

_____
_____

Now compile endorsements. Looking at each of your major areas of responsibility throughout your work history, write down any positive verbal or written commentary others have made on your performance.

_____
_____
_____

After rereading your answers, make three one-sentence statements that capture the essence of the professional you and your competitive difference.

_____

_____

_____

Take these three statements and rework them into one sentence. This is your competitive difference.

_____

Once you have completed the Competitive Difference Questionnaire and identified what your competitive differences are, you'll feel a new awareness of the *professional you*. You can integrate this new awareness and your competitive differences into your resume, and, in the process, give form to your brand. But before we do that, let's cover some final *professional brand* considerations.

A True and Truthful Brand

You have to be able to deliver on the brand you create. It must be based on your possession of the *technical skills* of your profession, those *transferable skills* that you take with you from job to job, and the *professional values* that imprint your approach to professional life.

It is all too easy to overpromise, and while an employer might be initially attracted by the pizzazz of your resume, whether or not you live up to its value proposition decides the length and quality of the relationship.

If a box of cereal doesn't live up to the brand's hype, you simply don't buy it again; but sell yourself into the wrong job with exaggerations or outright lies and it is likely to cost you that job, plus the possibility of collateral career damage that can follow you for years.

Benefits of a Defined Professional Brand

Understanding the skills and attributes that make for professional success might be your most immediately recognizable benefit. But your professional brand is also extremely valuable for your long-term survival and success. The fact that you know who you are, what you offer, and how you want to be perceived will differentiate you from others. And because you understand yourself and can communicate this understanding, you will have a professional presence.

Your Professional Brand and the Long Haul

Globalization has made your job less secure than ever, yet you are a financial entity that must survive over what will be at least a half-century of work life. You'll recall our earlier discussions about change being a constant in the modern career. So while you develop an initial professional brand as part of your job search strategy, you don't want to shelve it once you've landed a new job.

In this new, insecure world of work, it makes sense to maintain visibility within your profession. It is nothing more than intelligent market positioning for MeInc. The professional identity/brand built into your new resume will become part of the profile you keep posted on LinkedIn and your other professional networking sites. This increases your credibility and visibility within your profession as well as with the recruitment industry, making you more desirable as an employee and increasing your options.

CHAPTER

RESUME FORMATS

FIRST IMPRESSIONS ARE important. You have

obligation to package your professional

greatest benefit.

Everyone has different work experience: You may have worked for just one employer through-out your career, or you may have worked for five companies in ten years. You may have changed careers entirely, or you may have maintained a predictable career path, changing jobs but stay-ing within one profession or industry.

The look of your resume—the format you choose—depends on what your unique back-ground brings to the target job. There are three broadly defined resume formats, but their goals are the same:

1. To maximize your performance in the resume databases
2. To demonstrate your complete grasp of the job's deliverables
3. To create a professional brand for someone who lives and breathes this work
4. To showcase relevant achievements, attributes, and accumulation of expertise to the best advantage
5. To minimize any possible weaknesses

Resume experts acknowledge three major styles for presenting your credentials to a poten-tial employer: Chronological, Functional, and Combination. Your particular circumstances will determine the right format for you.

The Chronological Resume

The chronological resume is the most widely accepted format. It's what most of us think of when we think of resumes—a chronological listing of job titles and responsibilities. It starts with the current or most recent employment, then works backward to your first job.

This format is good for demonstrating your growth in a single profession. It is suitable for anyone with practical work experience who hasn't suffered prolonged periods of unemploy-ment. It is not always the best choice if you are just out of school or if you are changing careers, where it might draw attention to a lack of specific, relevant experience.

The distinguishing characteristic of the chronological resume is the way it ties your job responsibilities and achievements to specific employers, job titles, and dates.

This is the simplest resume to create:

PARAG GUPTA

104 W. Real Drive • Beaverton, OR 97006 • (503) 123-4286 • parag.gupta@technical.com

SYSTEMS ENGINEER: Motivated and driven IT Professional offering 9+ years of hands-on experience in designing, implementing, and enhancing systems to automate business operations. Demonstrated ability to develop high-performance systems, applications, databases, and interfaces.

- Part of TL9000 CND audit interviews that helped Technical get TL9000 certified, which is significant in Telecom industry. Skilled trainer and proven ability to lead many successful projects, like TSS, EMX, and TOL.
- Strategically manage time and expediently resolve problems for optimal productivity, improvement, and profitability; able to direct multiple tasks effectively.
- Strong technical background with a solid history of delivering outstanding customer service.
- Highly effective liaison and communication skills proven by effective interaction with management, users, team members, and vendors.

Technical Skills

Operating Systems:	Unix, Windows (2000, XP, 7), DOS
Languages:	C, C++, Java, Pascal, Assembly Languages (Z8000, 808x, DSP)
Methodologies:	TL9000, Digital Six Sigma
Software:	MS Office, Adobe FrameMaker, MATLAB
RDBMS:	DOORS, Oracle 7.x
Protocols:	TCP/IP, SS7 ISUP, A1, ANSI, TL1, SNMP
Tools:	Teamplay, ClearCase, ClearQuest, M-Gate keeper, Exceed, Visio, DocExpress, Compass
Other:	CDMA Telecom Standards – 3GPP2 (Including TIA/EIA-2001, TIA/EIA-41, TIA/EIA-664), ITU-T, AMPS

Professional Experience

Technical, Main Network Division, Hillsboro, OR   Jan 1999–Present

Principal Staff Engineer • Products Systems Engineering • Nov 2004–Present

- Known as "go-to" person for CDMA call processing and billing functional areas.
- Created customer requirements documents for Technical SoftSwitch (TSS) and SMS Gateway products. All deliverables done on/ahead schedule with high quality.
- Solely accountable for authoring and allocation, customer reviews, supporting fellow system engineers, development and test, and customer documentation teams.
- Support Product Management in RFPs, customer feature prioritization, impact statements, and budgetary estimates.
- Mentored junior engineers and 1 innovation disclosure patent submitted in 2007.
- Resolved deployed customer/internal requirements issues and contributed to Virtual Zero Defect quality goal.
- TOL process champion and part of CND focus group that contributed to reducing CRUD backlog (NPR) by 25% and cycle time (FRT) by 40%.
- Recognized as the TL9000 expert. Triage representative for switching and messaging products.
- Achieved "CND Quality Award" for contribution to quality improvement, May 2007.

Senior Staff Engineer • MSS Systems Engineering • May 2002–Oct 2004

- Led a team of 12 engineers for 3 major software releases of TSS product included around 80 features/enhancements to create T-Gate SE deliverables.

The Chronological Resume (page 2)

- Mentored newer engineers to get up to speed on TSS product.
- Created requirements for TSS product, 30 features/enhancements contributing to 5 major software releases. Recognized as overall product expert with specific focus on call processing and billing.
- Played integral role in successfully implementing proprietary commercial TSS billing system.
- Supported PdM organization by creating ROMs, technical support for RFPs (Vivo, Sprint, TELUS, TM, Tata, Inquam, Alaska, Reliance, Pakistan, PBTL, Mauritius, Telefonica, Brasicel, and Angola).
- Proactively identified functional areas of improvement for requirements coverage, contributed to resolving several faults, improved customer documentation, and provided reference for future releases as well as other customers.
- Received "Above and Beyond Performance Award" Oct 2003

Senior Software Engineer • EMX Development • Aug 2000–Apr 2002

- Successfully led and coordinated the cross-functional development teams, 30 engineers, to meet the scheduled design, code, and test completion dates ensuring Feature T-Gates are met.
- Feature Technical Lead for Concurrent Voice/Data Services feature, the largest revenue-generating feature for KDDI customer.
- Feature Lead for Paging Channel SMS feature. Created requirements and design; led implementation phase of five engineers' team; supported product, network, and release testing; and created customer reference documentation.
- Performed the role of functional area lead for Trunk Manager and A1 interface functional areas. Provided 2-day Technical Workshops for internal/customer knowledge sharing and functional area transition from Caltel.
- Provided customer site testing and FOA (First Office Application) support for major EMX releases and off-hours CNRC (Customer Networks Resolution Center) support.
- Received "Bravo Award" May 2001, Sep 2001, Jan 2002

Software Engineer • EMX Development • Jan 1999–Jul 2000

- Developed design and code for SMS feature as a Trunk Manager functional area lead for the largest FA impacted by the feature. Supported product, network, and release testing.
- Contributed to customer release documentation. Supported feature-level SMS testing at various internal labs and customer sites resulting in successful deployment at customer sites.
- Designed and coded phases for wiretap and virtual circuits feature development, initial assessment of internal and customer EMX PRs (problem reports) to route/classify issues and providing problem assessments for many of these PRs.
- Created an implementation process to serve as reference for new hires.
- Provided CNRC support during the Y2K transition.
- Received "Above and Beyond Performance Award" Jan 2000, Dec 2000 and "Certificate of Outstanding Achievement" Jun 1999

Education: Master of Science in Computer Engineering • University of Portland, Portland, OR • 1998
Bachelors of Engineering in Electronics • Technology and Science Institute, India •1996

Significant Trainings Include
- Open Source Software • WiMAX • Agile Management for Software Engineering
- WSG Requirements Process • Product Security

The Functional Resume

The functional resume format focuses on the professional skills you bring to a specific target job, rather than when, where, or how you acquired them. It also de-emphasizes employers and employment dates by their placement on the second page, which typically gets less attention than your lead page. Because the focus is on the skill rather than the context or time of its acquisition, job titles and employers can likewise play a lesser part in this format.

The functional format is still used. Although it is thought less effective than other formats, this may in part be attributable to the more challenging sells it is chosen for:

- Mature professionals with a storehouse of expertise and jobs pursuing encore careers
- Entry-level professionals whose skimpy experience might not justify a chronological resume
- For those in career transition who want to focus on skills rather than locus of the experience, because that experience was developed in a different professional context
- People returning to the workplace after a long absence

Though functional resumes are more freeform than chronological ones, they should share certain structural features:

Target Job Title

For any resume to be effective, it must be conceived with a specific target job in mind, and this is especially true for a functional resume. Because it focuses so strongly on skills and the ability to contribute in a particular direction, rather than on a directly relevant work history, you really must have an employment objective clearly in mind.

A Performance Profile/Performance Summary or Career Summary

Your target job should be followed by a short paragraph that captures your professional capabilities as they address the deliverables of the target job.

Core Competencies

A core competencies section in your functional resume will help its performance in databases, and the use of critical keywords early on shows that you have the essential skills for the job.

Performance Highlights

Based on your target job, this is where you identify the skills, behaviors, and accomplishments that best position you for the job. Notice how clearly these demonstrate competence in the example that follows.

Dates

If your employment history lacks continuity, a functional resume allows you to de-emphasize dates somewhat by their placement, but an absence of employment dates altogether will just draw attention to a potential problem. See Chapter 6 for more about how to handle employment dates.

Everything else related to functional resumes follows the rules outlined in Chapter 6.

A Functional Resume That Works

Functional resumes are not as popular as they once were, but in some circumstances, they really are the best choice. Following is a functional resume of someone applying for a job as an art gallery or museum curator whose only prior experience was as an art teacher. Read the first page and then ask yourself if you know what a good gallery director or museum curator needs to know. I'll give you a few more interesting insights after the example.

A couple of interesting observations about this resume:

- It is more informal in tone than many examples you will see in the book, but as it reflected someone in a profession where personality is a significant part of the job, there is nothing wrong with that. Given these considerations, I decided to give the resume a personal flavor, and the very first words of the performance profile/performance summary immediately draw the reader into a conversation with a passionate and committed professional: "My professional life is focused on art and all it embraces."
- There are professions where a less formal tone is more generally acceptable, usually education, the arts, and the caring professions.
- It is quite clear this person really understands the work of a curator. The first time it was used, this resume resulted in an interview within seventy-two hours, and a job offer was extended at the end of the first hour.
- Now for the kicker: The fact that this person had only been the arts department chair of a private elementary through middle school was never an issue, because he so clearly understood the demands of the target job. That was possible because his TJD research allowed the resume to be properly focused and prepared him for exactly the topics that would come up at the interview.

Charles Chalmers

Manhattan NY 11658 • (212) 555-2578 • fineartist@earthlink.net

Senior Curator

Performance Profile/Performance Summary

My professional life is focused on art in all it embraces: drawing, painting, sculpture, photography, cinema, video, audio, performance and digital art, art history, and criticism; my personal life is similarly committed. Recently relocated to Manhattan, I intend to make a contribution to the New York arts community that harnesses my knowledge, enthusiasm, and sensibilities.

Core Competencies

Photographer ~ editor ~ drawing ~ painting ~ sculpture ~ photography ~ cinema ~ video ~ audio ~ performance and digital art ~ art history and criticism ~ global artist networks ~ alumni groups ~ first-rank private collectors ~ social networking-themed, resourced, sequenced shows ~ campus & community involvement ~ education & outreach ~ installation-hang, light, and label-media kits ~ artist materials ~ Photoshop-art-staff management ~ curriculum development ~ art handlers-maintenance ~ printers ~ catering ~ graphics ~ portfolio prep-int/ext shows ~ theatre sets ~ streamed video gallery tours

Performance Highlights

ART HISTORY

Thorough knowledge of art history from caves of Lascaux through current artists such as Bruce Nauman, Jessica Stockholder, and Luc Tuymans. Film history from Lumiere Brothers to Almodovar. Current with key critical art and film theory. Ongoing workshops and lectures with the likes of Matthew Barney, Louise Bourgeoise, and Andy Goldsworthy.

RESEARCH NEW ARTISTS

Connected to cutting-edge art and artists through involvement with the art communities and galleries of New York and Boston and the faculty, student, and alumni networks of RISD, Columbia, Boston Museum School, New England School of Art & Design, and now Mass Art. Twenty years of Manhattan gallery openings and networking with artists at MOMA, PS1, Guggenheim, Whitney, Metropolitan, Film Forum, International Center for Photography workshops and lectures.

SOURCING ART WORK

Through local artists, regional and global artist networks, intercultural artist exchanges, alumni groups, first-rank private collectors, personal and family networks, and Internet calls for submissions.

ART AND THE COMMUNITY

Conception and launch of themed, resourced, and sequenced shows that invigorate campus and community involvement. Reconfigure existing art spaces to create dynamic dialogue with visitors. Education and outreach programs.

The Functional Resume (page 2)

ART INSTALLATION

Maintain fluidity of gallery space in preparing exhibitions with recognition of size/time considerations for the art, to insure a sympathetic environment for the presented works. Hang, light, and label shows in sequences that create dialogue between the works.

PUBLIC RELATIONS MATERIALS

Energizing invitations, comprehensive press kits, illustrated press releases, and artist binder materials. Sensitive to placing art in historical/cultural context. Photoshop.

Management experience

Fourteen years art-staff management experience, including curriculum development. Responsible for art instructors, art handlers, maintenance crews, and working with printers, catering, and graphic arts staff.

Professional experience

1994–2005 Chair of Visual Arts, The Green Briar School
Duties: Curriculum development, portfolio preparation, internal and external monthly shows, theatre sets, monthly video news show, taught art history and all the studio arts, managed staff of three.

1989–2004 President Art Workshops
Duties: Private art studio and art history curriculums, staff of four. Private groups to Manhattan museums and gallery tours.

1980–1989 Freelance artist, photographer, and editor
Highlights from the sublime to the ridiculous include: Taught photography at Trinity School, Manhattan; photographer for the Ramones; editor of *Pioneer*, insurance industry trade magazine; assistant to Claudia Weill, documentary filmmaker, director of "Girlfriends."

Education

MFA. Magna cum laude. Columbia University, 1983
Awards: ****** ***** Prize for film criticism
Taught undergraduate Intro to Film, under ****** ***** and ****** ******.

Subscriptions

Art in America, Art News, Art Forum, New York Times, Parkett, Sight & Sound, Film Comment, Modern Painters.

Memberships

MOMA/PS1, Whitney Museum of American Art, Guggenheim, Metropolitan Museum of Art, DIA.

Recent exhibitions

2004. Corcoran Center Gallery, Southampton, NY
2005. Corsair Gallery, 37 West 33rd St. NY
2006. Fuller Museum, Brockton MA
2002. 2007. Zeitgeist Gallery, Cambridge MA

- The second time this resume was used, a core competencies section was added to increase database visibility. In the middle of the 2008–10 recession, he was called by an executive recruiter, had two interviews, and was hired at a 50 percent increase in salary to run one of the nation's blue-chip galleries.

This functional resume was successful because the writer took the time to go through the TJD process and was then able to tell a captivating and believable story, demonstrating that he had exactly the credentials needed.

The Combination Resume

This format is fast becoming the resume of choice for performance in a database-dominated world. This format has all the flexibility and strength that comes from combining both the chronological and functional formats.

- It allows you maximum flexibility to demonstrate your thorough grasp of the job and its deliverables.
- It encourages greater data density and detail of information, which improves database retrieval performance.
- It offers more flexibility and scope for establishing a professional brand:

Target Job Title
(Here's the job I'm after.)

Performance Profile/Performance Summary
(This is a snapshot of what I can do.)

Core Competencies
(Here are the key professional skills that help me do my job well.)

Technology Competencies
(Optional: Here are the technical skills that help me do my job well.)

Performance Highlights
(Optional: outstanding achievements)

Professional Experience
(Where and when everything happened)

The following format takes more effort to create, but it is the most productive format in database performance, resonates most powerfully with human eyes, and gives the greatest scope for creating a strong professional brand, which we covered in Chapter 4.

Choose a Template

If you haven't already, now is a good time to start choosing a resume template. Go to the resume section, Chapter 10, to find examples suitable to your needs. You can get over 100 Microsoft Word resume templates in *Knock 'em Dead Resume Templates* at *www.knockemdead.com*.

It is common to look for resume templates that reflect someone in your profession. This is *wrong*! Resume templates have never been designed with particular professions or jobs in mind. There is no magically ordained format for resumes by profession. It doesn't matter at all if the accountant chooses the resume template of a geologist.

Choose your template based on its ability to accommodate your story in a visually appealing way.

The Combination Resume (page 1)

John William Wisher, MBA
1234 Bainbridge Blvd.
West Chicago, IL 60185

example@email.net

630.555.1234 630.555.2345

Expert leadership in cost effective supply chain, vendor, and project management within *Fortune* organizations.

EXECUTIVE PROFILE

A visionary, forward-thinking SUPPLY CHAIN AND LOGISTICS LEADER offering 20+ years of progressive growth and outstanding success streamlining operations across a wide range of industries. Excellent negotiation and relationship management skills with ability to inspire teams to outperform expectations. Proven record of delivering a synchronized supply chain approach through strategic models closely mirroring business plan to dramatically optimize ROI and manage risk.

Supply Chain Strategy:—Successfully led over 500 supply chain management initiatives across a wide spectrum of businesses, negotiating agreements from $5K to $27M. Implemented technology solutions and streamlined processes to reduce redundancies and staffing hours, improving both efficiency and productivity. Industries include: automotive and industrial manufacturing, consumer goods, government and defense, health care, high tech, and retail.

Industry Knowledge:—Extensive knowledge base developed from hands-on industry experience. Began career in dock operations with experience in Hub and Package Operations, multi-site retail operations management, to custom supply chain strategy development over twenty-one-year career with UPS.

Supply Chain Process Costing:—Built several information packets on total cost of ownership (TCO) and facilitated several C-level negotiations to identify and confirm opportunities. Worked to increase awareness among stakeholders on efficiencies and cost-saving measures ROI. Delivered $3.75M total cost savings to client base over three-year period.

Operations Reorganization:—Designed and implemented new sales force alignment and reporting structure; increased daily sales calls by 20%, reduced travel mileage 23%, and head count by nine; total annual cost savings of $920K.

Logistics:—Experienced across all modes of transportation: ocean, air freight, LTL, TL, mail services, and small package. Performs complex analysis to develop strategy based on cost and delivery requirements.

Project Management:—Implemented complete $1.2M redesign of 11 new UPS Customer Centers. Managed vendor and lease negotiations, developed budgets, training, and sales structure. All 11 centers up and operational on time and on budget.

Cost & Process Improvements

- Implemented complete warehouse redesign for a large optical distributor. Optimized warehouse operations through engineering a new warehouse design, integrating and automating technology, and synchronization of goods movement through ocean, air, ground, and mail services. Reduced transportation expense by 15%, increased production levels by 25%, reduced inventory by 15% and staffing by 20%.

- Built custom supply chain for a nationally recognized golf club manufacturer. Improved service levels by 30%, reduced damage by 45%, and integrated technology to support shipping process automation, reducing billing function staffing hours 50%.

Trust-Based Leadership

Vendor/Client Negotiations

Cross-Functional Collaboration

Supply Chain Mapping

Financial Logistics Analysis

Contingency Planning

Risk Management

Competitive Analysis

Haz Mat Compliance

Inventory Planning, Control, & Distribution

Recruiting/Training/Development

Project Management

Organizational Change Management

Distributive Computing

Budget Management

Labor Relations

John William Wisher, MBA

PROFESSIONAL BACKGROUND

United Parcel Service (UPS), Addison, IL   1986 to Present
World's largest package-delivery company and global leader in supply chain services, offering an extensive range of options for synchronizing the movement of goods, information, and funds. Serves more than 200 countries and territories worldwide and operates the largest franchise shipping chain, the UPS Store.

DIRECTOR/AREA MANAGER—SUPPLY CHAIN SALES, 2005–Present

Promoted to lead and develop a cross-functional sales force of 18 in consultative supply chain management services to Chicago-area businesses. Directs development of integrated supply chain management solutions across all modes of transportation, closely mirroring client business plans. Mentors team in Demand Responsive Model, a proven methodology to quickly align internal and external resources with changing market demands, situational requirements, and mission critical conditions. Manages $100M P&L.

Accomplishments:
• Implements over 100 multimillion-dollar supply chain integrations per year with 14% annual growth on 8% plan.
• Develops future organizational leaders; four staff members promoted through effective mentoring and development.
• Choreographed a supply chain movement from the Pacific Rim for a global fast-food chain to deliver 300k cartons to 15k locations all on the same day. Utilized modes of ocean, TL, air, and ground services, allowing for a national release synchronized to all locations on the same release date.
• Designed and implemented an automated reverse logistics program for a nationally recognized health food/supplement distributor. Automated returns process to reduce touches and costly staffing hours. Eliminated front-end phone contact using technology and web automation.

MARKETING MANAGER   2004 to 2005

Fast-tracked to streamline sales processes, increasing performance. Performed analysis of sales territory, historical data, operations alignment, reporting structure, and sales trends to devise solutions. Managed and coached area managers in business-plan development and execution of sales strategies. Delivered staff development in cost-reduction strategies and compliance requirements. Accountable for $500M P&L.

Accomplishments:
• Drove $500M+ in local market sales. Grew revenues 2004/2005 revenues 12% and 7% respectively.

RETAIL CHANNEL/OPERATIONS MANAGER   2002 to 2004

Charged with turning around this underperforming business unit. Managed development and implementation of new retail strategy across northern Illinois. Rebranded UPS Customer Centers and the UPS Store. Performed vendor negotiations and collaborated with nine regions to support additional implementations.

Accomplishments:
• Developed key revenue-generating initiatives across multiple channels. Attained 65% growth in discretionary sales. Several strategies adopted across the national organization.
• Re-engineered inventory for over 1,000 dropoff locations, reduced lease expenses by 45% and inventory levels by 40% through weekly measurement, inventory level development by SKU, order process automation, and order consolidation.
• Implemented new retail sales associate structure in 1,100 locations; scored highest national service levels by mystery shoppers.
• Selected as Corporate team member on Mail Boxes Etc. acquisition integration.

PROJECT MANAGER   2001 to 2002

Selected to support several underperforming business areas. Managed key segments of district business initiatives and compliance measures for 1,000 dropoff locations. Reported on status to corporate management. Supervised office staff of 16. Negotiated vendor and lease agreements.

Accomplishments:
• Rolled out and managed ongoing Haz Mat compliance program for all locations.
• Generated $6M in sales through cross-functional lead program and increased participation from 20% to 100%.
• Attained union workforce sponsorship of support-growth program through careful negotiations and persuasion.

SENIOR ACCOUNT MANAGER   1999 to 2001

Delivered $2.8M in growth on $1.1M plan, rated 3rd of 53 managers in revenue generation

ACCOUNT MANAGER   1997 to 1998

Top producer out of 53; $1.3M sales on $500K plan.

The Combination Resume (page 3)

John William Wisher, MBA

SERVICE PROVIDER 1994 to 1996
Top producer out of 53; $1.3M sales on $500K plan.

SUPERVISOR OF PACKAGE OPERATIONS 1994
Managed 65 full-time service providers. Performed post-routine analysis, operating strategy development, compliance, payroll, service failure recovery, and new technology implementation. Met 100% DOT and Haz Mat compliance. Reduced post-delivery staffing time by 50% and missed pickups by 65%.

SUPERVISOR OF HUB OPERATIONS 1988 to 1994
Managed up to 100 union employees and staff processing 75K pieces per day involving 40+ outbound bays. Performed complex staff scheduling and maintained low turnover rates. Designed new management reporting format, reducing administrative time by 20% and improved load quality by 30%.

OPERATIONS DOCK WORKER AND TRAINING LEAD 1986 to 1987

EDUCATION
MBA
National Louis University, Wheaton, IL, *4.0 GPA*

BA, Business, Supply Chain Management

Elmhurst College, Elmhurst, IL, *3.84 GPA, Magna cum laude*

Additional Specialized Courses:
• Supply Chain Mapping, 20 Hours
• Financial Logistics Analysis (FLOGAT), 10 Hours
• Hazardous Materials, 20 Hours
• Labor Relations, 30 Hours
• Managers Leadership School, 100 Hours
• Hazardous Materials, 20 Hours
• Managing from the Heart, 30 Hours

CHAPTER 6

THE SIMPLEST, SMARTEST, FASTEST WAY TO WRITE YOUR RESUME— KEEP IT SIMPLE, STUPID

THE MOST EFFECTIVE way to get a premium, powerful resume for a professional job in the shortest time with the least amount of hassle.

No one likes writing a resume, but you have to trust me when I tell you that there is no easier way than the way I am showing you. That shortcut you're thinking of? It won't work. If it did, I'd be telling you about it. This is the most streamlined way I know to give you a premium, powerful resume in the shortest time with the least amount of hassle.

Five Steps to a Great Resume

Your resume is a concise sales document that gives a snapshot of your professional life in a couple of short pages. A great finished product usually takes five steps:

1. A first draft to capture all the essentials on a basic resume template.
2. Two, three, five, or more gradually improving versions built over a week or more, as you tweak words and phrases; add and subtract; and cut, move, and paste until you cannot possibly improve it further.

    During this week or so, you should work on your resume for a couple of hours every day as you simultaneously organize, or reorganize, your job search. If you are smart enough to recognize that you need to rethink your resume to perform in the new world of work, commonsense also whispers that you probably need to retool your entire approach to job search.
3. A third draft to integrate your defined professional brand throughout the resume.
4. A fourth draft, where you paste your work so far into different templates and choose the one(s) best for you. As you do this, it is quite likely that you will still be tweaking a word here and there.
5. A final draft of your formatted resume where you do a grammatical edit and complete the polishing process.

Putting Together Your First Draft

With your completed TJD and Resume and Competitive Difference Questionnaires in hand, you know both *what the customer wants* and what you have to offer. Now you need to start assembling the pieces in a way that tells your story effectively.

To help you do this most efficiently, I've created a resume *Layout Template* for you. You use this to capture graphically and review the components your resume will contain. It is *not* intended as a template for your finished resume; it's just a gathering place for all the components of a cutting-edge resume. By using it, you'll become familiar with all the resume building blocks, and when the time comes to decide on a layout and template, everything will be ready to cut and paste.

Name

| Address | Telephone | E-mail address |

Target Job Title

A target job title, perhaps followed by an *optional* brand statement, as in the following example, helps database visibility and gives focus to the reader. The brief optional brand statement delivers value proposition you bring to the job, example:

Pharmaceutical Sales

Poised to outperform in pharmaceutical software sales repeating records of achievement with major pharmaceutical companies

Performance Profile/Performance Summary

What goes here? Take the most common requirements from your TJD and rewrite as a performance profile/performance summary. Helps database visibility and creates immediate resonance with reader's eyes. A maximum five lines of text can be followed by a second paragraph or list of bullets.

Core Competencies

A list of all the skills you identified in TJD. Repeat each skill listed here in context of the jobs where it was applied. This increases database visibility and gives reader immediate focus, "Oh s/he can talk about all of these things . . ." Example:

4-Handed Dentistry	Infection Control	Preventative Care
Oral Surgery/Extraction	Casts/Impressions	Emergency Treatment
Root Canals	Diagnostic X-Rays	Instrument Sterilization
Prosthetics/Restorations	Teeth Whitening	Radiology

Technical Competencies

An optional category depending on professional relevance.

Performance Highlights

An optional category depending on your experience.

Professional Experience

Employer's name	Dates
The company's focus	
Job Title	

If you are going to bold/caps anything, draw attention to what is most important: your job title.

Contact information at the top of each page. Keep your resume tightly edited but do not worry about page count. Reason: Jobs are more complex than they used to be, the additional info increases database performance, and readers won't mind as long as the resume is telling a relevant story.

Employer's name	Dates
The company's focus	
Job title	

Repeat employment history as necessary.

Education
May come earlier if these are critical professional credentials (as in medicine, law, etc.) that are especially relevant to job requirements, or highlight an important strength.

Licenses/Professional Accreditations
May come earlier if these credentials are critical credentials, especially relevant, or highlight an important strength.

Ongoing Professional Education

Professional Organizations/Affiliations

Publications, Patents, Speaking

Languages
Add them to the end of performance profile/performance summary and repeat them here.

Military Service

Extracurricular Interests
Add them here, if they relate to the job. Sports demonstrate fitness; chess, etc., denotes analytical skills; they can all be relevant.

(Closing brand statement)
Optional. If you use one, do *not* give it a heading,
as in the above parentheses. Example:
*"I believe that leadership by example and conscientious performance management
underlies my department's consistent customer satisfaction ratings."*

(References)
Never list references on your resume. Employers *assume* that your references are available, but it certainly doesn't hurt to end with a bold statement (but only if you have empty space at the end of the page and nothing else to add):

References Available on Request

Or

Excellent references available on request.

Or

My references will verify everything in this resume.

Why can't you choose a template right now? Because you select a template based on its layout and suitability to tell a particular story. This means you first have to determine all the components that will be in your story, and you don't know that till you've collected all the relevant information in one place. It's too soon to choose final templates at this point.

You will want to do this work on your computer. For a Microsoft Word version, go to the "Download" pages at *www.knockemdead.com* and download the Resume Layout Template. You can delete my commentary as you start to fill it out with your real-world experiences and information. The layout template is *not* intended as a final resume template, but as a tool to help you learn the component parts your resume needs to be maximally productive and to give you a sense of progress in the resume-development process. You'll find more than 100 resume templates on *www.knockemdead.com* in the e-book *Knock 'em Dead Resume Templates*.

How to Build Your Resume with the Resume Template Components

Name

Give your first and last name only, because that is the way you introduce yourself to someone in person. It isn't necessary to include your middle name(s), and unless you are known by your initials, don't use them on your resume.

It is not necessary to place Mr., Ms., Miss, or Mrs. before your name, unless yours is a unisex name like Jamie, Carroll, or Leslie; if you feel it necessary, it is acceptable to write Mr. Jamie Jones or Ms. Jamie Jackson. If you always add Jr. or III when you sign your name and that is the way you are addressed to avoid confusion, go ahead and use it.

Address

If you abbreviate—such as with *St.* or *Apt.*—be consistent. The state of your residence, however, is always abbreviated, for example: MN, WV, LA. The accepted format for laying out your address looks like this:

Maxwell Krieger
9 Central Avenue, Apartment 38
New York, NY 23456

or like this:

Maxwell Krieger
New York, NY 23456

But with a resume, if space is an issue, you can put your contact information on a single line:
Maxwell Krieger, New York, NY 23456

In an age of electronic communication, many people feel that street addresses are no longer necessary on a resume.

If you are employed and pursuing a confidential job search, it is acceptable to omit both your name and address. Your name would be replaced by a target job title and followed by e-mail and telephone contact information.

Telephone Number

Always include your area code and never use a work telephone number. Most telephone companies now have a master-ring feature, allowing you, at no extra charge, to have two or three different numbers on your phone line, each with a distinctive ring. It might not be a bad idea to use one of these available alternate numbers as your permanent career-management number. Then whenever it rings, you can be sure to finish crunching the potato chips before answering the call.

You should include your cell number, and if you don't have a master-ring system through your telephone provider, you might decide to use the cell number as your primary contact. Because we tend to answer our cell phones at all times, if a job call comes at a bad time, you should be prepared to say that you'd like to talk but will need to call back.

E-mail

Use your e-mail address as a job search marketing tool. Since the majority of job search communications are e-mail-based, it's the first thing any recruiter or potential employer sees, and it's a perfect opportunity for immediately positioning your credentials. In an Internet-based job search, your e-mail address is a powerful marketing tool, but for most job hunters it's a lost opportunity.

This might be a good time to retire those addresses like binkypoo@yahoo.com, bigboy@hotmail.com, *or* DDdoll@live.com, or at least restrict them to exclusively nonprofessional activities where they won't detract from your professional reputation.

Most e-mail hosts allow you to register a number of different e-mail addresses, so simply add an e-mail account devoted exclusively to your job search and career-management affairs.

Create an account name that reveals something about your professional profile, such as *SystemAnalyst@hotmail.com* or *TopAccountant@yahoo.com*.

This type of e-mail address acts as a headline to tell the reader who is writing, and to give some idea of what the communication is about. When names like *TopAccountant@yahoo.com* are already taken, you will be encouraged to accept something like *topaccountant1367@yahoo.com*. Before you accept this, try adding your area code (*TopAccountant516@yahoo.com*) or your zip code (*TopAccountant11579@yahoo.com*), both of which add information useful to an employer in your local target market but which usually won't mean much to someone outside of that market.

Using a profession-oriented e-mail address does double duty: It succinctly introduces the professional you, and it protects your identity. In a competitive job search, the little things can make a big difference; the way you introduce yourself is one of them. Finally, your e-mail address is an integral part of your contact information, and should always be hyperlinked on your resume so that a simple click will launch an e-mail so the reader can respond easily. It's another of those little things your competitors forget.

Target Job Title

Eighty percent of resumes lack a target job title, and this makes a resume less accessible to a harried recruiter who might spend as little as five seconds reviewing it before moving on to another candidate's resume where the writer has better focus and *communication skills*.

Recruiters use a target job title in database searches, so using one at the start of your resume helps it get pulled from a resume database for review by a recruiter. Additionally, once it is in front of human eyes, having a target job title gives both a recruiter and hiring manager immediate visual focus.

A target job title comes immediately after your contact information, at the top of your resume, and is most often centered on the page, is in a larger font than body copy, and is often in bold. It acts in the same way as a movie, TV show, and book or blog title: It draws the reader in by giving him a focus for what he is about to read.

The first thing any resume reader looks for is focus. A target job title explains what the resume is about. Decide on a target job title by taking all the title variations you collected in the TJD process. You should choose a common or generic target job title, something to widen your appeal. Here are some examples taken from finished resumes:

- **Certified Occupational Health Nurse Specialist**
- **Global Operations Executive**
- **Campaign Field Director**

- **Marketing Management**
- **Operations/Human Resources/Labor Relations/Staff Development**
- **Career Services Professional**
- **Operations Management**
- **Healthcare Review—Clinical Consultant**
- **Agricultural/Environmental Manager**
- **Horticultural Buying—International Experience**

Integrating a Professional Brand Into Your Resume

Your professional brand is communicated throughout your resume, but never more so than with your opening (and sometimes closing) brand statements. The first place you begin to establish a professional brand is with your target job title, where you consciously decide on the job that best allows you to package your skill sets and create a professional brand.

A target job title followed by a considered brand statement gives the reader an immediate focus on the resume's purpose and the type of person it represents. Your opening brand statement is a short phrase following the target job title that defines what you will bring to the job. It says, "These are the benefits my presence on your payroll will bring to your team and your company."

Opening Brand Statement

Notice how the following brand statements focus on the benefits brought to the job, but do not take up space identifying the specifics of how this was done. Professional brand statements often start with an action verb such as "Poised to," "Delivering," "Dedicated to," "Bringing," "Positioned to," or "Constructing":

Pharmaceutical Sales Management Professional

Poised to outperform in pharmaceutical software sales, repeating records of achievement with major pharmaceutical companies.

Senior Operations/Plant Management Professional

Dedicated to continuous improvement - Lean Six Sigma - Startup & turnaround operations - Mergers & change management - Process & productivity optimization - Logistics & supply chain

Bank Collections Management
Equipped to continue excelling in loss mitigation/collections/recovery management.

Mechanical/Design/Structural Engineer
Delivering high volume of complex structural and design projects for global companies in Manufacturing/Construction/Power Generation.

Account Management/Client Communications Manager
Reliably achieving performance improvement and compliance within Financial Services Industry.

Marketing Communications
Consistently delivering successful strategic marketing, media relations, & special events.

Administrative/Office Support Professional
Ready, willing, and competent; detail-oriented problem-solver; consistently forges effective working relationships with all publics.

Senior Engineering Executive
Bringing sound technical skills, strong business acumen, and real management skills to technical projects and personnel in a fast-paced environment.

Use Headlines to Guide the Reader

Headlines act like signposts, guiding a jaded and distracted reader through your resume. Your resume's job is to open as many doors for you as it can. It does this by making the information as accessible as possible to the target customer. Using headlines in your resume is both a visual and textual aid to comprehension, helping that tired-eyed, distracted reader absorb your message. Here are the headlines you will most likely use and the way they guide and make life easy for the reader:

Target Job Title
(Here's the job I'm after)

Performance Profile or **Performance/Career/Executive Summary**
(This is what I can do for you)

Core/Professional Competencies
(Here are all the key professional skills that help me do my job well)

Technology Competencies

(Here are the technology skills that help me do my job well)

Performance Highlights

(Here are some examples of my performance using the expertise you are interested in)

Professional Experience

(Where and when everything happened)

In little more than half a page, these headlines help the reader gain a quick grip on what you can bring to the table. Once you have a recruiter's attention, she will read your whole resume with serious attention.

Consistent Brand Messaging

Integrate your professional strengths, the building blocks of your brand, into the resume as you write it. As you revise and polish your resume, monitor and tweak your work to ensure that all the messaging supports the central concepts of your brand, especially in these sections of your resume:

- Performance Profile/Performance Summary
- Professional Competencies
- Performance/Career Highlights
- Professional Experience
- Closing Brand Statement

Performance Profile/Performance Summary

After your target job title and opening brand statement comes the performance profile/performance summary. The essence of every manager's (read: hiring authority's) job is performance management, and they spend a portion of every year thinking about and giving performance reviews. For that reason, this new and powerful headline will resonate with every manager. It speaks to your grasp of the job and your goal-orientation. It also encourages you to stay with the issues you know to be important to your target readers.

Take the major requirements from your TJD and turn them into 3–5 sentences, or no more than five lines without a paragraph break. It speaks to your grasp of the customer's priorities.

You can use headlines like Career/Professional/Executive Summary, but be aware that these traditional headlines encourage you to think about everything *you've* done rather than focus on customer needs.

Never Use Job Objective

Stay away from Job Objective (or Career Objective) if you can, for these reasons:

1. At this stage, no one cares what you want. The only issue is whether you can do the job.
2. Job Objective as a headline will not help your performance in database searches or resonate with recruiters' eyes, so you are wasting valuable selling space.

If you must use a Job Objective because you are at the start of your career and have no experience, that's okay—your competitors are in the same boat. Tilt the game in your favor by starting your objective with "The opportunity to" and then, referring to your TJD exercise, rewrite the target job's major priorities as your job objective. This will make a big difference in your resume's productivity.

Of the three traditional options for this important section of your resume—Career Summary, Job Objective, and Performance Profile/Performance Summary—you will find the "Performance Profile/Performance Summary" headline most productive. Recruiters and managers respond because it succinctly captures what you bring to the job.

How to Create a Performance Profile/Performance Summary

1. Take the 3–6 most important/common requirements identified in your TJD exercise and write 3–6 bulleted statements that capture your skills as they relate to the priorities identified in your TJD.
2. Combine all this information into just 3–5 short sentences. Together they will clearly show what you bring to the target job.
3. Check against your TJD to see that, wherever possible, you use the same words employers are using.
4. Dense blocks of text are hard on the eyes. If you have more than five lines, break the text into two paragraphs.

Your goal with a performance profile/performance summary is to demonstrate that you possess exactly the kinds of skills employers seek when hiring this type of person. It's a powerful way to open your resume both for its impact with the resume search engines and because it gives the reader the information they need: You're explaining what you bring to the table, based on their own prioritization of needs.

The finished product will be a performance profile/performance summary that captures the professional you in words most likely to be used in database searches and have a familiar ring to hiring managers' ears.

Using Keywords in a Performance Profile/Performance Summary

The words that employers use in job postings will be used by recruiters as search terms when they are searching the resume databases; so *using the same words in your resume as employers do in their job postings—words you know are important—will help get your resume pulled from the resume databases into which you load it.* Use them immediately, because search engine algorithms give weight to placement of words nearer the top of a document. Use as many keywords as you reasonably can in your performance profile/performance summary.

Here's a performance profile/performance summary for a Corporate Communications Management professional:

PERFORMANCE PROFILE/PERFORMANCE SUMMARY

9 years' strategic communications experience, developing high-impact and cost-efficient media outreach plans for consumer and business audiences in media, entertainment, and technology practice areas. Experienced in managing corporate and personal crisis communications. Goal- and deadline-oriented, with five years' experience managing internal and external communications. Adept at working with multiple teams and stakeholders.

Professional Competencies

A Professional/Core Competencies section is designed to capture all the skills you bring to your work in a succinct and easily accessible format; usually single words or short phrases in three or four columns. *Think of your core competencies section as an electronic business card that allows you to network with computers.* The positioning of likely keywords at the top of a document is favored by the search engines, and will help your resume's ranking in database searches; each one acts as an interest generator for the recruiter or hiring manager.

Recruiters and hiring managers appreciate a Professional Competencies section as a summary of the resume's focus. Each keyword or phrase acts as an affirmation of a skill area and possible topic of conversation. Confirming lots of topics to talk about so early in the resume is a big bonus for your candidacy. It acts as a preface to the body copy, in effect saying, "Hey, here are all the headlines. The stories behind them are immediately below," so the reader will pay closer attention.

There's no need to use articles or conjunctions. Just list the word, starting with a capital—"Forecasting," for example—or a phrase, such as "Financial modeling."

Here's an example of a Competencies section for a PR professional:

Professional Competencies

High-Tech Public Relations	Strong Editing Skills	Build & Lead Teams
Strategic Communications	Collateral Materials	Mentor
Executive Communications	New Business	Client Satisfaction
PR Messaging & Media Relations	Team Management	Organizational Skills
	Budget Management	Thought Leadership
Craft and Place Stories	Account Management	PR Counsel
Strong Writing Skills	Project Management	Social Media
Media Training	Detail Oriented	Leadership Branding
Multiple Projects	Acquisition	Story Telling
Story Placement	Positioning	Analyst Relations
Counsel Executives	Pitch Media	
Tactics	Market Research	

And an example from a Hospitality Management resume:

Core Competencies

• Revenue Optimization	• Team Building	• Operations Management
• Staff Development	• Time Management	• Policy & Procedures
• Spanish	• Productivity Growth	• Accounting/POS Support
• Customer Service	• Client Relations	• Inventory Control
• Brand Integrity	• Turnover Reduction	• Problem Solving
• P&L	• 250 Covers Daily	• Liquor Inventory
• Payroll	• 300 Pre-Theater	• Cash Reconciliation
• Food Cost Reduction	• Purchasing	• Administration
• Training Manuals	• POS Systems	• Marketing/Advertising
• Cost Containment	• Recruitment & Selection	

If you work in technology, or you have developed an extensive slate of technology competencies, you might choose to add a Technology Competencies section. It breaks up the page and it is easier to absorb when they are separated.

Here's an example of a separate Technology Competencies section:

Technology Competencies

Operating Systems:	Unix, Windows (2000, XP, 7), DOS
Languages:	C, C++, Java, Pascal, Assembly Languages (Z8000, 808x, DSP)
Methodologies:	TL9000, Digital Six Sigma
Software:	MS Office, Adobe FrameMaker, Matlab
RDBMS:	DOORS, Oracle 7.x
Protocols:	TCP/IP, SS7ISUP, A1, ANSI, TL1, SNMP
Tools:	Teamplay, ClearCase, ClearQuest, M-Gatekeeper, Exceed, Visio, DocExpress, Compass
Other:	CDMA Telecom Standards – 3GPP2 (Including TIA/EIA-2001, TIA-EIA-41, TIA/EIA-664), ITU-T, AMPS

Adding to Professional Competencies

Your resume is a living document, and its content may well change as your job search—and professional development projects—progresses. Whenever you come across keywords in job postings that reflect your capabilities, but which are not in your resume, it is time to add them. If nowhere else, at least put them in the Professional Competencies section.

Use Keywords Often

1. Give the most important of your professional competencies first in the performance profile/ performance summary section of your resume.
2. Include a complete list of your skills in the Professional Competencies section. It is the perfect spot to list the technical acronyms and professional jargon that speak to the range of your professional skills, especially if they won't fit into the Professional Experience section of your resume.
3. A Professional Competencies section should remind you to use as many of the keywords as you can in the Professional Experience part of your resume, where usage will show the context in which those skills were developed and applied.

This strategy will make your resume data dense for improved database performance, while also demonstrating that you have the relevant skills and putting them in context for the recruiter in a **visually accessible** manner. Yes, it will make your resume longer (we'll discuss this issue shortly); just know it has a much better chance of being pulled from the resume databases, and because its content is completely relevant to the needs of the job and readily accessible to the recruiter, you will get an improved response rate.

Make Room for Supporting Skills on Your Resume

If you want your resume pulled from the databases and read with serious attention, you know it needs to focus on the skills you bring to a single target job. However, employers still want to know about your supporting skills.

For example, a colleague and hiring manager in the IT world says, "I don't just want to see evidence that someone is a hotshot in, say, the .NET Framework; I also want to see that they can get around with other languages, so that I know (a) that they understand programming as distinct from just .NET, and (b) that if my company introduces a new programming language/development environment in the future, I have someone who will be able to handle that."

You can still get this important information about *supporting skills* into your resume, without taking up too much room, by adding them to your Professional Competencies section.

You'll start the section with those skills most important to your Target Job, but you can then add all those skills that support your all-around professionalism.

The appearance of these *supporting skills* in the Professional Competencies section can help your resume's performance in database searches, and it helps put your primary skills in the larger context of your complete professional abilities. And because they are supporting skills, it doesn't matter that you don't include them in the context of the jobs you've held.

Skills Prioritization

Your professional skills are most readily accessible when they appear in three or four columns. This section contains a list of your important professional skills and so needs to be near the top of your resume, for these reasons:

1. Coming after a Target Job Title and a Performance Summary that focuses on the skills you bring to the target job, skills reflect employer priorities. You are helping both the discoverability of your resume when it sits in resume databases and its impact upon knowledgeable readers.

2. The Applicant Tracking System (ATS) programs that recruiters use to search resume databases in turn use algorithms that reward relevant words near the front of a document as a means of judging that document's relevance to the recruiters' search terms. So your professional skills need to be relevant to the target job and come near the top of your resume—just as we have been suggesting for years. (This, perhaps, is because I have been using ATS systems since 1987 when they first came to the fore and have an understanding of how they work.)

3. A recent study showed that once a resume has been pulled from a resume database, recruiters spend an average of six seconds on a first-time scan of that resume. This means your qualifications have to jump out. You make them do so by using a Target Job Title, followed by a Performance Summary that reflects employer priorities as you determined in your TJD work, and followed in turn by a Professional Skills section that supports all the above claims of professional competency with a list of your relevant skills. This gives a recruiter plenty of time to see your abilities in that first six-second scan.

However there is another issue at play when it comes to the Professional Skills section of your resume. Ultimately it will be read by someone who really knows this job, who is aware of what's a "must-have" and what's a "nice to have."

The easiest way to explain this is with an example: A couple of years back we prepared a resume for a dental assistant, and she gave us a list of all the important technical skills of her job. We put these into three columns for visual accessibility, and something terrible jumped out at me: Her list started with "Teeth whitening" and ended with "Four-handed dentistry." What was so terrible about this? All the skills were there.

Yes they were, but in the West we read from left to right and top to bottom, so common sense says that the most important skills for a job should come before the less important skills. We immediately switched these phrases so that "Four-handed dentistry" (a highly marketable skill) came first and "Teeth whitening" (a more routine skill) came last.

Bear this story in mind when you are creating your own Professional Skills section: By prioritizing the skills you are subtly telling the man or woman who will ultimately hire you that you have a firm grasp of the relative importance of all the necessary professional skills of your work. That point adds to the clear focus and power of the opening first half page of your resume. If you follow these directions, the opening sections of your resume will show that:

- You can do the job
- Your skills list backs up your statements of ability
- You understand the relative importance of the component parts of your job.

The result is that in the first half page of your resume, and well within the framework of a six-second scan, you have gone a long way toward making the short list of candidates who will be brought in for interview.

Grids and Tables in Resume Formatting

A moment ago, I mentioned Applicant Tracking Systems. These came into being twenty-seven years ago to help recruiters find resumes in their growing databases. In the early days, the ATS programs had problems dealing with italics, lines, boxes, bolding, some kinds of bullets, the tables that give resume layout a precise snappy look, and some fonts; they also had difficulties reading a lot of various layouts.

We have come a long way in twenty-seven years. Just as you are not using the software you used in the mid 1980s (if you were alive and working then), neither are companies.

The colleagues whom I trust on these matters don't think these formatting issues are nearly of the importance they used to be. Personally, I don't think that the precise formatting that comes with the use of grids and tables matters at all.

For example, you can usually count on Europe and elsewhere to be behind the United States when it comes to technology (yes, I know there are exceptions but let's stick to the lesson point being made here). Last year we wrote a resume for a European Medicines Agency marketing guy living in Vienna, Austria. His resume was built with grids and tables; he uploaded it into fifteen then ultimately twenty-five databases and got interviews with all seven of his top target companies within two weeks. The formatting had no negative impact whatsoever. Common sense tells me that while corporations tend to keep up-to-date with new software releases, even when they don't, they certainly are not using twenty-seven-year-old software.

You can achieve the same look without formatting with grids and tables if you are feeling wary; it just takes longer, so ultimately the decision is up to you.

Performance/Career Highlights

In completing the resume questionnaire, you gathered evidence of achievements and contributions in your work and quantified them whenever you could. Now is the chance to choose 2–4 of these (depending on the depth of your experience) as standout contributions. Capture them in confident statements:

Performance Highlights

35% increase in on-time delivery + 20% reduction in client complaints

Effective Operations Management demands understanding every department's unique problems and timelines. Building these considerations into daily activities helped:

- Finance & Supply Chain, saved $55,000 in last three quarters
- Increased productivity, with a 35% increase in on-time delivery

These on-time delivery increases were achieved with improved communications, connecting Purchasing, Supply Chain, Customers, and Customer Service:

- Delivered 20% reduction in client complaints

Professional Experience

Company Names

Each job needs to be identified with an employer. There is no need to include specific contact information, although it can be useful to include the city and state. When working for a multidivision corporation, you may want to list the divisional employer.

Employment Dates

A resume without employment dates considerably underperforms a resume that has dates, and those dates need to be accurate because they can be checked. With a steady work history and no employment gaps, you can be very specific:

January 2007–September 2011

If you had an employment gap of six months in, say, 2008, you can disguise this:

MBO Inc.   2006–2008

XYZ Inc.   2008–present

I am *not* suggesting that you should lie about your work history, and you must be prepared to answer honestly and without hesitation if you are asked.

If you abbreviate employment dates, be sure to do so consistently. It is quite acceptable to list annual dates, rather than month and year. Remember, when references get checked, the first things verified are dates of employment and leaving salary; untruths in either of these areas are grounds for dismissal with cause, and that can dog your footsteps into the future.

Individual Jobs

Each section of the resume represents another opportunity to communicate your unique achievements and contributions. Replace time-worn descriptions in the Professional Experience section . . . :

- *Before:* Responsible for identifying and developing new accounts.
  . . . with strong action statements:
- *After:* Drove advances in market share and revitalized stalled business by persistently networking and pursuing forgotten market pockets—lost sales, smaller, untapped businesses/ prospects overlooked by competition.

The area where you address your responsibilities and achievements in each job, *as they relate to the customer's needs you identified during TJD,* is the meat of your resume. When working on this part of your resume, constantly refer to your TJD to remind yourself of the details target employers are most likely to want to read about and the keywords and phrases that will help your resume perform in recruiters' database searches.

The responsibilities and contributions you identify here are those functions that best relate to the needs of the target job. They do not necessarily correspond with how you spent the majority of your working day, nor are they related to how you might prefer to spend your working day. This can perhaps best be illustrated by showing you part of a resume that came to my desk recently. It is the work of a professional who listed her title and duties for one job like this:

"Motivated a sales staff of six, recruited, trained, managed. Hired to improve sales. Sales Manager increased sales."

The writer mistakenly listed everything in the reverse order of importance. She's not focused on the items' relative importance *to a future employer*, who, above all, will want to hire someone who can increase sales. She also wasted space stating the obvious about the reason she was hired as a sales manager: to improve sales. Let's look at what subsequent restructuring achieved:

Sales Manager: Hired to turn around stagnant sales force. Successfully recruited, trained, managed, and motivated sales staff of six. Result: 22 percent sales gain over first year. Notice how this is clearly focused on the essentials of any sales manager's job: to increase income for the company.

"Hired to turn around stagnant sales force.": Demonstrates her skills and responsibilities.

"Successfully recruited, trained, managed, and motivated sales staff of six. Result: 22 percent sales gain over first year.": Shows what she subsequently did with the sales staff, and exactly how well she did it.

By making these changes, her responsibilities and achievements become more important in the light of the problems they solved. Be sure to match your narrative to employers' needs and to the priorities of that target job. Avoid exaggeration of your accomplishments. It isn't necessary.

Achievements

Business has very limited interests. In fact, those interests can be reduced to a single phrase: making a profit. This is done in just three ways:

1. By *saving money* for the company
2. By *increasing productivity*, which in turn *saves money* and provides the opportunity to *make more money* in the time saved
3. By simply *earning money* for the company

That does not mean that you should address only these points in your resume and ignore valuable contributions that cannot be quantified. But it does mean that you should *try to quantify your achievements whenever you can.*

Pick 2–4 accomplishments for each job title and edit them down to bite-size chunks that read like a telegram. Write as if you had to pay for each entry by the word—this approach can help you pack a lot of information into a short space. The resulting abbreviated style will help convey a sense of immediacy to the reader. I'll use an example we can all relate to:

Responsible for new and used car sales. Earned "Salesman of the Year" awards, 2006 and 2007. Record holder: Most Cars Sold in One Year.

Here's another example from a fundraiser's resume:

- Created an annual giving program to raise operating funds. Raised $2,000,000.
- Targeted, cultivated, and solicited sources including individuals, corporations, foundations, and state and federal agencies. Raised $1,650,000.
- Raised funds for development of the Performing Arts School facility, capital expense, and music and dance programs. Raised $6,356,000.

Now, while you may tell the reader about these achievements, never explain how they were accomplished; the key phrase here is "specifically vague." The intent of your resume is to pique interest and to raise as many questions as you answer. Questions mean interest, interest means talking to you, and *getting conversations started is the primary goal of your resume!*

Prioritize your accomplishments, and quantify them whenever possible and appropriate.

You can cite achievements as part of a sentence/paragraph or as bullets, for example:

Collections:

Developed excellent rapport with customers while significantly shortening payout terms. Turned impending loss into profit. Personally salvaged and increased sales with two multimillion-dollar accounts by providing remedial action for their sales/financial problems.

Collections:
Developed excellent rapport with customers while significantly shortening payout terms:

- Evaluated sales performance; offered suggestions for financing/merchandising, turned impending loss into profit.
- Salvaged two multimillion-dollar problem accounts by providing remedial action for their sales/financial problems. Subsequently increased sales.

Whenever you can, keep each paragraph to a maximum of four or five lines. This ensures that the finished product has plenty of white space so that it is easy on the reader's eyes. If necessary, split one paragraph into two.

Endorsements and Excerpts from Performance Evaluations

You don't see these on resumes very often, but they can make a powerful addition. They are most effective when supporting quantified achievements. These endorsements are not necessary, though, and while they can make a good addition to your resume, they shouldn't be used to excess. One or two are adequate, although I have seen successful resumes where each job entry is finished with a complimentary endorsement.

Here are a couple of examples of how to do them well:

- Sales volume increased from $90 million to $175 million. Acknowledged as "the greatest single gain of the year."
- Earnings increased from $9 million to $18 million. Review stated, "Always has a view for the company bottom line."

Professional Performance

Year	Projection	Sales	Percentage
2011	$240,000	$425,000	177%
2010	$90,000	$106,200	128%
2009	$102,000	$114,000	121%
2008	$114,000	$123,120	117%
2007	$185,000	$192,816	109%
2006	$120,000	$121,000	102%

Charts and Graphs

A picture is worth a thousand words, so if you can use a graphic to make a point, it opens up the page and is infrequent enough to get attention. Here is an example of a graphic insert that shows increasing sales achievements. Compare this statement of achievement . . . :

Revenue Growth—Maintained consistent, year-over-year increase through fluctuating economies

. . . with:

Revenue Growth—Maintained consistent, year-over-year pattern of increasing revenues through robust and downturn economies, from $50,000 to $1.2 million as illustrated below:

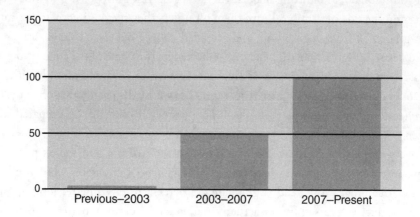

Avoid exaggerating your accomplishments. It isn't necessary.

Education

Educational history is normally placed wherever it helps your case the most. The exact positioning will vary according to the length of your professional experience, and the importance of your academic achievements to the job and your profession.

If you are recently out of school with little practical experience, your educational credentials might constitute your primary asset and should appear near the beginning of the resume.

After two or three years in the professional world, your academic credentials become less important in most professions, and move to the end of your resume. The exceptions are in professions where academic qualifications dominate—medicine and law, for example. The highest level of academic attainment always comes first: a doctorate, then a master's, followed by a bachelor's degree. For degreed professionals, there is no need to go back further into educational history; it is optional to list prep schools.

It is normal to abbreviate degrees (PhD, MA, BA, BS, etc.). In instances where educational attainment is paramount, it is acceptable to put that degree after your name. Traditionally, this has been the privilege of doctors and lawyers, but there is absolutely no reason that your name shouldn't be followed, for example, by MBA.

List scholarships and awards. More recent graduates will usually also list majors and minors (relevancy permitting—if it helps, use it; if it doesn't, don't). The case is a little more complicated for the seasoned professional. Many human resources people say it makes life easier for them if majors and minors are listed, so they can further sift and grade the applicants. That's good for them, but it might not be good for you. The resume needs to get you in the door, not slam it in your face. So, as omitting majors will never stop you from getting an interview, I suggest you err on the side of caution. Leave them off unless they speak directly to the target job.

If you graduated from high school and attended college but didn't graduate, you may be tempted to list your high school diploma first, followed by the name of the college you attended. That would give the wrong emphasis: It says you are a college dropout and identifies you as a high school graduate. In this instance, you would list your college and area of study, but omit any reference to graduation or earlier educational history. But again, be prepared to tell the truth when asked.

Employers really appreciate people who invest in their future and there's proof from the U.S. Department of Education to back it up. Of high school graduates who enrolled in any associate's degree program but didn't graduate, 48 percent received better job responsibilities and 29 percent received raises! If they actually graduated, it gets even better: 71 percent gained improved job responsibilities and 63 percent got raises.

Clearly, being enrolled in ongoing education looks good on a resume; you have nothing to lose and everything to gain by committing to your career. Being enrolled in courses toward a degree needn't be expensive, and all other things being equal when, say, a BS is required, "BS Accounting (Graduation anticipated Sept 2012)" can help you overcome an otherwise mandatory requirement.

Don't puff up your educational qualifications. Research has proven that three out of every ten resumes inflate educational qualifications. Consequently, verification of educational claims is quite common. If, after you have been hired, your employer discovers that you exaggerated your educational accomplishments, it could cost you your job.

Ongoing Professional Education

Identify all relevant professional training courses and seminars you've attended. It speaks to professional competency and demonstrates your commitment to your profession. It also shows that an employer thought you worthy of the investment. Technology is rapidly changing the nature of all work, so if you aren't learning new skills every year, you are being paid for an increasingly obsolescent skill set. Ongoing professional development is a smart career management strategy.

Accreditations, Professional Licenses, and Civil Service Grades

If licenses, accreditations, or civil service grades are mandatory requirements in your profession, you must feature them clearly. If you are close to gaining a particular accreditation or license you should identify it:

"Passed all parts of C.P.A. exam, September 2012 (expected certification March 2013)."

Civil service grades can be important if you are applying for jobs with government contractors, subcontractors, or any employers who do business with state or federal agencies.

Professional Associations

Membership in associations and societies related to your work demonstrates strong professional commitment, and offers great networking opportunities. See this year's edition of *Knock 'em Dead: The Ultimate Job Search Guide* for strategy and tactics in using these associations to find job opportunities. If you are not currently a member of one of your industry's professional associations, give serious consideration to joining.

Note the emphasis on "professional" in the heading. An employer is almost exclusively interested in your professional associations and societies. Omit references to any religious, political, or otherwise potentially controversial affiliations unless your *certain* knowledge of that company assures that such affiliations will be positively received.

An exception to this rule is found in those jobs where a wide circle of acquaintance is regarded as an asset. Some examples might include jobs in public relations, sales, marketing, real estate, and insurance. In these cases, include your membership/involvement with community/church organizations and the like, as your involvement demonstrates a professional who is also involved in the community and speaks to an outgoing personality with a wide circle of contacts.

By the same token, a seat on the town board, charitable cause involvement, or fundraising work are all activities that show a willingness to involve yourself and can demonstrate organizational abilities through titles held in those endeavors. Space permitting, these are all activities worthy of inclusion because they show you as a force for good in your community.

Companies that take their community responsibilities seriously often look for staff that feels and acts the same way. For instance, you could list yourself as:

American Heart Association: Area Fundraising Chair

If you are a recent entrant into the workplace, your meaningful extracurricular contributions are of even greater importance. List your position on the school newspaper or the student council, memberships in clubs, anything that demonstrates your potential as a productive employee. As your career progresses, however, prospective employers care less about your school life and more about your work life, so once you are two or three years into your career, the importance of these involvements should be replaced by similar activities in the adult world.

Publications, Patents, and Speaking

These three capabilities are rare and make powerful statements about creativity, organization, determination, and follow-through. They tell the reader that you invest considerable personal time and effort in your career and are therefore a cut above the competition.

Public speaking is respected in every profession because it is such a terrifying thing to do, and I say this as someone who has spoken all over the world for two decades! Publications are always respected but carry more weight in some professions (e.g., academia). You will notice in the resume examples in this book that the writers list dates and names of publications but do not often include copyright information or patent numbers, because it isn't necessary information for a resume. Here's an example of how to cite your publications:

"Radical Treatments for Chronic Pain." 2002. *Journal of American Medicine.*

"Pain: Is It Imagined or Real?" 2000. *Science & Health Magazine.*

Patents take years to achieve and cost a fortune in the process (I know; I have two optical patents). They speak to vision, creativity, attention to detail, and considerable tenacity. They are a definite plus in the technology and manufacturing fields.

> As you are piecing your resume together, it will almost certainly go beyond the one- and two-page mark. Do not worry about this. Traditional page count considerations are out of date, and besides, you haven't gotten to the editing stage yet.

Languages

With the current state of communications technology, all companies can have an international presence. Consequently, you should always cite your cultural awareness and language abilities. If you speak a foreign language, say so:

Fluent in Spanish and French
Read German
Read and write Serbo-Croatian
Conversational Mandarin

If you are targeting companies that have an international presence, I suggest you cite your linguistic abilities in your performance profile/performance summary and perhaps again at the end of the resume.

Military

Always list your military experience. Military experience speaks, amongst other things, to your determination, teamwork, goal-orientedness, and your understanding of *systems and procedures*. There are a number of major international corporations in which the senior ranks are heavily tilted toward men and women with a military background. In fact, the best boss I ever had was Colonel Peter Erbe, an ex-Airborne guy and one-time head of officer training at West Point. Everyone respects the commitment and the skills you developed in the military, and this can be a big plus in your career.

Personal Flexibility, Relocation

If you are open to relocation for the right opportunity, make it clear. It will never, in and of itself, get you an interview, but it won't hurt. Place this information within the first half page so that it is within scanning distance of your address.

Judgment Calls

Here are some areas that do not normally go into your resume, but might. Whether you include them or not will depend on your personal circumstances.

Summer and Part-Time Employment

This should only be included if you are just entering the work force or re-entering it after a substantial absence. The entry-level person can feel comfortable listing dates and places and times. The returnee should include the skills gained but minimize the part-time aspect of the experience.

Reason for Leaving

The topic is always covered during an interview, so why raise an issue that could have negative impact? You can usually use the space more productively, so your reason for leaving rarely belongs on a resume.

However, if you have frequently been caught in downsizings or mergers or recruited for more responsible positions, there can be a sound argument for listing these reasons to counteract the perception of your being a job hopper. You'll see examples in the resume section.

References

Employers assume that your references are available, and if they aren't available, boy, are you in trouble! However, there is a case for putting "References Available Upon Request" at the end of your resume. It may not be absolutely necessary to say that references are there for the asking, but those four extra words certainly don't do any harm and may help you stand out from the crowd. Including the phrase sends a little message: "Hey, look, I have no skeletons in my closet." But only if space allows—if you have to cut a line anywhere, this should be one of the first to go.

Never list the names of references on a resume: interviewers very rarely check them before meeting and developing a strong interest in you—it's too time-consuming. Additionally, the law (1970 Fair Credit and Reporting Act) forbids employers to check references without your written consent, so they have to meet you first in order to obtain your written permission.

FYI, you grant this permission when you fill out an application form. In fact, it is usually the reason you are given an application form to complete when you already have a perfectly good resume. There, at the bottom, just above the space for your signature, is a block of impossibly small type. Your signature below it grants permission for reference and credit checks.

Name Changes and Your References

If you have ever worked under a different surname, you must take this fact into account when giving your references. A recently divorced woman I know wasted a strong interview performance because she was using her maiden name on her resume and at the interview. She forgot to tell the employer that her references would, of course, remember her by a different last name. The results of this oversight were catastrophic: Three prior employers denied ever having heard of anyone by that name.

Marital Status

Some resume authorities think your marital status is important on the basis that it speaks to stability. However, with 50 percent of marriages ending in divorce and the average length of a marriage under fifteen years, your marital status will rarely win or deny you an interview, and as reference to marital status is illegal (1964 Civil Rights Act), it is safe to omit. There are some areas where these issues are occasionally thought to be a valid criterion for consideration: outside sales, trucking, and some churches.

Written Testimonials

It is best not to attach written testimonials to your resume. Of course, that doesn't mean that you shouldn't solicit such references: You might consider using them as a basis for those third-party endorsements we talked about earlier; then, if asked at the interview, you can produce the written testimonials to support the claims made on your resume. This way, you get to use them twice to good effect. Testimonials can be helpful if you are just entering the work force or are re-entering after a long absence; you can use the content of the testimonials to beef up your resume and your interview.

Personal Interests

If space permits, always include personal interests that reflect well on you as a professional and as a human being. References to personal activities that speak to your ethics (you volunteer for Hospice, for example) or are tied to the job in some way are the most effective.

A Korn Ferry study once showed that executives with team sports on their resumes averaged $3,000 a year more than their more sedentary counterparts. Now, that makes giving a line to your personal interests worthwhile, if they fit into certain broad categories. If you participate in team sports, determination activities (running, climbing, bicycling), and "strategy activities" (bridge, chess, Dungeons & Dragons), consider including something about them. Yes, poker involves critical thinking skills, but it's not worth the bad press your mention can get if the interviewer doesn't understand that it is a game of skill. The rule of thumb, as always, is only to include activities that can, in some way, contribute to your chances of being hired.

Fraternities and Sororities

Changing times have altered thinking about listing fraternities and sororities on resumes. In general, I recommend leaving them off. Unless your resume is tailored to individuals or companies where membership in such organizations will result in a case of "deep calling to deep": then, by all means, list it.

Closing Brand Statement

Using a closing brand statement provides a powerful reinforcement of the branding you have striven for throughout the document. A closing comment at the resume's end acts both as an exclamation point and a matching "bookend" for the brand statement at the beginning.

Most resumes are written in the third person, allowing you to talk about yourself with the semblance of objectivity. It can be effective to switch to a first-person voice to make it conversational and differentiate it from the voice of the rest of your resume.

For example:

I see performance management as a critical tool to ensure maximum profitability within the sales department; my consistency has always led to motivated, high-performance sales teams.

Or:

I understand customer service to be the company's face to the world, and I treat every customer interaction as critical to our success; leadership by example and conscientious performance management underlies my department's consistent customer satisfaction ratings.

Many people confuse the need for professionalism with stiff-necked formality. You'll find the most effective tone for a resume is one that mixes the formal with a little of the informal or conversational.

The effect of switching to a first-person voice at the end of the resume is that throughout the document a third party has been objectively discussing someone's professional background, and the first person jumps out at the end with a statement that shows your ownership of this document.

Integrating brand statements is a new idea and something many resumes do not have. Do it well and you can really stand out. But don't do it if you haven't fully defined your brand, or realize you have work to do before you have something worth branding.

You can also close with a third-party endorsement:

"I've never worked with a more ethical and conscientious auditor." —Petra Tompkins, Controller

Such an endorsement acts as a closing brand statement: a bold statement clarifying the value of the product (that's you, the brand). It's a great way to end a resume. If you have just the right kind of endorsement, this could be the perfect place to use it.

What Never Goes In

Some information just doesn't belong in a resume. Make the mistake of including it and at best your resume loses a little power, while at worst you fail to land the interview.

Personal Flexibility and Relocation Issues

If you are open to relocation for the right opportunity, make it clear, but conversely, *never state that you* aren't *open to relocation*. Let nothing stand in the way of generating job offers! You can always leverage a job offer you don't want into an offer you do. (Check out how in this year's edition of *Knock 'em Dead: The Ultimate Job Search Guide*.)

Titles Such As: Resume, CV, Curriculum Vitae, etc.

Their appearance on a properly structured resume is redundant. It makes clear that your resume needs more work. Such titles take up a whole line, one that could be used more productively. Use the space you save for information with greater impact, or buy yourself an extra line of white space to help your reader's eyes.

Availability

All jobs exist because there are problems that need solutions. For that reason, interviewers rarely have time for candidates who aren't readily available. If you are not ready to start work, then why are you wasting everyone's time? As a rule of thumb, let the subject of availability come up at the face-to-face meeting. After meeting you, an employer is more likely to be prepared to wait until you are available, but will usually pass on an interview if you cannot start now or in the reasonably near future—say, two to three weeks.

The only justification for including this (and then only in your cover letter) is that you expect to be finishing a project and moving on at such-and-such a time, and not before.

Salary

Leave out all references to salary, past and present—it is far too risky. Too high or too low a salary can knock you out of the running even before you hear the starting gun. Even in responding to a job posting that specifically requests salary requirements, don't give the information on your resume. A good resume will still get you the interview, and in the course of the discussions with the company, you'll talk about salary anyway. If you are obliged to give salary requirements, address them in your cover letter—and give a range; you may want to read the section on salary negotiation in the latest edition of *Knock 'em Dead: The Ultimate Job Search Guide*.

If you are obliged to give salary requirements, address them in your cover letter or use a separate Salary History page; you'll find an example in the samples chapter of this book, and you can find a template of this and more than 100 resume templates in the e-book *Knock 'em Dead Resume Templates* at *www.knockemdead.com*.

Age, Race, Religion, Sex, and National Origin

Government legislation was enacted in the 1960s and 1970s forbidding employment discrimination in these areas under most instances, so it is wisest to avoid reference to them unless they are deemed relevant to the job.

Photographs

In days of old, when men were bold and all our cars had fins, it was the thing to have a photograph in the top right-hand corner of the resume. Today, the fashion is against photographs. Obviously, careers in modeling, acting, and certain aspects of the media require headshots. In these professions, your appearance is an integral part of your product offering.

The place for your headshot is on your social networking profile on LinkedIn and other networking sites. We'll discuss your social networking profile as another version of your resume shortly.

Health/Physical Description

You are trying to get a job, not a date. Unless your physical appearance is immediately relevant to the job (gym instructor, model, actor, media personality), leave these issues out. If you need to demonstrate health, do it with your extracurricular interests.

CHAPTER 7

HOW TO GIVE YOUR RESUME PUNCH

FIRST IMPRESSIONS ARE important. Editing polishes your content and helps it deliver a greater punch.

The recruiters and hiring authorities who need to read and respond to your resume just hate the mind-numbing grind of it all. It's an activity that makes the eyes tired and the mind wander, so your resume needs to be visually accessible, as we have already discussed. Next, you need to make sure the words you use make sense, read intelligently, and pack a punch by speaking directly to your customers' needs.

You can assume that anyone who reads your resume has an open position to fill and is numb from reading resumes. Understanding exactly what this feels like will help you craft a finished resume that is most readily accessible to the tired eyes and distracted minds of recruiters and hiring authorities.

Imagine you are a recruiter for a moment. You read resumes for a good part of the day, every day. Today, you have just completed a resume database search and have twenty resumes to read. Now, if you didn't do this when I suggested it earlier, go read six resumes from the sample section without a break. Really try to understand each one, but don't spend more than sixty seconds on each.

Three things will happen in sequence: first a ringing in the ears, followed by fuzzy vision and an inability to concentrate. After about fifteen minutes at this, you'll realize why your focus on relevant content, clear layout, and compelling language for your resume are critical for getting it read and understood . . . and why those headlines are so appreciated.

Customize the Templates You Choose

While *Knock 'em Dead* resume layouts and templates are based on common sense and market-response monitoring, you are still free to customize layout. As a rule of thumb, the information most relevant to your candidacy should always come first. For example, when you have no experience, your degree might be your strongest qualification, so put it front and center. As experience increases with the passage of time, in most professions your education can become less important. This is why you will usually see education at the end of a resume, unless the job or the profession's particular demands require it up front. (There are some professions—medicine, education, and the law, for example—where essential academic and professional accreditations tend to be kept at the front of the resume. Bear this in mind if you work in one of these professions.)

However, the resume template you choose isn't sacrosanct; you can customize the layout to suit your needs. For example, you might decide that moving languages, special training, or other information typically found at the end of the resume increases the strength of your argument when placed first. If that makes sense, go ahead and do it.

Filling In the Template

Go through your chosen template and transfer the information you developed earlier, and almost immediately, you have a resume that begins to look like a finished product.

Tighten Up Sentences

Sentences gain power with action verbs. For example, a woman with ten years of law firm experience in a clerical position had written in her original resume:

I learned to use a new database.

After she thought about what was really involved, she gave this sentence more punch:

I analyzed and determined the need for a comprehensive upgrade of database, archival, and retrieval systems. I was responsible for selection and installation of "cloud-based" archival systems. Within one year, I had an integrated, company-wide archival system working.

Notice how verbs show that things happen when you are around the office; they bring action to a resume. Note that while they tell the reader what you did and how you did it, they also support the branding statements that can open and close your resume.

Now look at the above example when we add a third party:

I analyzed and determined the need for a comprehensive upgrade of database, archival, and retrieval systems. I was responsible for selection and installation of "cloud-based" archival systems. Within one year, I had an integrated, company-wide archival system working. A partner stated, "You brought us out of the dark ages, and in the process neither you nor the firm missed a beat!"

Now, while the content is clearly more powerful, the sentences are clunky, too wordy, and need tightening.

Tight Sentences Have Bigger Impact

Space is at a premium, and reader impact is your goal, so keep your sentences under about twenty words. Always aim for simplicity and clarity:

• Shorten sentences by cutting unnecessary words.
• Make two short sentences out of one long one. At the same time, you don't want the writing to sound choppy, so vary the length of sentences when you can.

You can also start with a short phrase and follow with a colon:

• Followed by bullets of information
• Each one supporting the original phrase

See how these techniques tighten the writing and enliven the reading process from our law firm example:

Analyzed and determined need for comprehensive upgrade of database, archival, and retrieval systems:

- *Responsible for hardware and software selection.*
- *Responsible for selection and installation of "cloud-based" archival systems.*
- *Responsible for compatible hardware and software upgrades.*
- *Trained users from managing partner through administrators.*
- *Achieved full upgrade, integration, and compliance in six months.*
- *Partner stated, "You brought us out of the dark ages, and neither you nor the firm missed a beat!"*

Notice in this example that by dropping personal pronouns and articles, the result is easier to read. It also speaks of a professional who knows the importance of *getting to relevant information fast.*

Big Words or Little Words?

Recruiters and hiring managers know every trick in the book; they've seen every eye-catching gimmick, and they're not impressed. Two of the biggest mistakes amateur (and professional) resume writers make is using:

1. Big words; in an effort to sound professional you end up sounding pompous and impenetrable.
2. Adjectives; when you use adjectives to describe yourself (excellent, superior, etc.), the recruiter will often discount them, muttering, "I'll be the judge of that." You'll see examples in the resume section, but notice that the use of superlatives is kept under control and backed up with hard facts.

The goal of your resume is to communicate quickly and efficiently, using short sentences and familiar words; they are easy to understand and communicate clearly and efficiently. Remember: Short words in short sentences in short paragraphs help tired eyes!

Voice and Tense

The voice you use in your resume depends on a few important factors: getting a lot said in a small space, being factual, and packaging yourself in the best way possible.

Sentences can be truncated (up to a point) by omitting pronouns—*I, you, he, she, it, they*—and articles—*a* or *the.* Dropping pronouns is a technique that saves space and allows you to brag about yourself without seeming boastful, because it gives the impression that another party is writing about you.

"I automated the office"—becomes, "Automated office." At the same time, writing in the first person makes you sound, well, personable. Use whatever works best for you. If you use personal pronouns, don't use them in every sentence—they get monotonous and take up valuable space on the page. Use a third-person voice throughout the resume, with a few final words in the first person as a closing brand statement at the end of the document to give an insight into your values. You saw an example of a functional resume with just such a personal tone that worked almost magically for its owner.

Using the third person and dropping pronouns and articles throughout the body of the resume saves space and gives you an authoritative tone.

Resume Length

The rule used to be one page for every ten years of experience, and never more than two pages. However, as jobs have gotten more complex, they require more explanation. *The length of your resume is less important than its relevance to the target job.* The first half to two-thirds of the first page of your resume should be tightly focused on a specific target job and include a Target Job Title, Performance Profile/Performance Summary, Professional Competencies, and perhaps Career Highlight sections. Do this and any reader can quickly see that you have the chops for the job.

If you are seen to be qualified, the reader will stay with you as you tell the story. Given the increasing complexity of jobs, the length and depth of your experience, and the need for data-dense resumes (which are overwhelmingly rewarded in database searches), it is idiotic to limit the length of your resume on the basis of outdated conventions from before the age of computers, let alone the Internet.

The worst—the most heinous crime of all—is to cram a seasoned professional's work history into tiny font sizes to get it onto one or two pages. Why? Here's a flash from reality: If you are a seasoned professional with a real track record requiring a complex skill-set and are climbing the ladder of success, it's likely your readers are also successful, seasoned professionals. Use tiny fonts and you annoy everyone whose eyesight has been weakened by prolonged computer use, and that means everyone. Busy senior managers simply won't read your resume because it speaks to poor judgment and communication skills, both of which are mandatory for seasoned professionals.

Let form follow function with your resume. If it takes three tightly edited pages to tell a properly focused story and make it readable, just do it.

What's the alternative? Leaving stuff out means your resume is less likely to get pulled from resume databases or sell the recruiter on your skills when it does get read.

Assuming your first page clearly demonstrates a thorough grasp of the target job, you can feel comfortable taking that second and third page, if necessary, to tell a concise story. In the resume sample chapter, you'll see examples of justifiably longer executive resumes, requiring greater length to convey a concise message of ability in a complex job.

Worrying too much about length considerations while you write is counterproductive. If the first page makes the right argument, the rest of your resume will be read with serious attention. A longer resume also means that much more space for selling your skills with relevant keywords and more opportunities to establish your brand. However, you should make every effort to maintain focus and an "if in doubt, leave it out" editing approach.

If you have more than twenty years under your belt, many older skills from the first part of your career are now irrelevant. On the whole, the rule of one page for every ten years is still a sensible *guideline*. The bottom line is that your resume can be as long as it needs to be to tell a concise and compelling story. I have never—ever—heard of a qualified candidate being rejected because her resume exceeded some arbitrary page count; it just doesn't happen.

Does My Resume Tell the Right Story?

As you write, rewrite, edit, and polish your resume, concentrate on the story your resume needs to tell. You can keep this focus in mind by regularly referring to your TJD, and then layering fact and illustration until the story is told. When the story is complete, begin to polish by asking yourself the following questions:

- Are my statements relevant to the target job?
- Where have I repeated myself?
- Can I cut out any paragraphs?
- Can I cut out any sentences?
- Can I shorten two sentences into one? If not, perhaps I can break that one long sentence into two short ones?
- Can I cut out any words?
- Can I cut out any pronouns?

If in doubt, leave it out—leave nothing but the focused story and action words!

Resumes Evolve in Layers

Resumes are written in layers. They don't spring fully formed in one draft from anyone's keyboard. They are the result of numerous drafts, each of which inches the product forward. As I was writing this edition of *Knock 'em Dead Resumes*, we worked with a public relations professional on her new resume. She did a complete resume questionnaire and TJD, and an initial resume layout template. Before we were finished, we had completed eight different versions, each evolving until we had a great finished product. It took about two and a half weeks, but then generated eight interviews in a week, proof again that 50 percent of the success of any project is in the preparation. You can see three of the eight evolving versions of this resume at the end of Chapter 2.

Proofreading Your Final Draft

Check your resume against the following points:

Contact Information

- Are your name, address, phone numbers, and e-mail address correct?
- Is your contact information on every page?
- Is the e-mail address hyperlinked, so that a reader of your resume can read it on his computer and reach out to you instantly?

Target Job Title

- Do you have a target job title that echoes the words and intent of the job titles you collected when deconstructing the target job?
- Is this followed by a short, one-sentence branding statement that captures the essence of the professional you? Only make brand statements when you really have something to brand.

Performance Profile/Performance Summary

- Does it give a concise synopsis of the professional you as it relates to the target job?
- Does the language reflect that of typical job postings for this job?
- Is it prioritized in the same way employers are prioritizing their needs in this job?
- Is it no more than five lines long, so it can be read easily? If more, can you cut it into two paragraphs or use bullets?
- Does it include reference to the *transferable skills* and *professional values* that are critical to success? If they don't fit here, make sure they are at least in the core competencies section.

Professional Competencies

- Is all spelling and capitalization correct?
- Are there any other keywords you should add?
- Do you have experience in each of the areas you've listed?
- Can you illustrate your experience in conversation?

Career Highlights

- If you included a Career/Performance Highlights section, do the entries support the central arguments of your resume?

Professional Experience

- Is your most relevant and qualifying work experience prioritized throughout the resume to correspond to the employers' needs as they have prioritized them?
- Have you avoided wasting space with unnecessarily detailed employer names and addresses?
- If employed, have you been discreet with the name of your current employer?
- Have you omitted any reference to reasons for leaving a particular job?
- Have you removed all references to past, current, or desired salaries?
- Have you removed references to your date of availability?

Education

- Is education placed in the appropriate position?
- Is your highest educational attainment shown first?
- Have you included professional courses that support your candidacy?

Chronology

- Is your work history in chronological order, with the most recent employment coming first?
- With a chronological or combination resume, does each company history start with details of your most senior position?
- Does your resume emphasize relevant experience, contributions, and achievements?
- Have you used one or more third-party endorsements of your work if they are available and relevant?
- Can you come up with a strong personal branding statement to end the resume? One that supports the focus and story you have told? Perhaps read your resume and decide which combination of your transferable skills are most relevant, and come up with a statement of how this selection of transferable skills allows you to perform in the way you do.
- Have you kept punch and focus by eliminating extraneous information?
- Have you included any volunteer, community service, or extracurricular activities that can lend strength to your candidacy?
- Have you left out lists of references and only mentioned the availability of references if there is nothing more valuable to fill up the space?
- Have you avoided treating your reader like a fool by heading your resume, "RESUME"?

Writing Style

- Have you substituted short words for long words?
- Have you used one word where previously there were two?
- Is your *average* sentence no more than twenty words? Have you shortened any sentence of more than twenty-five words or broken it into two?
- Have you kept paragraphs under five lines?
- Do your sentences begin, wherever possible, with powerful action verbs and phrases?
- Have you omitted articles and personal pronouns?

Spelling and Grammar

Incorrect spelling and poor grammar are guaranteed to annoy resume readers, besides drawing attention to your poor *written communication skills*. This is not a good opening statement in any job search. Spell checkers are *not* infallible. Check the spelling and grammar and then send your resume to the most literate person you know for input on grammar and spelling.

At *www.knockemdead.com*, our resume service offers a grammar, syntax, and spelling edit by a professional editor who also understands resumes. We will vet your resume and return it to you in thirty-six hours with tracked changes and suggestions. You need some distance from your creative efforts to gain detachment and objectivity. There is no hard-and-fast rule about how long it takes to come up with the finished product. Nevertheless, if you think you have finished, leave it alone, at least overnight. The next day, read your TJD document before reading your resume: then you will be able to read it with the mindset of a recruiter and see the parts that need tweaking.

CHAPTER 8

RESUME CUSTOMIZATION, ALTERNATIVE RESUMES, AND FORMATS NEEDED FOR AN EFFECTIVE JOB SEARCH

WITH JOB SEARCHING the way it is today, you will almost certainly need more than one resume for your job search, and you may need to repackage your background into three of four different delivery vehicles.

You'll probably need:

- Customized resumes for specific openings
- One or more resumes for other jobs you can do and want to pursue
- An ASCII resume
- A resume for your social networking site

And you might decide you need a *business card resume* and an HTML or *web-based resume*.

Customizing Your Resume for Specific Openings

Your resume is a living, breathing document, and the *primary* resume you so carefully developed is never really finished. It evolves throughout your job search as you learn more about the skills and experience your marketplace needs, and as you learn to express your possession of these skills and experiences in ways most accessible to your customer base.

Most important, it evolves every time you customize that resume in response to a particular job posting. Before sending your resume in response to any job opening, you should evaluate it against the job description, and tweak it *so that it speaks clearly and powerfully to the stated needs of that job.*

You will notice that the *transferable skills* we talk about throughout the *Knock 'em Dead* series (communication, critical thinking, multitasking, teamwork, etc.) crop up frequently in job postings:

"Work closely with" means you are a team player and work for the good of the team and the deliverables to which you are collectively committed.

"Communication skills" means you listen to understand and that you can take direction in all circumstances. It also refers to verbal and written skills, dress, body language, your social graces, and emotional maturity.

"Multitasking" does not mean you rush heedlessly from one emergency to the next; it means that you carefully order your activities based on sound time management and organizational skills.

"Problem-solving skills" means you think through the likely effects of your actions before taking them, and that you know your area of expertise well enough to identify, prevent, and solve the problems it generates on a daily basis.

Tweak Your Resume for *Keyword* Resonance

Match the job posting against your resume to see that the words you use to describe certain skills match the words the employer is using.

Then think through how the job posting requirement of, say, "work closely with others," applies to each of the employer's specific skill requirements that require you to interact with other people and other departments to get your work done. For example, an accountant working with accounts receivable might, on hearing "work closely with others," think about problem accounts and working with sales and the nonpaying customer, as well as working laterally and upward within the accounting department.

When you think through your work experience and discover achievements that speak directly to the stated needs of an employer, you can draw attention to your close match in either your resume or a cover letter.

Keywords in a Cover Letter

In a cover letter, these might appear as the company statement in quotation marks followed by an achievement in that area:

"Analytical/Critical thinking/Problem-solving skills"
- Thorough knowledge of the issues that impact productivity in Operations have resulted in a 35% increase in on-time delivery.

"Work closely with" and *"Communication skills"*
- Improvements in on-time delivery also made possible by improved communications with stakeholders: Purchasing, Supply Chain, Customer, and Customer Service; which also delivered a 20% reduction in client complaints.

"Multitasking"
- Effective Operations Management demands understanding every department's critical functions and timelines. Building these considerations into daily activities helped Finance & Supply Chain save $55,000 in last three quarters.

Keywords in a Resume

In a resume, you might decide to highlight such highly relevant achievements with a *Performance Highlights* or a *Career Highlights* section on your resume, coming right after the *Professional Competencies* section.

This section will comprise a short sequence of bulleted statements, each addressing one of the company's stated requirements, and so emphasizing the fit between the employer's needs and your capabilities. Use an example to illustrate if you can do so succinctly.

However, in your resume, space might be at more of a premium than in your cover letter, and so you would use the achievements without the quotes:

Performance Highlights
35% increase in on-time delivery + 20% reduction in client complaints

Effective Operations Management demands understanding every department's unique problems and timelines. Building these considerations into daily activities helped:

- Finance & Supply Chain, saved $55,000 in last three quarters
- Increased productivity, with a 35% increase in on-time delivery

These on-time delivery increases were achieved with improved communications, connecting Purchasing, Supply Chain, Customers, and Customer Service:

- Delivered 20% reduction in client complaints

A Job-Targeted Resume for That Other Job

With just a few years' experience in the professional world, most people reach a point where they have experience that qualifies them for more than one job. You built your *primary resume* around the job for which the odds are shortest. But that doesn't mean there aren't other jobs you can do and want to pursue.

After your primary resume is completed, it is fairly easy to create a resume for any additional job you want to pursue. Given your completed primary resume, you already have a template to start with; plus the dates, layout, chronology, contact information, and possibly the employers are all going to remain the same. There's a methodology, as I'm about to show you, that quickly helps you refocus and edit your primary resume into a resume for that second or third target job.

1. Save a duplicate copy of your primary resume, and save it under the new target job title, because although the job is different, a great deal of the information and resume layout will remain the same.
2. Complete a TJD exercise on the next target job.
3. On the duplicate copy of your resume, saved under the name of the second target job, use the new TJD to edit out irrelevant details and replace them with the higher-impact information that is more relevant to the new target job.
4. Edit and polish, and you have a customized resume for that second or third target job.

Social Networking Site Resume/Profile

Social networking has rapidly become integrated into all business activities and into the social activities of half the world. If you belong to the half of the world that isn't engaged with social media, a successful job search today demands that you'll have to change your thinking. Later in this chapter, I'll show you how to create a social networking resume/profile, and in the latest annual edition of *Knock 'em Dead: The Ultimate Job Search Guide*, I'll show you how to network effectively online.

The ASCII Resume and Where It Fits In

All companies, except the smallest locally owned and focused service/retail operations, use online recruitment as their primary staffing strategy. This means a predominantly online job search for most professionals.

An online job search means that your resume will probably have to exist in different formats for different situations, to give you the greatest visibility in your target markets. You will need to use different formats to achieve this.

ASCII, MSWord, PDF, and HTML Resumes

1. Microsoft Word or PDF files are referred to as *formatted*
2. ASCII is either plain text or with line breaks
3. Web-based/HTML

The above gobbledygook of techno-speak will all be made plain in the coming pages.

Formatted Resume

A formatted resume is your resume as created in a word-processing document, most often the ubiquitous Microsoft Word. When you attach your resume to an e-mail or print it out for distribution by traditional mail or to take to interviews, you can do it in either Microsoft Word or PDF format.

With PDF, the layout is fixed and will appear exactly as you send it, which can't always be said of Microsoft Word documents. Both ways are acceptable, and there are even people who attach their resume in both formats to give the reader a choice. I lean toward using PDF because the layout will never change no matter what. When sending an attached resume in Word or PDF by e-mail, you will mention the attachment in the body of your e-mail: "My resume is attached in a PDF document."

Plain Text or ASCII (American Standard Code for Information Interchange)

An ASCII resume looks like the average e-mail message you receive. You will see how to create two separate versions of an ASCII resume: one best suited for pasting into the body of an e-mail message after your signature, the other for cutting and pasting into resume-bank resume templates. You will likely need both.

The ASCII version of your resume is the simplest and least visually attractive; it is just the unadorned basics: letters, numbers, and a few symbols. ASCII resumes are important because *this is the only format that any and every computer can read*. The reader will not need a word-processing program such as Microsoft Word or WordPerfect, and software or printer compatibility isn't a consideration.

Web-Based or HTML Resume

A web-based/HTML resume is a "nice to have," not a "must-have." Don't even think about it until you have a properly constructed and branded resume that portrays you exactly as you wish to be seen. An HTML, web-based, or e-portfolio resume is one that can have additional features such as video and sound and can be uploaded in certain instances to resume banks and social networking sites, or even housed on the Internet at its own URL. There are some advantages to this. For example, if you work in arts, education, certain areas of communications, or technology, the ability to include audio and video clips, music, and pictures can be a plus. Likewise, if you are a web-page design professional or HTML guru, then by all means use the Internet to show your creative and technological abilities. If you are in a creative profession and would typically have a portfolio, a web resume can provide access to your work samples.

How to Convert Your Formatted Resume to ASCII

You start this simple process by opening the Microsoft Word–formatted version of your resume.

PATRICIA JOHNSON

1234 Murietta Ave. • Palmdale, CA 93550

Residence (661) 555-1234 • Mobile (661) 555-9876 • *PatJohnson@email.com*

FINANCE/ACCOUNTING PROFESSIONAL
Internal Auditor/Financial Analyst/Staff Accountant

Detail-oriented, problem solver with excellent analytical strengths and a track record of optimizing productivity, reducing costs, and increasing profit contributions. Well-developed team-building and leadership strengths with experience in training and coaching coworkers. Works well with public, clients, vendors, and coworkers at all levels. Highly motivated and goal orientated as demonstrated by completing studies toward BS in Finance, graduating with honors concurrent with full-time, progressive business experience.

—Core Competencies—

Research & Analysis/Accounts Receivable/Accounts Payable/Journal Entries/Bank Reconciliations
Payroll/Financial Statements/Auditing/General Ledger/Artist Contracts/Royalties/Escalation Clauses

PROFESSIONAL EXPERIENCE

MAJOR HOLLYWOOD STUDIO, Hollywood, CA • 2000 to Present

Achieved fast-track promotion to positions of increasing challenge and responsibility

Royalty Analyst—Music Group, Los Angeles, CA (2005–Present)

Process average of $8–9 million in payments monthly. Review artist contracts, licenses, and rate sheets to determine royalties due to producers and songwriters for leading record label. Ensure accuracy of statements sent to publishers in terms of units sold and rates applied. Research, resolve, and respond to all inquiries.

- Resolved longstanding problems substantially reducing publisher inquiries and complaints.
- Promoted to "Level 1" analyst within only one year and ahead of two staff members with longer tenure.
- Provided superior training to temporary employee that resulted in her being hired for permanent, Level 1 position after only three months.

Accounts Payable Analyst—Music & Video Distribution (2002–2005)

Processed high volume of utility bills, office equipment leases, shipping invoices, and office supplies for 12 regional branches. Assisted branches with proper invoice coding and resolving payment disputes with vendors.

- Identified longstanding duplicate payment that resulted in vendor refund of $12,000.
- Created contract-employment expenses spreadsheet; identified and resolved $24,000 in duplicate payments.
- Gained reputation for thoroughness and promptness in meeting all payment deadlines.
- Set up macro in accounts payable system that streamlined invoice payments.
- Consolidated vendor accounts, increasing productivity and reducing number of checks processed.

Accounts Receivable Analyst—Music & Video Distribution (2000–2002)

Processed incoming payments, received and posted daily check deposits, reviewed applications for vendor accounts, distributed accounting reports, and ordered office supplies. Handled rebillings of international accounts for shipments by various labels.

- Hired as permanent employee from temporary position after only three months.

Additional Experience: Billing Clerk/Accounting Clerk/Bookkeeper (*details available upon request*)

EDUCATION

BS in Finance; Graduated with Honors • CALIFORNIA STATE UNIVERSITY, Northridge, CA; 2005
Completed Studies Concurrent with Full-Time Employment

Computer Skills: Windows, Microsoft Office (Word, Excel, PowerPoint), Peachtree, J.D. Edwards, Tracs

Step One

Step one will convert the Word resume to an ASCII (or text) format. It will remove all graphic elements, standardize the font, and remove bolding, italics, and underlining. The purpose of this step is to produce a document that can be read by all operating systems (Mac, PC,

Linux, etc.), ISPs (Internet service providers), and resume-tracking software systems. You will use it for uploading and insertion into career and company websites. Here's how you do it:

1. Save resume using the "File/Save As" command.
2. In the "Save As" window, use an identifiable name such as (your name), E-Resume.
3. In "File Type" or "Format," scroll down and select "Plain Text" or "Text Only."
4. Make sure that "Insert Line Breaks" is *not* checked.
5. Make sure that "Allow Character Substitution" *is* checked.
6. Save and close.

Step Two

The purpose of step two is to make sure that the ASCII document is "clean" and that all information is left-justified to optimize readability by resume-tracking systems.

When you open the "E-Resume" file, all information will be in simple text and characters will show keyboard characters. Your resume will now look like this:

PATRICIA JOHNSON

1234 MURIETTA AVE. * PALMDALE, CA 93550

RESIDENCE (661) 555-1234 * MOBILE (661) 555-9876 * PATJOHNSON@EMAIL.COM

FINANCE/ACCOUNTING PROFESSIONAL

INTERNAL AUDITOR/FINANCIAL ANALYST/STAFF ACCOUNTANT

DETAIL-ORIENTED, PROBLEM SOLVER WITH EXCELLENT ANALYTICAL STRENGTHS AND A TRACK RECORD OF OPTIMIZING PRODUCTIVITY, REDUCING COSTS, AND INCREASING PROFIT CONTRIBUTIONS. WELL-DEVELOPED TEAM-BUILDING AND LEADERSHIP STRENGTHS WITH EXPERIENCE IN TRAINING AND COACHING COWORKERS. WORKS WELL WITH PUBLIC, CLIENTS, VENDORS, AND COWORKERS AT ALL LEVELS. HIGHLY MOTIVATED AND GOAL ORIENTATED AS DEMONSTRATED BY COMPLETING STUDIES TOWARD BS IN FINANCE, GRADUATING WITH HONORS CONCURRENT WITH FULL-TIME, PROGRESSIVE BUSINESS EXPERIENCE.

-CORE COMPETENCIES-

RESEARCH & ANALYSIS/ACCOUNTS RECEIVABLE/ACCOUNTS PAYABLE/JOURNAL ENTRIES/BANK RECONCILIATIONS

PAYROLL/FINANCIAL STATEMENTS/AUDITING/GENERAL LEDGER/ARTIST CONTRACTS/ROYALTIES/ ESCALATION CLAUSES

PROFESSIONAL EXPERIENCE

MAJOR HOLLYWOOD STUDIO, HOLLYWOOD, CA * 2000 TO PRESENT
ACHIEVED FAST-TRACK PROMOTION TO POSITIONS OF INCREASING CHALLENGE AND RESPONSIBILITY
ROYALTY ANALYST-MUSIC GROUP, LOS ANGELES, CA (2005-PRESENT)
PROCESS AVERAGE OF $8-9 MILLION IN PAYMENTS MONTHLY. REVIEW ARTIST CONTRACTS, LICENSES, AND RATE SHEETS TO DETERMINE ROYALTIES DUE TO PRODUCERS AND SONGWRITERS FOR LEADING RECORD LABEL. ENSURE ACCURACY OF STATEMENTS SENT TO PUBLISHERS IN TERMS OF UNITS SOLD AND RATES APPLIED. RESEARCH, RESOLVE, AND RESPOND TO ALL INQUIRIES.

* RESOLVED LONGSTANDING PROBLEMS SUBSTANTIALLY REDUCING PUBLISHER INQUIRIES AND COMPLAINTS.
* PROMOTED TO "LEVEL 1" ANALYST WITHIN ONLY ONE YEAR AND AHEAD OF TWO STAFF MEMBERS WITH LONGER TENURE.
* PROVIDED SUPERIOR TRAINING TO TEMPORARY EMPLOYEE THAT RESULTED IN HER BEING HIRED FOR PERMANENT, LEVEL 1 POSITION AFTER ONLY THREE MONTHS.

ACCOUNTS PAYABLE ANALYST-MUSIC & VIDEO DISTRIBUTION (2002-2005)
PROCESSED HIGH VOLUME OF UTILITY BILLS, OFFICE EQUIPMENT LEASES, SHIPPING INVOICES, AND OFFICE SUPPLIES FOR 12 REGIONAL BRANCHES. ASSISTED BRANCHES WITH PROPER INVOICE CODING AND RESOLVING PAYMENT DISPUTES WITH VENDORS.

* IDENTIFIED LONGSTANDING DUPLICATE PAYMENT THAT RESULTED IN VENDOR REFUND OF $12,000.
* CREATED CONTRACT-EMPLOYMENT EXPENSES SPREADSHEET; IDENTIFIED AND RESOLVED $24,000 IN DUPLICATE PAYMENTS.
* GAINED REPUTATION FOR THOROUGHNESS AND PROMPTNESS IN MEETING ALL PAYMENT DEADLINES.
* SET UP MACRO IN ACCOUNTS PAYABLE SYSTEM THAT STREAMLINED INVOICE PAYMENTS.
* CONSOLIDATED VENDOR ACCOUNTS, INCREASING PRODUCTIVITY AND REDUCING NUMBER OF CHECKS PROCESSED.

ACCOUNTS RECEIVABLE ANALYST-MUSIC & VIDEO DISTRIBUTION (2000-2002)
PROCESSED INCOMING PAYMENTS; RECEIVED AND POSTED DAILY CHECK DEPOSITS, REVIEWED APPLICATIONS FOR VENDOR ACCOUNTS; DISTRIBUTED ACCOUNTING REPORTS, AND ORDERED OFFICE SUPPLIES. HANDLED REBILLINGS OF INTERNATIONAL ACCOUNTS FOR SHIPMENTS BY VARIOUS LABELS.

* HIRED AS PERMANENT EMPLOYEE FROM TEMPORARY POSITION AFTER ONLY THREE MONTHS.

ADDITIONAL EXPERIENCE: BILLING CLERK/ACCOUNTING CLERK/BOOKKEEPER (DETAILS AVAILABLE UPON REQUEST)

EDUCATION

BS IN FINANCE; GRADUATED WITH HONORS * CALIFORNIA STATE UNIVERSITY, NORTHRIDGE, CA; 2005

COMPLETED STUDIES CONCURRENT WITH FULL-TIME EMPLOYMENT
COMPUTER SKILLS: WINDOWS, MICROSOFT OFFICE (WORD, EXCEL, POWERPOINT), PEACHTREE, J.D.
EDWARDS, TRACS

Now:

1. Set margins to 1" left, 2" right, 1" top and bottom.
2. Align all information to the left.
3. Check for unusual keyboard-character substitutions such as dollar signs. Usually the substitution will automatically default to asterisks, which is fine. Make changes as appropriate.
4. Correct any strange line breaks.
5. Separate sections using all caps for headings and lines composed of keyboard characters such as hyphens, equal signs, asterisks, tildes, etc.
6. Save, but don't close. Again, make sure that "Insert Line Breaks" is *not* checked and that "Allow Character Substitution" *is* checked.

Your e-resume will now look like this:

PATRICIA JOHNSON
1234 MURIETTA AVE.
PALMDALE, CA 93550
RESIDENCE (661) 555-1234
MOBILE (661) 555-9876
PATJOHNSON@EMAIL.COM
==
==
FINANCE/ACCOUNTING PROFESSIONAL
INTERNAL AUDITOR/FINANCIAL ANALYST/STAFF ACCOUNTANT
DETAIL-ORIENTED, PROBLEM SOLVER WITH EXCELLENT ANALYTICAL STRENGTHS AND A TRACK
RECORD OF OPTIMIZING PRODUCTIVITY, REDUCING COSTS, AND INCREASING PROFIT CONTRIBUTIONS.
WELL-DEVELOPED TEAM-BUILDING AND LEADERSHIP STRENGTHS WITH EXPERIENCE IN TRAINING AND
COACHING COWORKERS. WORKS WELL WITH PUBLIC, CLIENTS, VENDORS, AND COWORKERS AT ALL
LEVELS. HIGHLY MOTIVATED AND GOAL ORIENTATED AS DEMONSTRATED BY COMPLETING STUDIES
TOWARD BS IN FINANCE, GRADUATING WITH HONORS CONCURRENT WITH FULL-TIME, PROGRESSIVE
BUSINESS EXPERIENCE.
==
-CORE COMPETENCIES-
RESEARCH & ANALYSIS/ACCOUNTS RECEIVABLE/ACCOUNTS PAYABLE/JOURNAL ENTRIES/
BANK RECONCILIATIONS/PAYROLL/FINANCIAL STATEMENTS/AUDITING/GENERAL LEDGER/
ARTIST CONTRACTS/ROYALTIES/ESCALATION CLAUSES

===
===

PROFESSIONAL EXPERIENCE

MAJOR HOLLYWOOD STUDIO
HOLLYWOOD, CA
2000 TO PRESENT

ACHIEVED FAST-TRACK PROMOTION TO POSITIONS OF INCREASING CHALLENGE AND RESPONSIBILITY

~~ROYALTY ANALYST-MUSIC GROUP, LOS ANGELES, CA
~~(2005-PRESENT)

PROCESS AVERAGE OF $8-9 MILLION IN PAYMENTS MONTHLY. REVIEW ARTIST CONTRACTS, LICENSES, AND RATE SHEETS TO DETERMINE ROYALTIES DUE TO PRODUCERS AND SONGWRITERS FOR LEADING RECORD LABEL. ENSURE ACCURACY OF STATEMENTS SENT TO PUBLISHERS IN TERMS OF UNITS SOLD AND RATES APPLIED. RESEARCH, RESOLVE, AND RESPOND TO ALL INQUIRIES.

* RESOLVED LONGSTANDING PROBLEMS SUBSTANTIALLY REDUCING PUBLISHER INQUIRIES AND COMPLAINTS.

* PROMOTED TO "LEVEL 1" ANALYST WITHIN ONLY ONE YEAR AND AHEAD OF TWO STAFF MEMBERS WITH LONGER TENURE.

* PROVIDED SUPERIOR TRAINING TO TEMPORARY EMPLOYEE THAT RESULTED IN HER BEING HIRED FOR PERMANENT, LEVEL 1 POSITION AFTER ONLY THREE MONTHS.

~~ACCOUNTS PAYABLE ANALYST-MUSIC & VIDEO DISTRIBUTION
~~(2002-2005)

PROCESSED HIGH VOLUME OF UTILITY BILLS, OFFICE EQUIPMENT LEASES, SHIPPING INVOICES, AND OFFICE SUPPLIES FOR 12 REGIONAL BRANCHES. ASSISTED BRANCHES WITH PROPER INVOICE CODING AND RESOLVING PAYMENT DISPUTES WITH VENDORS.

* IDENTIFIED LONGSTANDING DUPLICATE PAYMENT THAT RESULTED IN VENDOR REFUND OF $12,000.

* CREATED CONTRACT-EMPLOYMENT EXPENSES SPREADSHEET; IDENTIFIED AND RESOLVED $24,000 IN DUPLICATE PAYMENTS.

* GAINED REPUTATION FOR THOROUGHNESS AND PROMPTNESS IN MEETING ALL PAYMENT DEADLINES.

* SET UP MACRO IN ACCOUNTS PAYABLE SYSTEM THAT STREAMLINED INVOICE PAYMENTS.

* CONSOLIDATED VENDOR ACCOUNTS, INCREASING PRODUCTIVITY AND REDUCING NUMBER OF CHECKS PROCESSED.

~~ACCOUNTS RECEIVABLE ANALYST-MUSIC & VIDEO DISTRIBUTION
~~(2000-2002)

PROCESSED INCOMING PAYMENTS; RECEIVED AND POSTED DAILY CHECK DEPOSITS, REVIEWED APPLICATIONS FOR VENDOR ACCOUNTS; DISTRIBUTED ACCOUNTING REPORTS AND ORDERED OFFICE SUPPLIES. HANDLED REBILLINGS OF INTERNATIONAL ACCOUNTS FOR SHIPMENTS BY VARIOUS LABELS. * HIRED AS PERMANENT EMPLOYEE FROM TEMPORARY POSITION AFTER ONLY THREE MONTHS.

ADDITIONAL EXPERIENCE: BILLING CLERK/ACCOUNTING CLERK/BOOKKEEPER
(DETAILS AVAILABLE UPON REQUEST)

==
==

EDUCATION

BS IN FINANCE; GRADUATED WITH HONORS
CALIFORNIA STATE UNIVERSITY
NORTHRIDGE, CA
2005
COMPLETED STUDIES CONCURRENT WITH FULL-TIME EMPLOYMENT
COMPUTER SKILLS: WINDOWS, MICROSOFT OFFICE (WORD, EXCEL, POWERPOINT), PEACHTREE, J.D. EDWARDS, TRACS

Step Three

Step three will create a resume that you can cut and paste directly into e-mails. While it appears to be the same as the previous version, in this step you will have line breaks at the end of each line. Since the margins have already been set at 1" left and 2" right, the new file *with* line breaks will contain lines having no more than 65 characters. This is the standard width of e-mail windows, and will fit into a standard screenshot. If you had cut and pasted the original e-resume into an e-mail without this step, the lines would have scrolled off the page and been hard to read.

1. Save again, using the "Save As" command, this time making sure that "Insert Line Breaks" *is* checked, as well as allowing character substitution. Use a save name such as (your name), e-mailResume.
2. This version will have line breaks and will fit a standard screenshot. Remember, this is the version to cut and paste directly *into* e-mail.

The resume will look like this:

PATRICIA JOHNSON
1234 Murietta Ave.
Palmdale, CA 93550
Residence (661) 555-1234
Mobile (661) 555-9876
PatJohnson@email.com
==
==
FINANCE/ACCOUNTING PROFESSIONAL
Internal Auditor/Financial Analyst/Staff Accountant
Detail-oriented, problem solver with excellent analytical strengths and a track record of optimizing productivity, reducing costs, and increasing profit contributions. Well-developed team-building and leadership strengths with experience in training and coaching coworkers. Works well with public, clients, vendors, and coworkers at all levels. Highly motivated and goal orientated as demonstrated by completing studies toward BS in Finance, graduating with honors concurrent with full-time, progressive business experience.
==
-Core Competencies-
Research & Analysis/Accounts Receivable/Accounts Payable/Journal Entries/Bank Reconciliations Payroll/Financial Statements/Auditing/General Ledger/Artist Contracts/Royalties/Escalation Clauses
==
==
PROFESSIONAL EXPERIENCE

MAJOR HOLLYWOOD STUDIO
Hollywood, CA
2000 to Present
Achieved fast-track promotion to positions of increasing challenge and responsibility
~~Royalty Analyst-Music Group, Los Angeles, CA
~~(2005-Present)
Process average of $8-9 million in payments monthly. Review artist contracts, licenses, and rate sheets to determine royalties due to producers and songwriters for leading record label. Ensure accuracy of statements sent to publishers in terms of units sold and rates applied. Research, resolve, and respond to all inquiries.

* Resolved longstanding problems substantially reducing publisher inquiries and complaints.

* Promoted to "Level 1" analyst within only one year and ahead of two staff members with longer tenure.
* Provided superior training to temporary employee that resulted in her being hired for permanent, Level 1 position after only three months.

~~Accounts Payable Analyst–Music & Video Distribution
~~(2002–2005)
Processed high volume of utility bills, office equipment leases, shipping invoices, and office supplies for 12 regional branches. Assisted branches with proper invoice coding and resolving payment disputes with vendors.

* Identified longstanding duplicate payment that resulted in vendor refund of $12,000.
* Created contract-employment expenses spreadsheet; identified and resolved $24,000 in duplicate payments.
* Gained reputation for thoroughness and promptness in meeting all payment deadlines.
* Set up macro in accounts payable system that streamlined invoice payments.
* Consolidated vendor accounts, increasing productivity and reducing number of checks processed.

~~Accounts Receivable Analyst–Music & Video Distribution
~~(2000–2002)
Processed incoming payments; received and posted daily check
deposits, reviewed applications for vendor accounts; distributed accounting reports, and ordered office supplies. Handled re-billings of international accounts for shipments by various labels.
* Hired as permanent employee from temporary position after only three months.

Additional Experience: Billing Clerk/Accounting Clerk/Bookkeeper (details available upon request)
==
==
EDUCATION

BS in Finance; Graduated with Honors
CALIFORNIA STATE UNIVERSITY
Northridge, CA
2005
Completed Studies Concurrent with Full-Time Employment
Computer Skills: Windows, Microsoft Office (Word, Excel, PowerPoint), Peachtree, J.D. Edwards, Tracs

You now have your very own ASCII resume for the resume databases. But remember that, since your resume is constantly evolving, you will have to repeat this conversion process regularly.

Social Networking Profile/Resume

Social networking has exploded on the Internet over the last few years, and using this approach in a job search has proved wildly successful for many people. Its impact has been further increased because recruiters see professional networking sites like LinkedIn as the perfect venue to find candidates: A long-time friend and recruiter of CFOs compared using LinkedIn for recruiting to "shooting fish in a barrel."

With well over 100 million professionals using LinkedIn for networking, you would be crazy to ignore it. There are two reasons for using a social networking site: to find people and to be found.

In both instances, you will need to create a profile of who you are. When you reach out to potential networking contacts, they are likely to check out your profile before responding. When recruiters and others are in turn looking for someone like you, the quality of that profile determines:

- Whether you will be found amongst those 100 million–plus users
- Whether the recruiter follows through with a contact

First Things First

But first things first: Upload your primary resume. This won't become your profile, but having it available gives you some visibility immediately. Use the application box.net to upload it: It works far better than the LinkedIn tool, which can create formatting problems. It is then available to a recruiter to download, print out, or forward. As a privacy issue, you may wish to remove your street address and just use the city of your residence as the geographical identifier.

How to Create a Killer LinkedIn Profile

The profile you create will give you visibility with search engines and enable others to find you: Remember that there could well be 150 million LinkedIn users by the time you read this! Also, recruiters and hiring managers who have already seen your resume increasingly like to check out your social profile(s) to find out more about you. This is why—once you are satisfied with your profile and *not* before—I suggested adding hyperlinks at the end of your resume.

Your LinkedIn profile, and any other social networking profiles you subsequently develop, are your public face and your most important passive marketing tool, so it deserves careful thought and effort. And with so many other profiles out there, you need to make sure yours is easily found and accessible.

Headline

The first thing anyone sees about you is your name and a brief headline. You can start with the Target Job Title from your *primary* resume, and then you have about ten words with which to describe who you are professionally. For maximum impact, check your TJD for the highest frequency keywords used to describe your job and use those, because they are the words most likely to be used by recruiters searching for someone like you.

Summary

You have a huge amount of space here and, consequently, your summary will probably grow over time as you develop the rest of your profile. The nature of a social networking site is social, so everything you write should be in the first person.

You need to give recruiters the right information to find you, but the nature of these sites is such that you can give more information and expand on the tight focus you use in a job-targeted resume. Start by adding those five or so lines from your *primary* resume's performance profile/performance summary. Add to it with any additional information from the performance profiles/performance summaries of additional resumes, including anything that might be relevant from your old *general* resume.

Some people writing on this topic suggest writing about your interests here. I strongly disagree. This information is irrelevant to all but the most interested parties and giving it to them upfront is likely to cost you readers. LinkedIn has provided a space for this in your profile, and those personal interests should appear in the proper place: at the end of your profile.

Work Experience

Like a traditional chronological resume, the experience section of your profile begins with your current job and work. Again, you can cut-and-paste the entry from your primary resume first, then add to this with additional information from subsequent resumes.

While the rule of thumb for social networking is a first-person voice, you might want to stick with the attenuated third-person voice you used in your resume; it is more immediate and allows you to speak for yourself without seeming self-congratulatory.

When everything is pasted in, review the entry and see if there is additional experience you would like to add. There is plenty of space here, so as long as your entries for each job start with the most important information from your *primary* resume, you can add additional supporting information at the end of each entry.

Whatever you do, don't cheap out and just list your current job: It can give the appearance that this is all the experience you have. LinkedIn tells us that you are twelve times more likely to be found by recruiters when you have more than one job listed, perhaps because those other jobs allow you to weight your profile with enough relevant keywords to be found in recruiters' database searches.

Professional and Technology Competencies

Adding a Professional Competencies and/or Technology Competencies section to your LinkedIn profile has the same benefits as adding it to your resume: It makes your profile more visible in database searches and your skills more readily accessible to readers.

Click on *Edit Profile*, then look for the *Add Skills* link. You can paste up to fifty skills in the dialog box.

Education

Cut-and-paste the information from your resume. However, unlike your resume, you might want to consider listing high school as well: LinkedIn says that this increases your networking opportunities, and it makes sense in this context.

Certifications

Add all your professional certifications, and because this is a networking site, you can add certifications related to activities outside of your professional life, such as your scuba diving or ballroom dancing certifications.

Interests

Finally, the place where it is appropriate to add something about your outside interests! If someone has read this far, learning that I enjoy history, historical fiction, kayaking, ballroom dancing, am an obsessed collector of phonographs, prohibition-era cocktail shakers, art-deco chrome, and am the world's worst bass player might be of interest, because it gives me an additional dimension; but coming earlier in my profile it would only be a distraction.

Associations and Awards

Include membership in any associations or societies. List profession-related organizations and professional awards first, then follow with groups and awards related to your personal interests.

Reading List

If you list anything here, I would be sure to include at least 50 percent profession-oriented materials.

Headshot

While a headshot on a resume is inappropriate, it is pretty much expected with a social networking profile. Springing for a professional headshot is the best option, but if this isn't possible, you can probably do a passable job with the help of a friend.

Review professional-looking headshots on LinkedIn, because you'll be looking at the size yours will be, and you can evaluate what works and what doesn't. You'll notice the distance they seem to be taken from and the plain, light-colored backgrounds that seem most popular. You'll notice that almost everyone is looking directly into the camera and is smiling to some degree.

Spelling, Punctuation, and Grammar

The same considerations you applied to spelling, punctuation, and grammar in your resume also apply here. If you have problems creating your profile or editing it, at *www.knockemdead .com,* we create LinkedIn profiles for our resume clients and also offer a separate social networking profile editing service, similar to the one we offer for resumes.

Save Your Work

As with all things computer-related, if you don't back up your work, somewhere along the line you are going to lose it. My recommendation is to save everything in a Microsoft Word document, *and to back up that document.*

LinkedIn Networking Tactics

You can learn much more about networking and how to leverage your social networking presence in the latest annual edition of *Knock 'em Dead: The Ultimate Job Search Guide.*

HTML/Multimedia Resume Considerations

An HTML or multimedia resume can be a sensible option if you work in a field where visuals and sound and/or graphics represent critical skills. About 50 percent of resume banks and social networking sites accept HTML resumes; plus a simple HTML resume can be created by using the "Save as HTML" command, which you can access in Microsoft Word when you save and name your documents.

If you want to create a small website, you can create a much richer experience for the viewer, adding audio and video and other bells and whistles if they will help. You can add a hyperlink in your standard resume, or in your cover letter/e-mail, that takes the reader to your web-hosted resume. This has the advantage of allowing the viewer to see your background positioned exactly as you wish it to be, with the enrichment of additional media.

HTML and Multimedia Design Considerations

- Don't be seduced by design capabilities for the sake of their flashiness; remember the needs of your customer and your communication goals. Use technology to make life easier for the visitor. For example, your e-mail address can be a hyperlink, so that clicking on it immediately launches the user's e-mail to contact you.
- If the HTML resume ends up being a complex document with graphics, sound, and video, layout is going to be a major consideration. You don't want the mission-critical topics—performance profile/performance summary, core and technical competencies, education, work samples, etc.—to get lost in the glitz. It is all too easy to get caught up in the aforementioned glitz of building a website, because it's just a convenient and fun way to put off the real grunt work of building your resume.

- Provide a hyperlink that allows the user to print out that beautifully formatted PDF version of your resume.
- Don't start from ground zero; find an example you like and copy it.

Is an Interactive Portfolio/Web-Based Resume a Waste of Time?

Much depends on your situation and what you are trying to sell and to whom. It's a nice thing for anyone to have, but not mandatory unless:

- Your profession is web-based
- Your work involves visual and auditory components
- Your work is technology-based with a communications component
- Demonstrating technological savvy is a plus for your branding

Since an online portfolio is the most complex resume document you can create, you want the core content of the site to be finished before you start creating this version with all its bells and whistles. The most practical approach is to get your Microsoft Word resume completed, along with the necessary ASCII text versions. Once you've done your due diligence as you develop the other versions, and have your job search up to speed, you can decide if you need to develop this third variation.

Some disadvantages include:

- Adding the graphics and visuals and video and audio is a time-consuming process, and can be expensive if you hire someone to do it for you; most professionals don't need to present themselves in this way.
- If you want an HTML or web-based resume, you'll need to build a website or have one built. This website will then have to be hosted somewhere and you'll have registration fees and hosting fees and announcement fees (elementary optimization); if this is a foreign language to you, as a website owner you'll have to learn it, because all these things cost money. Apart from paying to have such a site built, these costs are usually small, but they are ongoing and add up over time.
- If you want to build it yourself without any experience, there is a learning curve involved.
- Because the content is more complex, these documents take longer to open and work through, so the content needs to be compelling if you are going to hold anyone's attention.
- You will build a web-based resume because you hope to *send* people to see it. You can't expect recruiters to flock to it, since there is fierce competition to achieve a reasonable search ranking in the world of resumes. So unless you spend a small fortune on optimization, you can't realistically expect much traffic; it is more a place to which you send recruiters.

For most people, having a LinkedIn Profile will be quite adequate.

The Business Card Resume

The first time you hear about a business card resume, it can sound like a gimmick, and you should know better than to waste valuable job search time pursuing gimmicks. That said, business cards are an accepted sales tool the world over, and for a job hunter they're so much less intrusive than carrying around a wad of resumes under your arm.

If you want to try a business card resume, you must consider the severely limited space available to you and use that space wisely:

Front of the Card

- List critical information: Your name, Target Job Title, telephone number, and e-mail address.
- Use legible, business-like (Times Roman, Arial) fonts.
- Make it readable. Limit the word count so that you can maximize font size to increase readability; better to have one legible e-mail address than add a social network address and have them both be illegible.
- No one in a position to hire you can read an 8-point font, and reminding someone that they are old and have failing eyesight . . . not a good sales pitch.

Back of the Card

Space is minimal, so less is more and readability is everything; the words you choose must communicate *both* your understanding of the job and your ability to deliver when you are doing that job.

1. Repeat your Target Job Title.
2. This is followed by a two-word headline on the next line: Performance Profile/Performance Summary.
3. Follow this with a single short sentence that addresses the #1 deliverable of your target job. The #1 deliverable in your job (and all jobs) is—say it with me now—the identification, prevention, and solution of problems within a specific area of professional expertise. It is ultimately what we all get hired to do.

4. Finish with a social network address that delivers a comprehensive professional profile to any interested reader, such as your LinkedIn profile, your web-based resume, or any other URL that delivers the full story on your professional capabilities.

As an example we can all relate to, an accounting professional who worked in accounts receivable might have the rear side of a business card resume that looks something like this:

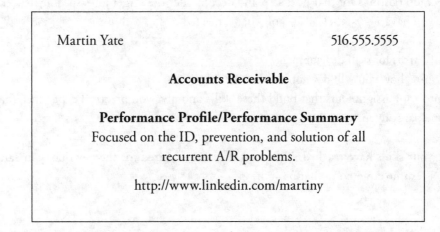

Martin Yate   516.555.5555

Accounts Receivable

Performance Profile/Performance Summary
Focused on the ID, prevention, and solution of all
recurrent A/R problems.

http://www.linkedin.com/martiny

Notice that by starting this mini-resume with a verb, you not only show understanding of what is at the heart of this job, you also deliver a powerful personal brand statement by telling the reader what to expect.

Resume for Promotions

We tend to think of our resume as a tool to get a new job at another company, and forget that we can use it to get a promotion where we already are.

You need a job-targeted resume for pursuing internal promotions because:

- No one is paying as much attention to you as you would like.
- It shows an employer you are serious about growth.
- It's a powerful way to get yourself viewed in a different light.
- It puts you on a par with external candidates who will have job-targeted resumes.
- It puts you ahead of these candidates, because you are a known quantity.
- When you have the required skills, it's much easier to get promoted from within.

Promotions come to those who earn them, not as a reward for watching the clock for three years. Thinking through what's really needed for your next step up the ladder, building the skills to earn that promotion, and then creating a resume that positions you for the job, is smart strategic thinking.

Your promotion campaign starts with determining a specific target job for the next logical step up the ladder, and then understanding the requirements for someone holding that job title.

Collect job postings for that next step and deconstruct the target job's specific deliverables. Once you have a crystal-clear idea of what is needed to succeed in the target job:

- Identify areas for skill development.
- Determine how you will develop these skills.
- Volunteer for assignments that build these skills and give you practical experience that can become part of your resume.

Once your skills have reached 70 percent of those required for the new job, you can start building a resume targeted to that promotion.

Proofread and Test-E-mail All Versions of Your Resume

Before you send any version of your resume, proofread it carefully. Send your electronic cover letters and resume attachments to yourself and to a friend or family member. Ask them for printouts of your practice e-mail messages and resumes to ensure that what you intended to send is actually what was received, and can be printed out. Often, this exercise will help you find mistakes, bloopers, or larger problems incurred during the conversion process. If you find typos at this late stage, reward yourself with a smack upside the head for being sloppy. The most common and annoying problem is that the contact information you carefully put at the top of the second page now appears halfway down it; these are the important mistakes you can easily catch with this exercise.

CHAPTER 9
READY TO LAUNCH

WHY EVERYONE HATES reading resumes and what you can do about it. Here are some powerful construction strategies to make your resume simultaneously information-dense and visually accessible to tired, distracted recruiters and hiring managers.

You are in the home stretch, giving your resume the final polish before releasing it to a very discriminating public. It has to be:

- Job-focused and data-dense to beat out the competition in the resume database wars.
- Typographically clean, and visually accessible to accommodate the recruiters' initial scan.
- Headline-rich and textually concise to deliver a compelling message.

Make this happen and your resume will get pulled for review from the resume databases. It will then get serious attention from recruiters and hiring managers.

The Importance of Immediate Impact

Your resume will get between five and forty seconds of initial attention, and the more accessible it is to the tired and distracted eyes of recruiters and hiring managers, the closer the attention it will receive. You'll improve the chances that your resume will receive attention if you:

1. *Make it readable.* Stop worrying about page count. In resumes, as in everything, *form follows function*; use the space you need to tell the story you need to tell. Use 11- and 12-point fonts that are easier on adult eyes. You do not have to use 9- and 10-point fonts only a twenty-year-old can read in order to cram everything on one or two pages. (Tip: Twenty-year-olds are almost never in a position to hire you.)
2. *Check your headlines.* They help a reader achieve and maintain focus. The first page of your resume always needs to start off strong, and there is no better way of doing this than with headlines that help accessibility and comprehension.

Target Job Title
(What the resume is about)

Performance Profile/Performance Summary
(A snapshot of what I can do)

Professional Competencies
(The key professional skills that help me do my job well)

Technology Competencies
(Optional: the technical skills that help me do my job well)

Performance Highlights

(Optional: my outstanding achievements as they relate to the job)

Professional Experience

(Where and when everything happened)

3. *Check Professional Competencies and Technology Competencies.* These are the hard skills that enable you to do what you do. Each word or phrase should act as a headline of capability and topic for discussion.
4. *Performance/Career Highlights.* This is an optional section, provided that your experience has the achievements to support it.

A first page with these headlines and job-focused content in readable fonts will draw in the reader.

Fonts and Font Sizes

You can use one font throughout your resume, but never use more than two fonts in your resume: one for headlines and the other for the body copy. The most popular fonts for business communication are Arial and Times or Times New Roman. They probably look boring because you are so used to seeing them, but you see them so much because they are clear and very readable. Bottom line: They work. The biggest criticism of these fonts is their lack of flair and design value. Below are some other fonts that are good for headlines and body copy, since they are readable and almost universally recognized by printers (obviously a plus if you plan on having someone actually read your resume). I mentioned some acceptable fonts earlier. The nature of each font is unique and the actual size of each is going to vary. Don't be a slave to 12-point: Sometimes 11-point might work with a particular font. Just don't use a smaller font size to keep your resume to one or two pages. Your resume must be easily readable by those tired and distracted eyes.

Avoid or minimize capitalized text, as it's tough on the eyes. Many people think it makes a powerful statement when used in headlines, but all it does is cause eyestrain and give the reader the impression that you are shouting.

Good for headlines:
Arial
Times/Times New Roman
Century Gothic

Verdana
Gill Sans
Lucida Sans

Good for body copy:
Arial
Times/Times New Roman
Garamond
Georgia
Goudy Old Style

Each of the above is in 12-point font, but you can see that the nature of each font is unique and the actual size of each is going to vary.

Avoid "script" fonts that look similar to handwriting. While they look attractive to the occasional reader, they are harder on the eyes of people who read any amount of business correspondence. That said, in the resumes later in this book you will see examples of just this sort of font. For example, the arts, education, and (sometimes) health care are areas where the warmer and more personal look of a script font can work and still present a professional-looking resume. Use with discretion.

Avoid Typos Like the Plague!

Resumes that are riddled with misspeltings get siht-canned *fast*. How annoying is that last sentence? You have a spellchecker; use it.

A couple of years back, I counseled an executive vice president in the $400k-per-year range. He was having problems getting in front of the right people. The first paragraph of his resume stated that he was an executive with "superior communication skills." Unfortunately, the other twelve words of the sentence contained a spelling error! Fortunately, we caught it. In an age of spellcheckers, this sloppiness isn't acceptable at any level.

A word of caution: The spellchecker can't catch everything, so you'll have to do some editing work yourself. For example, spellcheck won't catch the common mistyping of "form" for "from" because "form" is a word. Similarly, your spellchecker can't help you, but educated people will immediately recognize a cretin who doesn't know *too* from *to* and *two*, *your* from *you're*, or *it's* from *its*.

Once you decide on font(s), stick with them. More than two fonts will be vaguely disquieting to the reader. You can do plenty to liven up the visual impact of the page and create emphasis with **bold**, *italic*, ***bold italic***, underlining, sizing of words, and highlighting, used judiciously.

Remember that spellcheckers aren't infallible either and will confuse words and their appropriate usage, so get someone you trust to check it over as well. You can also use our *Knock 'em Dead* editor for a typographical and grammar check; just come to the resume services page at the website.

Proofing the Print Resume

Even in the age of e-mail and databases, you will need print versions of your resume. For example, you should always take printed copies to your interviews: This guarantees each interviewer will have your background laid out in the way you want it. Print it out now to ensure that the onscreen layout matches that of the printed document. Make sure the pagination of the printed copy works the way you intend. Double check the printed copy for:

- Layout and balance
- Typos and grammatical errors
- Punctuation and capitalization
- Page alignment errors
- That everything has been underlined, capitalized, bolded, italicized, and indented exactly as you intended

Print it out on as many different printers as you reasonably can. Why? Depending on the printer, you can find fonts performing differently; that's one of the reasons for using Times and Arial: They print without problems on every printer.

Appearance Checklist

Let the resume rest overnight or longer, then pick it up and review it with fresh eyes, immediately after you have reread your TJD.

- What's your immediate reaction to it? Is it clear who and what this document is about? Does it clearly address the needs of your TJD? Are the lines clean?
- Does the copy under each of your headlines tell a convincing story?
- Does the first page of the resume identify you as someone clearly capable of delivering on the job's requirements?
- Have you used only one side of the page?
- Are your fonts readable, in the 11- to 12-point range?

- Does the layout accommodate the reader's needs, rather than outmoded concerns on resume length?
- Are your paragraphs no more than five lines long? Are your sentences fewer than twenty words long?
- Are your sentences short on personal pronouns and long on action verbs?
- Is there plenty of white space around important areas, such as Target Job Title and your Opening and Closing Brand Statements? Recruiters and managers may be reviewing resumes on handheld devices, and plenty of space helps readability.

The Final Product

The paper version of your resume should be printed on standard 8½" x 11" (letter-size) paper. Paper comes in different weights and textures; good resume-quality paper has a weight designation of between 20 and 25 pounds. Lighter paper feels flimsy and curls; heavier paper is unwieldy. Most office supply stores carry paper and envelopes packaged as kits for resumes and cover letters.

As for paper color, white, pale gray, and cream are the prime choices. They are straightforward, no-nonsense colors that speak directly to your professionalism, assuming you want to be perceived as straightforward and no-nonsense. I'm assured that some of the pale pastel shades can be both attractive and effective. Personally, I think that on a first meeting, most professionals don't come off as strongly as they might when dressed in pink.

Cover letter stationery should have the same contact information as your resume and should *always* match the color and weight of the paper used. Again, it's part of the professional branding issue that underlies all the little things you pay attention to in a job search.

Set up letterhead for your cover letter stationery, using the same fonts you used on the resume. The coordinated paper size, color, weight, and fonts will give you a cohesive look.

CHAPTER 10
THE RESUMES

I HAVE INCLUDED resumes from a wide range of jobs so that you will be able to find a resume telling a story similar to yours. However, *resume layouts are tailored not to the job but to the person and their story.* So when you see a resume layout that works for you, use it: Don't be restrained because the example is of someone in another profession.

Chantile Fausett

500 La Villa • Brentwood, New York 11717 • (631) 555-2233 • ERNurse@med.net

CLINICAL NURSE ASSISTANT
ER...Shock/Trauma...Immediate Care...Triage

Performance Profile/Performance Summary

- Two years' experience as a Clinical Nurse Assistant in ER, Shock/Trauma, Immediate Care, and Triage units.
- Maintain strong observation, assessment, and intervention skills essential to providing competent patient care.
- Advocate for patients/family rights; effectively communicate a patient's needs and concerns to medical team.
- Hardworking and energetic; adapt easily to change, stressful environments, and flexible work schedules.

Education

Western Community College, Brentwood, NY   2007–Present
Liberal Arts Program with a concentration in Nursing
Coursework: Anatomy and Physiology, Chemistry, Psychology, Sociology, Statistics

North Brentwood School of Nursing, Brentwood, NY   2006
Clinical Assistant Skills Upgrade Program

Licenses & Certifications

New York State Certified Clinical Nurse Assistant   2002
Basic EKG and Phlebotomy

Professional Experience

North Brentwood Hospital, Brentwood, New York   4/01–Present
Clinical Nurse Assistant

- Work with a team of nurses and physicians throughout Emergency Room, Shock/Trauma, Immediate Care, and Triage departments for Brentwood Hospital, one of the only Level I Trauma hospitals on Long Island.
- Care for up to 200 patients per shift within a 29-bed Emergency Room Unit, and for patients in 7-bed Trauma Unit; assist with intubating of patients, life support systems, and general post-mortem procedures.
- Provide direct patient care in areas of vital signs, phlebotomy, EKGs, treatment of surgical wounds, gynecological examinations, Activities of Daily Living, and patient transportation within the hospital.
- Prepare patients for transfer to all critical care units, demonstrating quick thinking skills and ability to multitask while remaining focused and calm under pressure.
- Under the direction of the staff nurse, perform initial assessments of patients upon admission to Triage unit, and establish a Plan-of-Care for all patients.

Clinical Nurse Assistant continued

- Assist orthopedic physicians with splinting, casting, positioning, and set-up of tractions.
- Closely monitor and report changes in patients' conditions and malfunctioning of medical equipment.
- Precept new CNAs exercising strong leadership skills, ability to prioritize and delegate assignments.
- Prepare and maintain sanitary conditions of patients' rooms in full compliance with regulatory guidelines.
- Worked alongside pharmacists at Brentwood Hospital and One Way Pharmacy, overseeing the counting, verification, and logging of pharmaceuticals for the fulfillment of 200-350 daily prescriptions.
- Provided customer service, processed payments, and coordinated pickups, drop-offs, and refills.

Prior Positions at Brentwood
Hospital Attendant; Pharmacist Assistant Evening/Night Shifts
Provided excellence in customer service, processed payments, and coordinated pickups,
drop-offs, and refills.

One Way Pharmacy, West Islip, NY   6/99–10/00
Pharmacist Assistant

Safeway Transportation, Islip, NY   5/98–06/98
Customer Service Representative

Paulina Rodriquez
CDA, EFDA, CPR certified
Little Rock, AR 72201   501.555-2394   toothfairy@aol.com

DENTAL ASSISTANT
ORAL SURGERY ▪ PERIODONTICS ▪ ENDODONTICS ▪ ORTHODONTICS
"Professional, poised, calm and competent"

Performance Summary
Skilled, energetic, and flexible, with experience in 4-handed dentistry, radiology, sterilization, laboratory, and office duties. Adept at earning patients' trust and confidence. Demonstrated initiative and commitment, and a proven asset to a growing practice.

Core Dental Skills

➢ 4-Handed Dentistry	➢ Infection Control	➢ Preventative Care
➢ Oral Surgery/Extraction	➢ Casts/Impressions	➢ Emergency Treatment
➢ Root Canals	➢ Diagnostic X-Rays	➢ Instrument Sterilization
➢ Prosthetics/Restorations	➢ Teeth Whitening	➢ Radiology
➢ Tray Setups	➢ Dental Records	➢ Dental Histories
➢ Patient Prep	➢ Supplies	➢ Autoclave/Ultrasound
➢ Policies and Procedures	➢ Lab/Office Duties	➢ Patient Education

Chair-side Experience
Prepare patients for procedures – ensure comfort and develop trust; calm distressed patients; instruct patients on postoperative and general oral health care; take and record medical and dental histories.
Oversee cleanliness of operatories and instruments; ensure safe/sanitary conditions using autoclave, ultrasound, and dry heat instrument sterilization.
- Prepare tray setups for dental procedures. Obtain dental records prior to appointment.
- Assist dentist with extractions, fillings, and sealants. Take casts and impressions for prosthetics/restorations.

Laboratory Experience
- Prepare materials for impressions and restorations.
- Pour models and make casts.
- Expose radiographs and process X-ray film.

Office Experience
- Greet patients; arrange and confirm appointments; keep treatment records.
- Order dental supplies and materials; maintain stock in accordance with budgets.
- Develop and document policies and procedures. Share best practices with staff.

Professional History

Dr. George Rose, Little Rock   January 2002 – Present
Chair-side Assistant

Dr. George Rose, Little Rock   Jan 2002 – Present
Chair-side Assistant
Dr. Victoria Mercer, Little Rock   Sept 2001 – Dec 2001
Student Intern/Chair-side Assistant
Dr. John Mann, Little Rock   October 2001
Student Intern/Nitrous Oxide/Oxygen Administration

Education
B.B.A. University of Tacoma, Tacoma, WA   May 1990

Professional Development
American Red Cross   2002 – 2004
  ➢ CPR Certification – Adult, Infant, and Child
ADA Continuing Education Recognition Program   2003
  ➢ Tooth Bleaching, Home Study Educators
Little Rock Community College   2002
  ➢ Certified Dental Assistant
University of Arkansas School of Dentistry   2002
  ➢ Expanded Function Dental Assistant (EFDA)
  ➢ Schuster Center for Professional Development   2001 – 2004
  ➢ Colorado Radiology Certification   2001
  ➢ Nitrous Oxide/Oxygen Administration Certification   2001
  ➢ Photocopier Technician Certification   1993
ADA Midwinter Dental Conventions   2000 – 2003

Excellent references available on request.

JESSICA BUSH

35 W. Castle Drive ◆ Buck Head, GA 34203 ◆ 404-671-3308 ◆
JBPharma@gmail.com

Pharmacy Operations

Performance Summary

Licensed pharmacist dedicated to pursuing the highest quality of pharmacist's care. 14+ years' experience in pharmacy and pharmacy practice settings, including retail, hospital, sales, and long-term care. In-depth knowledge of all pharmaceutical operations, including drug distribution systems, drug utilization evaluation, equipment and delivery systems, emerging medications, and multi-state pharmacy regulations.

- Calm, flexible, and focused in deadline-driven, fast-paced, and urgent environments.
- Accurate and detail oriented with superior organizational skills.
- Services delivered with a sense of timeliness, accountability, and integrity.
- Proven ability to quickly resolve problems and implement solutions while moving seamlessly from strategy to operations.
- Superb interpersonal skills, with ability to build and maintain strategic business/client relationships while interfacing positively with people of all levels and backgrounds.

Professional Competencies

- ✓ Customer Development/Service
- ✓ Marketing & Sales
- ✓ Problem Resolution
- ✓ Multi-site Management
- ✓ Training/Development
- ✓ Innovation
- ✓ Presentations
- ✓ Coaching
- ✓ Negotiation
- ✓ Project Management
- ✓ Reports
- ✓ Long-Term Care
- ✓ Technically Adept
- ✓ Financial Reporting
- ✓ Relationship Building

Professional Experience

JustCare, Inc., Atlanta, GA
2010 – Present
Regional provider of a broad array of pharmacy-related products to hospitals, outpatient surgery clinics, and long-term care facilities.

Divisional Director of Florida Operations   2012 – Present
Responsible for operational management of all Florida accounts, including pharmacies in 42 client facilities. Assist in division's multi-pharmacy budgeting process of $500M in annual sales and approximately two million dispensed prescriptions.

- Cost savings of $250K annually with new stat delivery reduction initiatives.
- Developed key performance indicator dashboard to conduct weekly and monthly reviews of site efficiency and service levels.
- Identified and provided assistance and upgrades for under-performing pharmacies.
- Increased pharmacy performance: 8% increase in revenue, 4% increase in operating profit.
- Partner with Divisional Compliance Officer to identify regulatory goals and corresponding operational processes and best practices.

160

- Establish and execute operational best practices and standards and performance improvement plans to facilitate high-level, consistent patient care through provision of pharmaceuticals in challenged pharmacy sites.
- Research, evaluate, and implement new technologies, including eMARs, CPOE, e-Prescribing, and automation across 42 client sites.

JustCare, Inc., Gainesville, FL

Regional Manager Florida Operations   2010 – 2012

Accountable for multi-site management of 37 client pharmacies and annualized revenue of $377M.

- Managed 37 client pharmacies to ensure financial and operational success as well as compliance with federal, state, and local regulations.
- Assisted in consolidating Rite Aid SeniorMed subsidiary acquisition, capturing additional $37M in annual revenue.
- Implemented hub/spoke model for Florida pharmacies, resulting in efficiencies and significant cost reductions.
- Secured $5.5M in annualized revenue as part of Kroger pharmacy acquisition integration in Orlando.
- Key Account Manager for Top Shelf Healthcare Management, with eight long-term nursing facilities and annualized revenue of $4.2M, plus five assisted living facilities for New Life Management with $2.2M in annual revenue.

Eli Lilly and Company, Indianapolis, IN

Sales Representative   2001 – 2010

- Managed finance and budgets to achieve corporate goals, and ensured regulatory compliance of pharmacies for annual State Board of Pharmacy inspection. Recruited, selected, trained, and coached all personnel.
- Increased productivity by coordinating training, implementation, and evaluation of IV program - $400K.

CVS, Gainesville, FL   1999 – 2001
Pharmacy Manager

CVS, Hilton Head, SC   1997 – 1999
Pharmacy Manager

Education

BS, Pharmacy, University of Georgia

Professional Development

Corporate Finance, Armstrong Atlantic, Savannah, GA

Microsoft Office Certificate, Penn-Foster

Professional Licenses

South Carolina–registered Pharmacist License #345875

Professional Organizations/Affiliations

Florida Pharmacy Association

Lao Tzu
813-555-3333
1000 Orange Circle, Tampa, FL 33602 legalnurse@earthlink.net

NURSE/NURSE CONSULTANT
Legal Nurse Consultant ... Registered Nurse

EDUCATION

Legal Nurse Consultant Certification Program - Current
Kaplan College, West Palm Beach, Florida

Associate in Science in Nursing (R.N.) - 2004
St. Petersburg Community College, St. Petersburg, Florida

Associate in Science in EMS Management - 2001
EMT and Paramedic Certification Program
St. Petersburg Community College, St. Petersburg, Florida

CERTIFICATIONS / TRAINING

Advanced Cardiac Life Support (ACLS)
Pediatric Advanced Life Support (PALS)
EMT-Tactical, Counter-Narcotics Tactical Operations
Introduction to Chemical, Biological, & Radiological Defense

PROFESSIONAL EXPERIENCE

Registered Nurse, - Emergency Room, Radiology Specialist
MEASE HOSPITAL, Clearwater, Florida
2004-Present
General nursing duties within a critical care setting.

Rescue Lieutenant - Firefighter - SWAT Paramedic
PINELLAS COUNTY FIRE RESCUE, Tampa, Florida
1999 to 2004
Directed field medical patient care and supervision.

Hospital Corpsman, 2nd Class, Fleet Marine Force
UNITED STATES NAVAL RESERVE, Jacksonville, Florida
1996 to 1999
Provided field medical patient care and coordinated urinalysis,
immunization, and annual medical/dental screening programs.

Emergency Medical Services Lab Supervisor
HILLSBOROUGH COMMUNITY COLLEGE, Tampa, Florida
1993 to 1996
Monitored and assessed student progress.

QUALIFICATIONS SUMMARY

Competent and knowledgeable medical professional with more than 10 years of increasingly responsible experience. Effective critical thinking, problem solving, and interpersonal skills.

EXPERTISE

- *Legal Nurse Consultant:*

- *Direct initial client assessments to identify potential liability*

- *Organize and review medical charts and records*

- *Review surgeon and expert witness depositions*

Nursing Expertise:

- *Direct patient care and advocacy*

- *Triage*

Gayle Ramirez-Chung

Trenton, NJ 08601 609.555.2894 ophthalmictech@sbcglobal.net

OPHTHALMIC TECHNICIAN/DOCTOR ASSISTANT
Building organizational value by assisting with diagnostic and treatment-oriented procedures

Technical Skills:

Precise Refracting/Work Up
Scribing
Goniometry
Sterile Techniques

Procedures & Treatments:

· Chalazion Surgery
Glaucoma Treatments
Conjunctivitis
Diabetes Monitoring
Retinopathy of Prematurity
Macular Degeneration
Strabismus
Cataracts
Palsy
NLD Obstruction
Blepharplasty

Equipment:

A Scans
Lasers
Tonometry
Slit Lamp
Lensonetry
Keratometer
Visual Fields
Topography

Performance Summary

Personable and capable professional experienced in conducting diagnostic tests; measuring and recording vision; testing eye muscle function; inserting, removing, and caring for contact lenses; and applying eye dressings. Competently assist physicians during surgery, maintain optical and surgical instruments, and administer eye medications. Extensive knowledge in ophthalmic medications dealing with glaucoma, cataract surgery, and a wide variety of other diagnoses.

Professional Experience

AUGUSTA EYE ASSOCIATES, Decatur, Georgia — since 2006
Hired as a **Technician/Assistant** for a cornea specialist in a large ophthalmic practice. Performed histories, vision screenings, pupil exams, and precise manifest refractions. Assisted with a variety of surgical procedures. Quickly built trust and rapport and streamlined processes to ensure physician efficiency.

GUGGINO FAMILY EYE CENTER, Atlanta, Georgia — 2002 to 2006
Taught customer service techniques and promoted twice within two months to an **Ophthalmic Doctor Assistant** for a pediatric neurology ophthalmologist performing scribing, taking histories, preparing patients for examination, and educating patients on treatment procedures.

DAVEL COMMUNICATIONS, Atlanta, Georgia — 1999 to 2002
Recruited as a **Regional Account Manager** and promoted within 3 months of hire to **National Account Manager**. Maintained a 100% satisfied customer retention rate.

CHILI'S BAR & GRILL, Decatur, Georgia — 1994 to 1998
Hired as a **Hostess** and quickly promoted to **Server**.

Education

Bachelor of Science, Organizational Communication — 1998
University of Georgia, Athens, Georgia

Certification
Certified Ophthalmic Assistant (COA) — expected July 2003

Cheryl Bloom, R.N.

Monrovia, NY 95777   (315) 555-3854   nurseone@earthlink.net

Registered Nurse

Performance Profile/Performance Summary

> ➤ Strongly motivated graduate with experience in hospital, sub-acute, and other health care settings.
> ➤ Clinical skills combine with dedication to excellent patient care, compassion, and professionalism to integrate patients' medical and emotional care.
> ➤ Able to relate to patients quickly and work effectively with physicians, peers, and other health care professionals. Conscientious, team-oriented, and eager to learn.

Education, Licensure and Certification

Registered Nurse, New York State License	2009
B.A. in Nursing	2008
Chenneworth College, Croton, NY	
Certified Nursing Assistant, New York Nursing Assistant Registry	2005
Basic Life Support with Automatic External Defibrillator, American Heart Association	
CPR, American Heart Association	
Additional: Math and Sciences courses, Flynn Community College, Monrovia, NY	

Core Skills

- Physical Assessments	- Dispensing Medications, Intravenous Therapy
- Vital Signs/Blood Glucose	- Documentation, Care Maps
- Catheter Insertion	- Nasopharengeal & Oral Suctioning
- Finger Sticks	- Application of Dressings, Wound Care
- Patient & Family Education	- Cast Care, Pin Care
--Tracheostomy Care	- Traction Care

Clinical Training

Acquired hands-on clinical experience and knowledge in nursing procedures while completing several rotations at the following facilities. Experience with patients ranging from pediatric to geriatric.

Medical-Surgical	Rockport General Hospital
OB/GYN	Melville Memorial Hospital
Pediatric	Montessori School
Gerontology	Evergreen Health Care Center, Mediplex, Kimberly Hall, Meadowbrook

Professional Experience

Patient Care Technician – Jackson Memorial Hospital, Croton, NY   2003-Present

Provide post-operative care to patients on an 80-bed Medical-Surgical Unit. Diverse responsibilities include: monitoring vital signs, blood glucose, and tube intake/output, collecting specimens, assisting with personal hygiene and feeding, and recording patient status. Transport patients to medical procedures and operate portable electrocardiogram. Educate patients and family members on home care.

Current Professional References Available

RICHARD ISAACS, RN, BSN

Springwater, New York 14560   585-555-6184   abcdefg@email.com

---

RN, BSN

DISASTER RESPONSE • ACUTE & CRITICAL PATIENT CARE • MEDICAL/SURGICAL CARE
Pediatrics/Geriatrics/Post-Surgical/Nuclear & Biological Hazards

Performance Profile/Performance Summary

10 years' intensive experience in fast-paced military hospital environments, including supervisory responsibilities for support staff in a variety of clinical settings. Proven capacity to function effectively in crisis situations, plus natural ability to relate to patients from diverse cultural backgrounds and age groups.
Specialized response training for mass casualty, nuclear and biological exposure, and infectious diseases such as Typhoid, Meningitis, Tuberculosis, AIDS, and other contagions.

Core Competencies

RN	BSN	Medical	Surgical	ICU
Outpatient	Terminal	Oncology	Acute	Infectious Disease
Telemetry	Burns	Cardiac	BLS/ACLS	Mass Casualty
Typhoid	Tuberculosis	Meningitis	Field Hospital	Shipboard Hospital
AIDS	PALS I	IVCS	Pediatrics	Geriatrics
Incarceration	Humanitarian	Anesthesia	Biological Hazard	Nuclear Hazard
Care	Response	Recovery	Response	Response

Primary Clinical Experience

LIEUTENANT, UNITED STATES NAVY   2001 - Present
US Naval Hospital; Tokyo, Japan   May 2005 - Present
Infants through geriatrics, broad range of infectious diseases and physical injuries.
Staff Nurse/Charge Nurse - Adult & Pediatric Care

- Provide bedside care to patients; administer medications and implement physician orders.
- Confer with physicians and other care team members on patient treatment plans.
- Address the needs of patients in isolation with Typhoid, Meningitis, and other contagious diseases.
- Train and provide leadership for staff of seven RNs and LPNs in Charge Nurse role.
- Participate in field exercises to maintain readiness for combat deployment in support of Marine units.

Key Accomplishment
Restructured medical supplies inventory and wrote new Standard Operating Procedures (SOPs) to improve departmental efficiencies.

Staff Nurse/Division Officer - Post Anesthesia Care Unit   May 2001 - May 2005

- Served needs of post-operative patients, addressing special concerns of post-anesthesia recovery.
- Otherwise supported surgical teams in treating patients with a broad range of medical conditions.

US Naval Hospital; Annapolis, MD   1998 - April 2001
Patient base included military dependents and retirees, as well as active military personnel and VIP patients.
Staff Nurse - Medical/Telemetry Acute Care Unit
- Addressed acute care needs of medical patients, including oncology and infectious disease patients.
- Cared for patients in isolation wards with tuberculosis, AIDS, and other contagious diseases.
- Monitored cardiac activity of patients using state-of-the-art telemetry technology.

Key Accomplishment
Selected to serve as part of Humanitarian Relief Response Team.

Additional Clinical Experience

LONG ISLAND GENERAL HOSPITAL; Riverhead, NY   1994 - 1998
Suburban/rural facility (eastern Long Island, NY) providing full range of medical services.
Staff Nurse/Charge Nurse - Medical/Surgical Unit
- Provided direct patient care including telemetry monitoring.
- Served needs of incarcerated individuals in conjunction with Suffolk County (NY) Sheriff's Office.

EXPOSERVE MEDICAL SERVICES; Annapolis, MD   1998 - 2001
Per Diem Registered Nurse - Maryland Children's Center
Served the needs of pediatric patients in a clinical outpatient setting.

HEARTLAND NURSING SERVICES; Riverhead, New York
Per Diem Registered Nurse   1994 - 1998
- Cared for burn victims, cardiac patients, post-surgical patients, ICU patients, and the terminally ill.

Education

MICHIGAN STATE UNIVERSITY; East Lansing, Michigan
Master of Science, Community Service   *Anticipated May 2011*

STATE UNIVERSITY OF NEW YORK AT ALBANY; Albany, New York
Bachelor of Science, Nursing   May 1994
Sigma Theta Tau Honorary/Gold Key Award/Silver Key Award

JOHNSON & WALES UNIVERSITY; Providence, Rhode Island
Associate of Science, Hotel & Restaurant Management   June 1987

Certifications and Specialized Training

Registered Nurse
Advanced Cardiac Life Support (ACLS); Basic Life Support (BLS)
Pediatric Advanced Life Support (PALS I)
Intravenous Conscious Sedation (IVCS)
Nuclear & Biological Hazard Medical Training
Mass Casualty Training; Field Hospital Training; Shipboard Hospital Training
Suturing; Chest Tube Insertion

References Provided

Mickey Dolenz, RN

San Francisco, CA 94117   415.555.1230   chargenurse@juno.com

Registered Nurse

PERFORMANCE PROFILE/PERFORMANCE SUMMARY
10+ years' experience in health care and nursing profession, recent RN graduate. Comprehensive knowledge of nursing procedures and commitment to delivering quality patient care. Successful in managing time and prioritizing tasks. Communicate well with staff, family, and patients. Punctual, reliable, and able to be counted on in a crisis.

EDUCATION, LICENSURE & CERTIFICATIONS
Bachelor of Science in Nursing, May, 2003
University of California, San Francisco, School of Nursing, San Francisco, CA
License # 123-4567
Associates in Science, Nurse Education, 1994
Evergreen Valley College, San Jose, CA
Licensed Practical Nurse, California
License # 123-4567
CPR, The American Heart Association, 1994

Professional Experience

MENDELSOHN HOUSE – San Francisco, CA   1998–2001
Charge Nurse

Provided quality patient care in a 200-bed residential nursing facility. Supervised Certified Nursing Assistants, Rehabilitation Aides, and assisted in training new licensed staff. Performed patient assessments, developed care plans, and coordinated with other disciplines including physical therapy, occupational therapy, dietary, activities, and consulted with psychologists, pharmacists, and social workers regularly. Distributed medications, as indicated by physicians; ordered and documented labs by lab cards.
- ❑ Supervised night shift as the only licensed nurse on duty.
- ❑ Provided patient care in Medicare Unit, observing patients' progress with medication, treatment, and rehabilitation; reviewed shift documentation, ensuring accuracy and completeness of forms and monthly summaries.
- ❑ Resolved pharmacy problems relating to delays and reimbursement issues and ensured compliance with documentation requirements.
- ❑ Received rarely issued management recognition award for excellence in nursing, flexibility, and willingness to work varied shifts to accommodate scheduling needs.

EL CAMINO HEALTHCARE – Mountain View, CA   1996–1998
Nurse

Provided outsourced nursing care in various settings: Medsurg, Detox, Special Needs, School, Long-Term Care, Group Home, Adult Care.

VALLENCIA VILLA– San Jose, CA   1990–1996
Charge Nurse (1994–1996); Certified Nurses Aid (1990–1994)

Supervised staff of six CNAs, and one Rehabilitation Aide, in providing nursing care for two floors, 35 patients each. Monitored blood glucose, labs, therapeutic drug levels and equipment; performed assessments, treatments, and documentation. Organized staff/patient assignments and patient care.

Pat Richardson

Tulip House
Baton Rouge, LA 70801

225.555.1234
trauma_nurse@comcast.net

TRAUMA COORDINATOR
Bilingual Registered Staff Nurse

Performance Profile/Performance Summary

13+ years' experience with principles, methods, and procedures of ER and trauma care. Currently in charge of 40 nurses in 43-bed emergency room. Nurse Staff Counsel for Emergency Department. Dedicated, resourceful, background in Training, Mentoring, and Support. Experience in coordinating and executing outreach programs. *Fluent Spanish.*

Core Competencies

* Extreme Trauma
* Scheduling
* JCAHO
* Program Development
* Quality Assurance

* ER
* Community Outreach
* Data Analysis
* Conflict Resolution
* Public speaking

* Training & Development
* Trauma Procedure Standards
* Emergency Medical Processes
* Local/ State/Fed Regulation
* Systems & Procedures

Education & Credentials

Bachelor of Science in Nursing
Baton Rouge Christian University, LA

Anticipated Feb 2011

Associates Degree in Science
Eastern New Mexico University, Roswell, NM

1999

Certifications

ACLS, BLS, PALS, TNCC, ENPC
Member, Emergency Nurse Association

PROFESSIONAL EXPERIENCE

COVENANT MEDICAL CENTER – Lubbock, TX

2001 – Present

Staff Registered Nurse
43-bed Emergency Room (over 40 nurses at any given time), perform Relief Charge Nurse duties at least once per week. Match patients with nurses at various levels and direct ambulances to different stations.

➢ Senior nurse within unit, serve as official mentor for organization
➢ Trainer for new graduates
➢ Resolution specialist to address conflicts between staff members
➢ Nurse Staff Counsel for the Emergency Department over the past 2 years

Continued

168

Contributions & Achievements

Implementing strategies for upholding high level of morale within under-staffed, stressful situations while maintaining optimal emergency and trauma care.

> Assisted unit in ensuring fulfillment of standards for JCAHO, as well as improving Quality Assurance and Safety objectives.

> Coordinated successful, well-received Injury Prevention Outreach Program. Health Fairs and work with local fire departments (spanning from Ransom Canyon to Levelland) to disseminate information regarding fireworks safety measures.

> Served as key member of Student Advocacy Subcommittee, ensuring proper training for high school, nursing, and EMT students. Took on educator role with students circulating through ER, contributing to improved capabilities.

> Earned "Excellent" ratings on performance evaluations and received acknowledgement from multiple patients for high level of care and personal attention. Leveraged bilingual background to serve Spanish-speaking population.

Eastern New Mexico Medical Center, Roswell, NM   1997-2001

Staff Registered Nurse

Performed various nursing duties, including those revolving around Emergency Room. Participated in extreme trauma cases.

Affiliations

Member, Emergency Nurse Association

> Currently serve as Injury Prevention Chairperson for local and state chapters
> Attended National ENA Convention for the past 3 years

1234 Dove Lake Road
Athens, Ohio 45701
740.555.3996
sjkramer@hotmail.com

Shannon J. Kramer
Elementary School Teacher

Career Summary

♦ Self-directed, resourceful, and enthusiastic teaching professional with a genuine interest in fostering students' cognitive and social growth

♦ Skilled in the design of developmentally appropriate, enriching, innovative and hands-on activities and lessons to meet social and emotional needs of students as well as state standards

♦ Combine strong passion for literacy, motivation, and inspiration to create a fun and challenging learning environment with strong connections to community

♦ Active team member effectively communicating and collaborating with all levels of staff to ensure optimum learning environment for students

Education

OHIO UNIVERSITY, Athens, Ohio (November 1999)
Bachelor of Science in Elementary Education • Reading Endorsement

Certification

State of Ohio Five-Year Professional License (1-8) with K-12 Reading Endorsement (Effective June 2007)

Related Teaching Experience

First and Second Grade Multi-Age Teacher
HIGHLAND PARK ELEMENTARY SCHOOL, Grove City, Ohio
August 2007–Present

♦ Integrated first and second grade curriculum while establishing an independent, self-directed multi-age classroom. Conducted Developmental Reading Assessments (DRAs) as well as other routine assessments setting individual student performance goals based on results. Successfully implemented new science curriculum. Developed home/school relationships with communication through weekly newsletters and grading period conferences. Utilized a variety of teaching methods including Guided Imagery, Process Drama, and hands-on sensory activities to facilitate learning process.

Long Term Substitute/First Grade Classroom
BARRINGTON ELEMENTARY SCHOOL, Upper Arlington, Ohio
February–June 2000

♦ Developed and implemented weekly lesson plans and units in absence of regular classroom teacher. Created and fostered a child-centered, literacy-rich environment. Established individual student goals across curriculum. Scheduled daily parent involvement and held parent/teacher conferences.

1234 Dove Lake Road
Athens, Ohio 45701
740.555.3996
sjkramer@hotmail.com

Shannon J. Kramer
Page 2
Elementary School Teacher

Excerpts from Letters of Recommendation (cont'd)

"... you have established expectations for behavior, and have structured the environment for student success ... children are becoming very self directed and competent ..."
 - Dr. Peggy Rainfield
 Former Principal
 Highland Elementary School

♦ ♦ ♦

"... a gentle, kind, and nurturing individual ... she accepts every student for his/her needs ... shows this through her positive interaction with children ... values children's opinions and ideas... her values of a child-centered, hands-on learning environment were evident through her classroom organization and method of instruction ..."
 - Mary McDonald
 Second Grade Teacher
 Highland Elementary School

Related Teaching Experience (cont'd)

Student Teacher
BARRINGTON ELEMENTARY SCHOOL, Upper Arlington, Ohio

Fall 1999

♦ Assumed full teaching responsibility in first-grade classroom developing, planning, and implementing weekly lesson plans and units. Assisted cooperating teacher with assessments. Completed DRA and Everyday Math training; integrated Everyday Mathematics into lesson plans. Attended staff meetings, parent information night, and parent/teacher conferences.

Ohio University Literacy Partnership (400 hours)
CHAUNCEY ELEMENTARY SCHOOL, Chauncey, Ohio

September 1998–June 1999

♦ Collaborated with both 2nd- and 6th-grade teachers and students in challenging school demographic of 30% IEP and 25% identified students. Taught individual, small group, and whole class assignments. Created and taught lessons using rich text aligned with thematic units. Used various reading assessments to set reading goals, develop lessons with appropriate reading strategies to support students' literacy growth, and track progress throughout the year.

Technology Skills

Competent in both Microsoft Windows and Macintosh OS X operating systems and the following software packages:

♦ Microsoft Word and PowerPoint

♦ WordPerfect

♦ AutoCAD

♦ Scholastic Reading Inventory

♦ Power Media Plus

♦ Chalk waves

♦ Internet and e-mail packages

♦ Working knowledge of Quicken

Onethia Stevens

Indianapolis, IN 46201   317.555.2957   problemsolver@gmail.com

Entry-Level Computer Technician/Software Customer Service

Lifetime computer nerd, dedicated online gamer with 1 year of intense formal training, offers real skills, enthusiasm, and dedication. Self-starter with proven coaching chops and these formal skills:

EDUCATION

The Computer Learning Center, Skillman, NJ   2008 – 2009
Computer Coursework completed in:

- ✓ Networking Essentials
- ✓ A+ Certification
- ✓ MS Office Advanced 2009
- ✓ MS Office Basic 2009
- ✓ Beginning Access 2009
- ✓ TCP/IP Protocol
- ✓ Beginning Windows NTX
- ✓ Administering Windows NTX
- ✓ Windows NTX Core Technologies
- ✓ Windows NTX Support by Enterprise
- ✓ Business on the Internet
- ✓ Beginning FrontPage 2009

Montclair University, Montclair, NJ   2006 – 2007
General first-year courses in Bachelor's Degree program
(24 credits).

EMPLOYMENT

A Cut Above, Montclair, NJ   2008 – 2009
Receptionist/Cashier
Worked full-time to fund computer education & care for sibling

- Successfully handled front desk and three incoming telephone lines for busy, upscale hair salon. Greeted and logged-in steady stream of customers, coordinating appointments with hairdresser availability.

- Developed cooperative, team-oriented working relationships with owners and co-workers in this 12-station salon.

- Managed customer problems and complaints with tact and attention to prompt customer service. Received team and customer service awards.

- Gained experience in opening and closing procedures, cash register receipts, counter sales, light bookkeeping, and telephone follow-up.

Pro Soccer Camp, Princeton, NJ   Summers 2005– 2007
Trainer/Coach

- Assisted Woman's Soccer Coach in 200-participant soccer camp. Asked to return as trainer for 3 seasons. Worked with individuals, as well as teams, to improve their attitude and resulting soccer performance.

ACTIVITIES

Jersey Waves Soccer Semi-Pro Team   2004 – 2007
Team consistently ranked in top 10 semi-pro teams in the nation.

- ✓ River Crossing High School Soccer Team   1998 – 2000
- ✓ Captain of team that won State Soccer Title   1999
- ✓ Recognized as one of the top two mid-fielders in the state in 1998

Bernard Rice

5523 Ficus Lane, Apt. 14
Los Angeles, California 90049

(310) 555-1923
financialsales@ameritech.com

FINANCIAL SALES/PORTFOLIO MANAGEMENT
Strengths in Research/Analysis/Client Relations/Financial Planning

Performance Profile/Performance Summary

Recent graduate Bachelor of Science in Business Economics; Minor in Accounting GPA: 3.8. Worked throughout college to partially self-finance education. Proven leadership strengths and ability to manage multiple responsibilities in a fast-paced environment. Well-organized with attention to detail. Proficient in oral and written *Spanish*, including business terminology.

Core Competencies

- ✓ Market Research
- ✓ Project Management
- ✓ E-commerce
- ✓ Financial Planning
- ✓ Account Compliance
- ✓ IRS Audits
- ✓ Excel
- ✓ Access
- ✓ QuickBooks

- ✓ Competitive Intelligence
- ✓ Budget Management
- ✓ Website Maintenance
- ✓ Accounting
- ✓ Money/Account Transfers
- ✓ Personal Tax Returns
- ✓ Word
- ✓ Outlook
- ✓ Turbo Tax

- ✓ Strategic Planning
- ✓ Team Building/Leadership
- ✓ Client Relations
- ✓ Portfolio Management
- ✓ Tax Accounting
- ✓ Corporate Tax Returns
- ✓ PowerPoint
- ✓ Peachtree

Education

University of Southern California, Los Angeles, CA   12/2009
Bachelor of Science in Business Economics; Minor in Accounting   GPA: 3.8

Campus Leadership

Treasurer President—Student Accounting Society
Vice President—Business-Economics Society
Volunteer Income Tax Assistance (V.I.T.A.) for low-income families—IRS
Treasurer—Alpha Beta Gamma Fraternity

Professional Experience

PORTER WARNER, INC., Century City, CA   Jan. 2008 to Nov. 2009
Portfolio Manager/Finance Assistant to Senior Portfolio Managers
(Concurrent with Studies)

Set up and managed client accounts to ensure compliance with established policies and procedures. Collaborated with other financial institutions to facilitate money and account transfers. Conducted in-depth research utilizing Internet, Bloomberg, and direct corporate contacts.
- Implemented and maintained detailed database to accurately track clients and prospects.
- Streamlined client communication process.
- Collaborated with support staff to maintain account compliance and reduce missing documents.

INTERNAL REVENUE SERVICE, Los Angeles, CA   2005, 2006, 2007, 2008
Volunteer Income Tax Assistance (V.I.T.A.) (*Tax Seasons, concurrent with studies*)

IRS *continued*

- Prepared income tax returns for low-income families and students; provided step-by-step instruction to guide taxpayers in filling out future returns.

ZEMAN & YOUNG, C.P.A., Los Angeles, CA   Oct. 2004 to Jan. 2006
Jr. Accountant *(Concurrent with Studies)*

Prepared individual and corporate income tax returns; audited company records to identify fraud; investigated, compiled, and summarized data to support records for IRS audit.

- Maintained client books through financial statement preparation.
- Prepared investment proposal for start-up company.

Additional Relevant Experience

Camp Counselor   *Summers 2001 to 2003*

Foreign Languages

Proficient in oral and written Spanish, including business terminology

Community Activities

Little League Coach, Big Brothers

Computer Skills

Microsoft Word, Excel, PowerPoint, Access, Outlook, Peachtree, QuickBooks, Turbo Tax

*Professional references
from both public and private sectors
available upon request*

Herb Ritts, PMP

25 Hawthorne Dr.,   201.555.2315   ITmanager@earthlink.net
Mahwah, NJ 07430

Information Management

"Breathing technology since birth"

Performance Profile/Performance Summary

Hands-on technology manager with multi-faceted experience in mainframe and client server environments with multi-relational databases; Informix, Oracle Sybase, and SQL.

Strong background in relational database management, performance tuning, and high-availability techniques. Skilled project manager with ability to obtain project requirements and implement solutions that drive bottom line.

Talented in providing technology risk management. Leverages wide-ranging talents in computer technology, staff leadership, and SDLC to effectively manage organizational change, mitigate risk, infuse new ideas, and deliver large-company capabilities.

➤ Excellent ability to analyze business needs and implement cost-effective solutions meeting business objectives.
➤ Solid record of achievement building and aligning organizations with strategic IT business objectives to achieve dramatic bottom-line results.
➤ Expertise providing project management, technology expertise, and staff leadership.
➤ Demonstrated talents in database architecture, design, and maintenance.
➤ Performed technology management, including configuration, release, and risk management.

Core Competencies

✓ Project Management	✓ Process Management	✓ Development Lifecycle
✓ Staff Leadership	✓ SOX Compliancy	✓ DRM
✓ Vendor Management	✓ ETL Solutions	✓ Database Administration
✓ Application Testing	✓ Telecom Systems	✓ CRM
✓ Audits	✓ Technology Planning	✓ Release & Change Mgmnt
✓ Relational Databases	✓ Informix	✓ Org. Change Mgmnt
✓ Oracle Sybase	✓ SQL	✓ Performance Tuning
✓ Risk Management	✓ SDLC	✓ Database Security

Professional Experience

XYZ FINANCE COMPANY, Parsippany, NJ   2003 – Present
Consumer division of 100 billion dollar bank: auto leasing & home mortgages

Application System Team Manager

Team leadership and project management for timely completion of IT projects ranging from $50K to $1.5M. Directs and mentors four Application/Database Designers, providing prototype, design, development, and implementation of database architecture and strategies and 24/7 support of databases and applications.

Herb Ritts	201.555.2315	ITmanager@earthlink.net	Page 2

Application System Team Manager *continued*

Oversees organizational change management functions, providing support and approval of over 100 change requests in one release cycle.

Designs and implements ETL solutions for XML-based interface of Origination data. Assists audit organizations, providing engineering and architecture changes to necessary applications, databases, and servers for SOX Compliancy.

SME for origination data and ensures persistence of data across downstream systems. Provides 24/7 support for back applications.

Accomplishments:
- Increased client leads by 20% through development and implementation of lead registration system.
- Directed team in development and implementation of Disaster Recovery Planning efforts, providing quick restoration of critical applications.
- Spearheaded major 18-month application and database design project for implementation of application and database security ensuring SOX compliancy for entire organization with budget of $1.5M.

"The son of a technology pioneer, I have lived technology and psychology since birth, and bring a depth of understanding beyond my chronological experience."

Premier references available on request.

Max Beeker MCSE, CCNA

80 Hill Street ♦ Bronx, NY 10451 ♦ 718.555.4567 ♦ network_admin@hotmail.com

Network Administrator/Programmer

$300,000+ cost reduction and improved operational efficiencies

Performance Summary

Certified Network Systems Specialist with extensive technical experience in network administration and programming. Experienced with: installation, configuration, maintenance, troubleshooting, design, and conversion. Excellent organizational, team-building, and communication skills.

Core Skills

- MCSE+1
- Certified Linux Administrator
- Network Administrator
- Domain servers
- Router Configuration
- Workstations
- CCNA
- C Programmer
- Windows NT/2000
- Network Firewalls
- Network conversions
- Software and Hardware Configuration
- Mail systems
- MS-SQL
- LAN/WAN
- Sys Integration
- Internet

Professional Experience

CW Associates, New York, NY   2002 - Present
Network Administrator/Programmer

Researched and implemented $300,000+ cost-saving technology programs and operating systems. Oversaw and supervised network conversions from *FileMaker Pro, Lasso and Webstar to MS-SQL, Php, and Apache.*

Customized and monitored company search engines. Configured, installed, and maintained Company *VPN, Cisco Pix Firewalls and Routers.* Updated company electronic mail system from QuickMail to CommuniGatePro.

Networking Worldwide, New York, NY   1999 –2002
Network Administrator

Designed, installed, and configured computers and peripherals. Maintained and repaired hardware, software, and operating systems. Troubleshot and resolved application and e-mail system issues. Managed four domain servers.

Education & Training

Columbia University, New York, NY
- **MS in Computer Science**   2002
- **BS in Computer Science**   2001
- **Microsoft Systems Certified Engineer**   2000
- **Cisco Certified Network Associate**   2000

Superior references available on request.

DAVID J. WAGNER, MCP
217 Magnolia Court, Oakland, NJ 07436
(201) 555-1239 Home • (201) 555-9374 Mobile • djwagner@csn.com

Networks/Systems
Hardware Configuration:
Windows, UNIX, Cisco
Software Configuration
Systems Integration
Systems Configuration
Router Configuration
Intrusion Detection
Systems
Frame Relay Networking
Network Planning
Network Firewalls
Peer-to-peer Networks
Ethernet Networks
Telephony & Fiber Optics
Internet Information Server
Switches & Hubs
ISDN/T1 Lines
Media & Peripherals
Voice & Data
TCP/IP
Project Management
Technology Consulting
Technology Management
Networking Infrastructures
Systems Implementation
Virtual Team Leadership
Relationship Management
Advanced
Communications
Telecommunications
Security Analysis
Security Development
Applications Development
Evaluation & Testing
Troubleshooting
Resource Utilization
Inventory Management
Technology Training
End-User Training
Knowledge Transfer
Executive Presentations
Strategic Planning
Project Team Development
Team Building
Client Relations
Quality Assurance
Problem Solving

TEAM LEADER • PROJECT MANAGER • DEPARTMENT MANAGER
Network Administration • Systems Security Technology

Microsoft Certified Professional. A+ Certification.
Accomplished technology consultant and project manager adept in desktop and network security/systems architecture planning, design, installation, configuration, maintenance, and smooth project delivery.
Accustomed to supporting multi-user networks, as well as leading high-performance technology and telecommunications solutions. Successfully employ technology to improve operations efficiency, reduce costs, and meet reliability and security goals and deadlines.
Proven track record in team leadership and training, supplying a balanced mix of analytical, management, coaching, and technical skills.

PROFESSIONAL EXPERIENCE

Senior Computer Scientist 2003 – present
S5 Systems Group (US Army technology consulting firm), Stockton, NJ

Technical Lead – Army Computer Systems Office (2004 – present)
Focus: Rollout of Army Partnership Tool Suite (APTS) system, implementing new functionality into live networks and systems.
Lead Consultant and liaison (chosen by government project manager) in 7-member cross-functional team deploying integrated networks, systems, and technologies. Introduced real-time, peer-to-peer collaboration via new application, bringing far-flung team together and eliminating disconnects.
Key player in development, testing, and implementation process, including custom tool suite development, to fit client needs. Integrate configuration and supply installation support for pioneering technology collaboration.

Lead Network Engineer
Information Systems Engineering Office (2003 – 2004)
Focus: $24 million Communications Update & Planning System (CUPS).
Evaluated, selected, and integrated advanced communications and networking products for the Communications Collaboration Team.

Key role (network engineer/administrator/technician) leading 6-member team. Honed end-to-end project management and presentation skills.
Pioneered first-ever use of security hardware/software, including intrusion detection systems (IDS), Cisco routers, and network management apps.
Designed robust, mobile communications (and upgrades) to facilitate efficient network convergence and bandwidth utilization. Developed network management tools for real-time monitoring and troubleshooting.
Field-tested flying local area network (FLAN), utilizing wireless Ethernet technology, which interconnected en route aircraft to ground-based units.
Proposed equipment purchasing savings of $2.5 – $6 million through services analysis, reducing duplication of physical space and equipment.
Introduced new traffic routing method (tech) utilizing a defense satellite channel for communications, enabling net-meeting in worldwide locations.
continued

DAVID J. WAGNER, MCP
(201) 555-1239 Home • djwagner@csn.com

Hardware:
Sun Microsystems
IBM PCs & compatibles
SCSI & IDE Hard Drives
Cisco Routers & Switches
3COM Switches & Hubs
Ascend Pipeline Series
Netgear Hubs
RAID Arrays (Sun)
Ethernet NICs
Printers, Scanners
CD-ROMs, Modems
CD-R & CD-RW Drives
Sound Cards, TV Cards
Tape Drives
Software (UNIX):
Solaris, Linux
HP UNIX, SCO UNIX
Cisco Works Essentials
BIND 4 & 9 (DNS)
X-Windows, Open
Windows
SSH, Lynx, Pine, ELM
sh, csh, bash
ftp servers & clients
Eagle Raptor Firewall
Apache, Sendmail, IRC
Software (PC):
Windows, DOS
Novell Netware
MS Office, MS Outlook
WordPerfect, FrontPage
IRC, IE, Netscape
FTP Servers & Clients
Norton, Cisco
HyperTerminal, Kermit
HP Openview
Cisco Works Essentials
Carbon Copy
Seagate Backup Exec.
SCO Xvision
Software (Cisco IOS):
Internetworking OS
Network Address Trans.
Access Lists
Context Based Access
Intrusion Detection
Remote Syslog Logging
Routing Protocols

Signal Officer   1994 – present
113th Signal Battalion, NJ Army NG, Stockton, NJ

Platoon Leader – Mobile Subscriber Equipment Company. Lead, develop, and motivate 40 soldiers. Oversee inventory management of $4.8 million in vehicles, weaponry, security, and communications equipment.
Mission – establish mobile subscriber equipment network (mobile phone network for combat soldiers in the field).

Computer Scientist   2001 – 2003
Computer Development Services, Inc., Oakland, NJ

Lead technical consultant – Computer Services Security Branch (US Army) for setup, testing, and evaluation of networks/systems security technologies. Established configuration, installation procedures, and network topologies for all support tasks. Tech reports used as management measurement tool.
Designed secure test bed network/domain on UNIX, Windows, and Cisco IOS providing e-mail, DNS, firewalls, routing, file serving, and accounting.
Selected to serve as test bed manager for dry run and official testing, personally resolving testing challenges and intrusion issues.

Systems Administrator   2000 – 2001
Technical Solutions & Services Corporation, Oakland, NJ

Installation, configuration, and troubleshooting software (UNIX, Linux, Windows, Solaris) on HP workstations, Toshiba laptops, and servers (Compaq, Diversified, HP, Sun). Prepared backups on multiple platforms and provided 24/7 technical support to data warehousing center.
Oversaw corporate telecomm system, LAN physical extension, and technical purchasing (POs, quoting, authorizations, and receiving).

Technology Consultant   1999 – 2000
Campbell & Cohen (legal firm), Trenton, NJ

Systems and network troubleshooting (Windows & Novell Netware) at multiple locations. Peer-to-peer training. Proposed LAN and equipment recommendations to stay ahead of the curve, which were implemented.

Systems Instructor/Client Support   1998 – 1999
Healthcare Information Group, Oakland, NJ

EDUCATION & CERTIFICATIONS
MS, Telecommunications Management, Rutgers University – in progress
BS, Accounting, The College of New Jersey, Ewing, NJ – 1998

Microsoft Certified Professional – Windows NT, Network Essentials
A+ Certification – Computer and Network Repair
Cisco Switching 2.0 & Routing 2.0 – towards CCNP in progress
Building Scalable Cisco Networks (BSCN) course – in-house training

PROFESSIONAL ASSOCIATIONS
Institute of Electrical & Electronics Engineers (IEEE)

JOHN A. CHRISTOPHER

11 Barbara Lane • Simi Valley, California 93063 • (805) 555-3787 • fax (805) 555-9741 jacla@aol.com

Applications

Adaptec Easy CD Creator
Adaptec Direct CD
Carbon Copy
Cc Mail
Clarify
HP Colorado Backup
MS Active Sync
MS Office Professional
MS Outlook 98 and 2003
MS Internet Explorer
NetAccess Internet
Netscape
Norton Ghost
Partition Magic
PC Anywhere
Rainbow
Reflection 1
Reflection X
Remedy-ARS
Symantec Norton Antivirus
Visio
Windows CE

Operating Systems

Microsoft Windows 2000
Microsoft Windows NT 4.0
Workstation and Server
Microsoft Windows ME
Microsoft Windows 95, 98
Cisco Router/Switch IOS
MS-DOS
UNIX

Hardware

Intel-based Desktops
Intel-based Mobile
Computers
HP Colorado Tape Backup
Cisco 2500 Series Router
Hewlett Packard Pro Curve
Switches
CD Writer

Protocols & Services
TCP/IP
DHCP
DNS
NetBEUI
Remote Access Service
WINS

Networking
Ethernet
Token Ring
Microsoft Networking

Network Architecture Specialist
Cisco Certified Network Associate

Performance Profile

Results-driven, self-motivated professional with solid experience supporting hundreds of users in multiple departments in the corporate environment. Recognized for outstanding support and services, process development, and project management. Able to manage multiple projects simultaneously and move quickly among projects. Capable of leading or collaborating. Areas of expertise include:

- Network architectures and networking components
- Software and operating system deployment in corporate environments
- PC hardware installation/repair and disk imaging
- Troubleshoot complex operating system problems
- Call tracking, case management, solution integration

Accomplishments

- Reduced help desk calls by developing end-user training and knowledge database.
- Led migration for 3000+ client/server email accounts from HP Open Mail to MS Exchange.
- Developed data collection protocol for BLM Natural Resource Inventory.
- Mentored teammates on technical materials and procedures.
- Built relationships to quickly resolve business critical issues.

Certifications

Technical Certification for MS Network Support Program, 9/02
CCNA – Cisco Certified Network Associate, 8/02

Work History

Technical Support Engineer, ABC Technologies (Holt Services), 4/07 – Present
E-mail Migration Specialist, ABC Technologies (Holt Services), 11/02 – 4/07
PC Technician, RBM (The Cameo Group) 5/02 – 11/02
Customer Support Specialist, Center Partners, 9/01 – 5/02
Recycle Technician, RBM (WasteNot Recycling), 2/01 – 9/01
Soil Scientist, Bureau of Land Management, 5/00 – 10/00

Education

B.S., Soil Science: Environmental Mgt. – CA Polytechnic State University, 12/00
Pacific Institute Workshop – Goal Setting, Achievement, Motivation, 1/01
A.A., Mathematics, Mira Costa College, 7/97

Awards and Honors

ABC Shining Star Award for Outstanding Customer Service, October '04
Outstanding Services to Technical Services Division, January '03
High Quality Customer Service Award, RBM Technical Support March & April '02

BRENDA R. HINESVILE

Phone: (214) 555-7856   4658 Lovers Lane   SoftArchitect@yahoo.com

Dallas, TX 75240

Technology Strategist/Senior Software Architect
Solid Leadership – Software Architecture – Mobile Application Development – Internet Marketing

PERFORMANCE PROFILE

Proven Leadership — Rare blend of theoretical and practical understanding of open-source applications and server environments. Leadership and hands-on experience in regulated financial services and mobile software industries.

Senior-Level Software Professional — Strong leader. 12+ years of experience developing and managing open-source software. Successful in building solid technology platforms and leading technology organizations. Career includes senior-level positions, contributing to corporate, board, and division-level strategic planning, policy formation, and decision making.

CORE COMPETENCIES

Software Development	Management Leadership	System Administration
▪ Advanced Objective-C on iPhone OS	▪ Personnel Recruiting/Management	▪ Server & Network Administration
▪ Advanced C/C++ on OS X, BSD, Linux	▪ Regulatory Accountability/Compliance	▪ Extensive Work in UNIX Shells
▪ UNIX Systems Programming	▪ Translation/Communication of Technology Needs & Issues	▪ Expert in Terminal Environments
▪ Application Architecture & Design	▪ Process & Policy Creation & Implementation	▪ Thorough Knowledge of OS Internals
▪ Network & Security Protocols	▪ P&L Accountability	▪ FFIEC Technology Regulations
▪ Mobile Hardware/Software Limitations		▪ Web and Server Security
		▪ Network Protocol Analysis

PROFESSIONAL ACHIEVEMENTS

➢ **Developed iPhone App for commercial transportation industry**   2009 to 2010

- Ranked #2 on App Store top free business apps, June 2010.
- Featured on App Store – New and Noteworthy, June 2010.
- Featured in numerous freight publications and Dallas Morning News.
- Online Gallery, HD Screencasts, technical overview available on Project URL.

➢ **Contributed Documentation to iPlone – Open Source CMS**   2009 to 2010

- How to configure a Plone 3 production server with Squid and Apache 2 + SSL on a FreeBSD 7 server with PF, the packet filter. Comprehensive instructions for secure installation.

Developed Open Source Enterprise Software for Federal Savings Bank   2003 to 2008

- Deployed loan pricing and eligibility software across nationwide network on hardened Linux servers.
- Designed extensive schema in PostgreSQL, C++ DFA for parsers, and TCL for dynamic content.
- Achieved near 100% system uptime and significantly increased bank profit margins.
- 500+ mortgage programs, 50K+ underwriting/pricing rules, $1M daily changing mortgage interest rates.

Migrated Bank Infrastructure to Open Source Platforms   2003 to 2005

- Deployed, managed Open Source mail/web servers on hardened Linux at SAS 70 Type II data center.
- Drastically reduced costs, near 100% uptime, and significantly mitigated security/regulatory risks.
- Developed CRM on Open Source CMS and deployed across nation-wide branch network.
- Deployed Open Source mail/web clients on corporate workstations – trained IT department on Linux server administration and workstation software management.

➤ **Led Startup of IT Department for Federal Savings Bank**   2003 to 2005

- Established bank's online presence and branded "Cofedbank".
- Integrated custom CRM with Google Adwords to track lead conversion quality and ratios.
- Provided technical, financial, and managerial oversight of bank's technology infrastructure.
- Ensured compliance with FFIEC Regulations.

PROFESSIONAL EXPERIENCE

LEAD SOFTWARE ARCHITECT/DEVELOPER
APPLICANDY, LLC - MOBILE APPLICATION DEVELOPMENT, DALLAS, TX
2009 to Present

Designed and developed iPhone application, iLogMiles, for commercial transportation industry. Led project, including all development, and provided training on software standards, Apple guidelines, and Internet marketing. Closely followed agile design principles.
Designed and managed website and web application framework.

- "App released for the iTruckers on the road" – Today's Trucking Magazine, April 2010.
- "New iPhone App Provides Daily Log Book" – Heavy Duty Trucking Magazine, April 2010.
- "Amid industry discussion…, smartphone logging apps proliferate" – Overdrive Magazine, April 2010.
- "Two Dallas iPhone/iPad app developers hit milestones with iLogMiles . . ." – Dallas Morning News, April 2010.
- "Software developers keep churning out the apps" – Dallas Morning News, March 2010.

PRESIDENT/SOFTWARE CONSULTANT
HINESVILLE MORTGAGE & INVESTMENT CO., DALLAS, TX
2008 to 2009

Consulting services for regulated banks and financial institutions – Enterprise software architecture, capital markets consulting - Mark to Market, Fall-Out analysis, and Hedged Pipeline analysis reports. Deployed Plone on hardened FreeBSD server at SAS 70 Type II data center.

VP — INFORMATION TECHNOLOGY/MANAGING DIRECTOR
COLORADO FEDERAL SAVINGS BANK (COFEDBANK), DALLAS, TX
2003 to 2008

Led and managed technology department and created tech strategy for bank. Architect and manager of technology infrastructure, including migration strategies for accounting and loan origination systems. Trained personnel on network protocols, system admin, server security, and data modeling. Performed technology assessments of prospective acquisitions. Managed project life cycles for several software interfaces. Performed database migrations, server installations, server upgrades, performance tuning, and security assessments. Managed vendor contracts.

Brenda Hinesville Droid: (214) 555-5687 iPhone: (214) 555-7856 SoftArchitect@yahoo.com

OPEN SOURCE DEVELOPER, DALLAS, TX   1996 to 2002

UNIX systems programming on Solaris, Open/FreeBSD, RH/Slackware Linux.
Developed thread-safe, streams library in C++. The library is an extension of the C++ iostreams hierarchy. Customized
streams provide support for sockets, shared memory, pipes, and text files. Project URL - http://mls.sourceforge.net

C++ and UNIX TUTOR
COLLIN COUNTY COMMUNITY COLLEGE, PLANO, TX   2000 to 2001

Tutored 200+ students in C++ and UNIX courses.

SOFTWARE DEVELOPER
MORTGAGE PORTFOLIO SERVICES, DALLAS, TX   2001 to 2002

Designed, developed, and deployed mortgage lock platform using CGI and C++.

EDUCATION

BS — Computer Science, University of Texas at Dallas, Dallas, TX   2002

- Graduate-level coursework in Computer Science
- Emphasis on operating system architecture and database design

Member of iEEE Computer Society

Notable Conferences: Apple World Wide Developer Conference; Apple iPhone Tech Talk – San Jose, 2009.

Administering Linux in Production Environments – USENIX; Online Analytics – Omniture Inc.; Search

Engine Strategies – Chicago, 2006.

Alleah Williams

939B Tree Tops Villas   (650) 878-9887
Mountain View, CA 94040   awilliams.engineer@gmail.com

Data Center Engineer
Performance Summary

5 years' experience in data center management and technical support. Storage engineer at a dedicated high-security site with 800 enterprise servers for secure messaging services. Server technology and hardware replacement and upgrades: Hard Drive, CPU, RAM, etc.

Technology Skills

Hitachi Data Systems (HDS)	Event Monitoring Service (EMS)	System Security
Preventive Maintenance	Electromagnetic Interference (EMI)	Disaster Recovery, Backups
C-class Blade Installation	Hardware Upgrades	Application Support
Troubleshooting	Cabling and Testing	SN8000 B-series Brocade SAN
Rack layout, IO Card Layout	Diagnose and Repair Systems	Cooling System/Air Distribution

Hardware: Hitachi Data Systems (HDS, P9500), HP 9000 Servers and Workstations, Itanium and Intel-based Blade Servers, C-class Blade Enclosure, SN8000 B-series Brocade SAN Switches (DCX).
Operating Systems: Windows, HP UX, Brocade Fabric OS.
Applications: Remote Web Console (Hitachi Data Systems), Virtual Connect Support Utility, Brocade Fabric Manager, ICE (support ticket documentation tool), SanXpert, Support Tools Manager (STM).

Professional Experience

Hitachi Systems, San Jose, CA   2010–Current
Data Center Engineer
Conducted reactive field repairs and support for enterprise-level HP servers and storage. Troubleshoot and resolve problems quickly to ensure uninterrupted operating capability.

- Provide 24/7 data center engineering support for global financial services industry.
- Improved processes and performance in a deadline-driven environment.
- Proven ability to effectively coordinate with external vendors and internal staff; works well with others in a team environment.
- Implemented customer problem structure/flow, increasing responsiveness and decreasing resolution time.
- Responsible for improving technical protocols with real-time data collection.

Education & Professional Development

San Jose State University, San Jose CA   2010
BS in Business Management

San Francisco Community College, S.F., CA   2008
AAS in Computer Science
HIPAA Privacy and Security Awareness   2014
3PAR InServ Storage Server Hardware Introduction   2014
HP StorageWorks VLS and D2D Solutions   2013

Impeccable references available

Regina Boyd PMP

39 Saddle Court
Menlo Park, CA 94027

Mobile: 650-878-4596
projectmanager@gmail.com

IT Project Management

Performance Summary

15 years' experience in IT Project Management, from requirements identification through creation and implementation of project teams in multi-vendor environments. Extensive project management experience in IT services, financial services, and H/C. Skilled in creating and presenting reports to senior management. Demonstrated experience in integrating strategies, innovation, technology, and team building to achieve successful and profitable ventures.

——Professional Skills——

Project/Portfolio Management	Project Scope Management	Requirements Analysis	Project/Portfolio Governance
Stakeholder Management	Matrix Team Leadership	Partnership Management	Cross-Functional Teams
Project Status Reporting	Financial Management	Conflict Management	Capacity Planning
Team Development	Coaching and Mentoring	Lean Six Sigma	SDLC/Agile Methodology
Systems Conversion	Vendor Management	Product Launch	Systems Integrations

Professional Experience

Memory Experts, Mountain View, CA 2009 to present
IT Project Management Consultant
Delivered high-level project management and technology needs analysis. Served as Senior Project Manager.

Projects and Accomplishments:

- Directed the implementation of $23 million Document Management systems for law enforcement agency. Included user interface, image capture, storage, batch, and bar code processing throughout multiple regions.

- Led cross-functional teams of business and IT professionals to implement defined benefit solutions at *Fortune* 500 client. Mentored Junior PMs to assume more visible roles and navigate internal and client matrix structures. Managed client engagements and project budget to within 5% of plan.

- Managed the implementation of $20 million Inter-Plan Teleprocessing System Conversion of VSAM & IMS to DB2, with enabling infrastructure for front-end and web services, partnering with over 100 businesses and technology experts utilizing SDLC and Agile methodologies.

Fort Knox Finance Systems, Cupertino, CA 1997 to 2009
A financial service division of a premier eCommerce organization.
Technical Project Manager
Hired to lead development of new software releases to bring the company into new technology. Charged with planning, management, and delivery of $2 million to $5 million project initiatives with teams of up to 30 staff members. Led customer conferences and brainstorming sessions to gather requirements. Ensured adherence with quality assurance standards by directing test plan creation. Validated unit and system test results and assisted in creating systems, user, and marketing documentation.

Education and Complementary Experience

Certified Project Management Professional (PMP), Project Management Institute 2003

Bachelor of Science, Electrical Engineering, Berkeley, CA 1997

Bachelor of Science, Information Systems, UCLA 1996

REGINA PIERCE

1900 Paramont Way
Toledo, OH 43606
Phone: 419.555.0423
Email: softwaremagic@juno.com

• SOFTWARE DESIGN ENGINEER •
DELIVERING SOFTWARE TO REDUCE COSTS AND INCREASE EFFICIENCIES

Performance Profile. Detail–oriented Systems Software Engineer with 8+ years of successful experience in designing, developing, and implementing software solutions to support business objectives. Keen **problem-solving skills** evidenced by the implementation of innovative technologies across dissimilar architectures and multiple platforms to provide quality product functionality. An **effective communicator** who can easily interface with end-users, technical teams, and professionals on all levels.

Technology Expertise Includes:

- Astute strategic understanding of mainframe, client/server, and Internet environments.
- Experience in Object-Oriented design and development.
- Empirical knowledge of all system development life cycle phases and a structured approach to project management. Accurately develop end–user documentation.
- Proven ability to acquire knowledge rapidly and to apply new technologies for process improvement.
- Functional knowledge of the finance, billing, and operations areas of **Customer Information Systems**.

Key Project Management & Leadership

ERNST & YOUNG – * LEAD TECHNICAL ANALYST *

Customer Information System for Southeastern Utility Company

Challenge: To identify and resolve critical errors of newly developed software in the Primary Test region before migrating online and batch programs to Regression Testing region.

Action: Extensively used problem-solving skills while interacting with eight-member team, Software Engineers, Data Conversion, project manager, and end-users to understand client requirements. Executed and analyzed test suites resulting in quality assessments that verified product requirements and high-quality code.

Result: Delivered high-quality software that exceeded client expectations and was specifically requested to stay on as Technical Analyst of the Regression Test Team, supporting both test teams through first-site implementation.

ERNST & YOUNG – * CUSTOM DEVELOPMENT LEAD/SUPERVISOR*
Customization of Client/Server Customer Information System

Challenge: To resolve technical issues of Open Client architecture that were slowing progress on the development of a $1.8M CIS system at a Canadian utility company; to develop a detailed design of Powerbuilder software modifications in the Operations area.

Action: (1) Supervised two developers in identifying the cause of the Open Client issues and in the completion of software modifications to resolve those issues.

(2) Developed detailed design of Powerbuilder software modifications to increase functionality and efficiency.

Result: My team successfully identified and resolved the Open Client issues ahead of schedule, streamlining the rest of the project back to schedule.

COMPUTER TECHNOLOGIES

Languages*: SQL, SQL*Plus, PL/SQL, Transact SQL, C, Java, HTML, COBOL, Pascal, Scheme ▪ **Databases***: Oracle 8.x, DB2, Sybase, MS Access ▪ **Environments***: Microsoft Windows 95/98/NT/2000, DOS, UNIX, VMS, CICS ▪ **CASE Tools***: ADW 1.6, ADW 2.7▪ **Development Tools***: JDeveloper v.2.0, Oracle Designer v.6.0, Oracle Developer 2000 v.2.0, Oracle Forms v.5.0, Oracle Reports v.2.5, Dream Weaver 3.0 ▪ **Methodologies:** Oracle's Applications Implementation Methodology (AIM) & Custom Development Methodology (CDM); Ernst & Young's Application Implementation Methodology (SMM).

Raj Chimesh

104 W. Real Drive • Beaverton, OR 97006 • (503) 555-4286 • systemsraj@sbcglobal.net

SYSTEMS ENGINEER

Performance Profile/Performance Summary

IT Professional offering 9+ years of hands–on experience in design, implementation, and enhancement of business systems automation. Demonstrated ability to develop high-performance systems, applications, databases, and interfaces.

➢ Part of TL9000 CND audit interviews which helped Technical get crucial TL9000 certification. Skilled trainer and proven ability to lead many successful projects, such as TSS, EMX, and TOL.

➢ Strategically manage time and expediently resolve problems for optimal productivity, improvement, and profitability; able to direct multiple tasks effectively.

➢ Strong technical background with a solid history of delivering outstanding customer service.

➢ Highly effective liaison and communication skills proven by effective interaction with management, users, team members, and vendors.

Technical Skills

Operating Systems:	Unix, Windows (2000, XP), DOS
Languages:	C, C++, Java, Pascal, Assembly Languages (Z8000, 808x, DSP)
Methodologies:	TL9000, Digital Six Sigma
Software:	MS Office, Adobe Framemaker, Matlab
RDBMS:	DOORS, Oracle 7.x
Protocols:	TCP/IP, SS7 ISUP, A1, ANSI, TL1, SNMP
Tools:	Teamplay, Clearcase, Clearquest, M-Gatekeeper, Exceed, Visio, DocExpress, Compass
Other:	CDMA Telecom Standards – 3GPP2 (Including TIA/EIA-2001, TIA/EIA-41, TIA/EIA-664), ITU-T, AMPS

Significant Training

Open Source Software	WiMAX	Agile Management for Software Engineering
WSG Requirements Process	Product Security	Fagan Inspection and Moderation

PROFESSIONAL EXPERIENCE

Technical, Main Network Division, Hillsboro, OR   Jan 1999 – Present
Principal Staff Engineer • Products Systems Engineering   Nov 2004 – Present

✓ Known as "go-to" person for CDMA call processing and billing functional areas.

✓ Create customer requirements documents for Technical SoftSwitch (TSS) and SMS Gateway products. All deliverables done on/ahead schedule with high quality.

✓ Solely accountable for authoring and allocation, customer reviews, supporting fellow system engineers, development, and test and customer documentation teams.

✓ Support Product Management in RFPs, customer feature prioritization, impact statements, and budgetary estimates.

✓ Mentored junior engineers; one innovation disclosure patent submitted in 2007.

✓ Resolve deployed customer/internal requirements issues and contribute to Virtual Zero Defect quality goal.

✓ TOL process champion and part of CND focus group that contributed to reducing CRUD backlog (NPR) by 25% and cycle time (FRT) by 40%.

✓ Recognized as the TL9000 expert. Triage representative for switching and messaging products.

✓ *Achieved 'CND Quality Award' for contribution to quality improvement in May 2007.*

Senior Staff Engineer • MSS Systems Engineering   May 2002 – Oct 2004

✓ Led a team of 12 engineers for 3 major software releases of TSS product, included around 80 features/enhancements to create T-Gate SE deliverables.

✓ Mentored newer engineers to get up to speed on TSS product.

Continued

Senior Staff Engineer · MSS Systems Engineering (continued)

- ✓ Created requirements for TSS product, 30 features/enhancements contributing to 5 major software releases. *Recognized as overall product expert with specific focus on call processing and billing.*
- ✓ Played integral role in successfully implementing proprietary commercial TSS billing system.
- ✓ Supported PdM organization by creating ROMs, technical support for RFPs (Vivo, Sprint, TELUS, TM, Tata, Inquam, Alaska, Reliance, Pakistan, PBTL, Mauritius, Telefonica, Brasicel, and Angola).
- ✓ Proactively identified functional areas of improvement for requirements coverage, contributed to resolving several faults, improved customer documentation, and provided reference for future releases as well as other customers.
- ✓ *Received 'Above and Beyond Performance Award' – Oct 2003*

Senior Staff Engineer · MSS Systems Engineering   Aug 2000 – Apr 2002

- ✓ Successfully led and coordinated the cross-functional development teams, 30 engineers, to meet the scheduled design, code, and test completion dates ensuring Feature T-Gates are met.
- ✓ Feature Technical Lead for Concurrent Voice/Data Services feature, the largest revenue-generating feature for KDDI customer.
- ✓ Feature Lead for Paging Channel SMS feature. Created requirements and design, led implementation phase of five engineers' team, supported product, network, and release testing, and created customer reference documentation.
- ✓ Performed the role of functional area lead for Trunk Manager and A1 interface functional areas. Provided 2-day Technical Workshops for internal/customer knowledge sharing and functional area transition from Caltel.
- ✓ Provided customer site testing and FOA (First Office Application) support for major EMX releases and off-hours CNRC (Customer Networks Resolution Center) support.
- ✓ *Received 'Bravo Award' – May 2001, Sep 2001, Jan 2002*

Software Engineer · EMX Development   Jan 1999 – Jul 2000

- ✓ Developed design and code for SMS feature as a Trunk Manager functional area lead for the largest FA impacted by the feature. Supported product, network, and release testing.
- ✓ Contributed to customer release documentation. Supported feature-level SMS testing at various internal labs and customer sites resulting in successful deployment at customer sites.
- ✓ Designed and coded phases for wiretap and virtual circuits feature development, as well as initial assessment of internal and customer EMX PRs (problem reports) to route/classify issues, and provided problem assessments for many of these PRs.
- ✓ Created an implementation process to serve as reference for new hires.
- ✓ Provided CNRC support during the Y2K transition.
- ✓ *Received 'Above and Beyond Performance Award' – Jan 2000, Dec 2000 and 'Certificate of Outstanding Achievement' – Jun 1999*

Education

University of Portland, Portland, OR   1998

Master of Science in Computer Engineering

Technology and Science Institute, India   1996

Bachelors of Engineering in Electronics

LIANE ORTIZ

Stevens Point, WI 54481   (715) 555-1654   TechSupport@gmail.com

App Support/Tech Support/Desktop Support

Performance Summary

Technologically sophisticated, bilingual (Spanish/English) IT Support & Training Specialist with hands-on experience in project life-cycle management for technical and intranet applications, website development and maintenance, and workgroup support. Proven desktop and network troubleshooting skills. Expertise in:

☑ Help Desk & Hardware Support	☑ First-Level PC Support	☑ Project
☑ System Upgrades	☑ LAN / WAN Architecture	☑ Escalation
☑ Peer-to-Peer User Groups	☑ Web Content Upgrades	☑ Customer Service

Technology Profile

Networking LAN/WAN, Windows 2000/NT 4.0 Server, Windows 95 Server, TCP/IP, SQL Server

Operating Systems Windows 95/98/2000/XP, Windows 2000/NT 4.0 Server, DOS 6.0

Programming HTML code, CGI, Java, JavaScript, C Programming, RPG 400, SQL, Visual Basic 5.0, Visual InterDev 6.0, AS/400, ASP code

Applications

Dream Weaver	Acrobat 8	Excel	PowerPoint
GroupWise	Flash	Access	Flash 4.0
Page mill	Lotus Suite	WinZip	PDF
Corel Suite	Photoshop	Kodak	WinZip

Professional Experience

WISCONSIN STATE TREASURY DEPT., DIV. OF TAXATION,	2002–Present
Senior Technician, MIS – Technical Support	2005–Present

Promoted to provide help desk support for 2000+ end-users (including remote users) in 9 locations throughout Wisconsin, as well as project management team leadership for special technical assignments. First point of contact for support incidents, as well as end-user training.

- **Help Desk.** Ensure effective "one-stop" technical support for mainframe, WAN, LAN, and remote system. Install and update software, and set up, configure, and troubleshoot Reach Center equipment. Track and de-escalate technology and workflow problems, and assist Desktop Support Group and other IT groups.

- **Website Development.** Project managed Division of Taxation's website redesign to text-only version, enabling fast and easy access for all users, including vision impaired. Supervised staff of 8.

- **Intranet Development.** Key player in creation, launch, and maintenance of Division of Taxation intranet site, providing management with easily retrievable, up-to-date information for operations decisions. Initiated, created, and maintain Access users group intranet to facilitate informationsharing and learning.

- **Project Management.** Led WIX CD-ROM project for 2 years, delivering interactive CD-ROMs with 1000+ tax-law-verified documents for simplified tax preparation (tax years 2001 & 2002) on schedule.

- **ASP Development.** Played pivotal role in beta-test programming and development of causal sales application (upgraded Alpha 4 database into back-end of Access 2000 and SQL Server, front-end into Internet Explorer via ASP programming).

- **End-User Training.** Expanded Reach Center offerings by designing, developing, and delivering advanced programs and manuals for MS Office, GroupWise, Novell Network, and Internet, making information easily understood and usable. Manage all Access courses and training; supervise 5 adjunct team instructors.

Technical Assistant, MIS – Technical Support   2001-2005

First-level technical support for software installation, as well as setup and configuration of new equipment used in Division of Taxation (PCs, laptops, printers, scanners, projectors, digital & video).

- **IT Software Training.** Designed curriculum and materials, and delivered technical training, for introductory programs in Microsoft Office Suite (Word, Excel, Access), as well as Windows 95, keeping staff motivated and focused while improving job satisfaction and productivity.

- **Website Support.** Functioned as Web Editor for Division of Taxation's Internet/Intranet website, proofing and updating website information on a daily basis.

- **Database Maintenance.** Upgraded and maintained link-shared employee Access database with Chief of Staff's office, ensuring data integrity for training. Created database reports for management evaluation.

- **Technical Development Project.** Pioneered development and implementation of storage, archive, and retrieval system for electronic presentations used throughout Division of Taxation.

Principal Clerk – Technical Education   1998–2001

Promoted to provide installation, configuration, and troubleshooting support for new equipment and software in REACH Center, as well as evaluation and modification of skills assessment.

- **Training Center Database.** Initiated and implemented data-gathering system in Access to compile, store, and retrieve statistics on computer training classes. Researched and wrote monthly reports used to evaluate training trends and staff training needs.

- **WI Saver Rebate Program.** Key team participant in initial, large-scale data compilation for WI Saver Rebate Program, including retrieval, distribution, quality control, and storage of data.

Senior Clerk Typist, Clerk Typist – Corporation Business Tax   1995–1997

Assisted auditors by researching taxpayer information on mainframe, ordered work files for Supervising Auditor using HLLAPI information system, and prepared report statistics using Excel spreadsheets.

WISCONSIN STATE DEPT. OF BANKING, Madison, WI   1993–1998
Data Entry Specialist/Legal Secretary

Front office support for attorneys and accountants: records management, legal document preparation, purchasing, and equipment maintenance. Used IS software for research and to process taxpayer complaints.

FIRST AMERICAN BANK, Stevens Point   1988-1993
Customer Service Representative

Instructed employees in use of computerized banking systems and procedures. Audited financial reports and balance sheets. Cash management responsibility exceeded $100,000.

Education

Instructor Certification, **HRDI, Blue Bell, PA – 2000**
Courses: Curriculum Design, Performance Consulting, Training Presentations, Design Surveys and Questions, Determining Training Needs, and Active Techniques for Teaching.

Certificate in Computer Programming, The Computer Institute, Madison, WI – 1999
Courses: HTML, CGI, Java Programming, JavaScript Programming, RPG 400, C Programming, SQL, Visual Basic 5.0, AS/400 Subfiles & Common Language Queries, MS Office, Windows NT 4.0

Ongoing Professional and Technical Development in-house and at vendor locations (1995–present)

Superior references available on request.

Jesus Zamudio

Pittsboro, WA 12345   (888) 555-2200   **programswell@yahoo.com**

Web Developer/Programmer/Database Programmer

"If it's grown wild and beyond control

I will tame and teach your website or database new manners"

Jesus Zamudio The Site Whisperer

Performance Profile/Performance Summary

➢ 14 years of innovation in Web Development and Programming for high profile technical companies and governmental organizations. Skilled problem-solver with fast learning curve for cutting-edge technologies.

➢ Polished communication, presentation, training, and client-relations skills. Able to relate effectively to people at all levels and convey complex technical information in an understandable manner.

➢ Experienced in all aspects of architecture and accessibility techniques. Hands-on knowledge of Section 508 and W3C Standards.

Technical Skills

Languages	HTML, XHTML DHTML CSS Stylesheets, ColdFusion, Fusebox, Perl, JavaScript, CGI Scripting, XSSI, Java, Java Servlets, JSP, JDBC, Swing
Database Applications	SQL, SQL/PL, Oracle, Access, Database Design and Architecture
Software	Dreamweaver, Flash, Fireworks, Adobe PhotoShop
Operating Systems	Unix and Windows 95/98/2000/NT

Professional Experience

Excel Systems/EPA – Research Triangle Park, WA   2003 - Present

Web Developer/IT Specialist

Manage the maintenance, development, and enhancement of a Coldfusion application that interfaces with an Oracle database.
Create, update, and maintain 11,000 web pages/templates while ensuring compliance with section 508 and EPA web guidelines.
Perform Java Script and PDF conversions; create high quality graphics; produce content; integrate dynamic popup menus; update employee web-based information.

➢ Managed the complete conversion of 20,000 EPA web pages to meet section 508 website guidelines in both appearance and compatibility.
➢ Instrumental in successfully meeting all critical and stringent deadlines.
➢ Recognized by management for advanced skill level and efficiency.

Jesus Zamudio (888) 555-2200 **programswell@yahoo.com** Page 2

Django Systems Pittsboro WA 2002 - 2003

Web Developer/IT Specialist

Oversaw all aspects of client website development. Performed a wide range of design and coding projects utilizing HTML, DHTML, XHTML, JavaScript, and Flash. Updated and maintained content and graphics for both new and previously existing sites.

> ➤ Spearheaded and managed all business, technical, and client-relations functions.
> ➤ Developed and launched numerous high-impact websites in addition to successfully re-designing existing sites to create additional market exposure.

MCTC – Research Triangle Park, WA WA 1999 - 2002

Junior Systems Programmer/Analyst

Hired to develop and code web-based applications and user interfaces in transmitting/integrating data with Oracle databases for a comprehensive governmental occupational network database. Served as a member of a technical team in developing multiple web, database, data search, and retrieval applications.

> ➤ Recruited for a part-time position, promoted to full-time.
> ➤ Pioneered the research and development of guidelines for people with disabilities.

Marketing/Technical Support Assistant, URKG CORPORATION – Morton, WA (1997 to 1998)

Educational & Training

MS Computer Information Technology (Expected 5/03), REGIS UNIVERSITY – Colorado Springs, CO (GPA 3.96)

Bachelor of Arts in Sociology (1997), UNIVERSITY OF NORTH CAROLINA – Chapel Hill, NC (GPA 3.7)

Information Systems Programming (1999), DURHAM TECHNICAL COMMUNITY COLLEGE – Durham, NC (GPA 4.0)

HTML   Advanced HTML   Advanced Online Java Script Training   Sun's sl285 Hands-on Java Workshop   XML Certification Training   Applied Systems Analysis and Design   Object-Oriented Software

"Websites and databases have personalities: those of their designers –
that's why they're often cranky. I can give them the performance
and accessibility your users want and deserve"

Jesus Zamudio

SHARON WISE

Plymouth, MI 48170   734.555.0487   child_guidance@gmail.com

School Guidance Counselor
"I bring competence and team spirit, caring and a smile."

Performance Profile/Performance Summary

Dedicated elementary, middle, and high school guidance counselor, skilled at providing positive direction for students' academic, social, and emotional well-being. Work effectively with children with ADHD, and with multicultural and diverse populations.

Core Counseling Skills

Guidance Curriculum: Classroom Guidance Lessons; Career Awareness; Conflict Resolution/Social Skills; Developmental Awareness

Individual Planning: Student Assessments; Student Placement & Scheduling; New Student Transition; Academic & Career Advisement

Responsive Services: Mental Health; Family & Teacher Consulting; Crisis Intervention & Grief Management; Psycho-Educational Support Groups

Systems Support: Program Evaluation; Program Development & Coordination; Needs Assessment; Committee Participation

Education & Certification

MA, *School Counseling*, UNIVERSITY OF DETROIT-MERCY, Detroit, MI
MA, *Teaching*, MARYGROVE COLLEGE, Detroit, MI
BA, *Teaching - Social Studies/French*, MICHIGAN STATE UNIVERSITY, East Lansing, MI
Certified - *Counseling* - K-12 - State of Michigan
Certified - *Social Studies & French* - grades 7-12 - State of Michigan
Certified - *LLPC* - expected completion 7/03

Professional Experience

HARTLAND COMMUNITY SCHOOLS, Hartland, MI   2007 - 2010
SCHOOL COUNSELOR

Provide individual and small-group counseling sessions and large-group counseling presentations within classroom and guidance office environments for a school with 800 students. Participate in parent/teacher meetings to discuss and develop emotional and behavioral strategies for students with physical, mental, and emotional challenges.

- Developed 45-minute Bully-Proofing classes and presented them to each of 30 classes in the building.
- Wrote a monthly article for the school newsletter on a topic of relevance.
- Facilitated students participating in the Midwest talent search for the Gifted & Talented program.
- Held orientation for new students and their parents, providing them with a schedule of classes and showing them around the building.
- Created 30-minute Career Awareness/Exploration sessions so students would become exposed to various career options. Organized a Career Day, arranging for 40 speakers in various fields to talk with the students about their profession.
- Facilitated support groups dealing with social and coping skills, and conducted needs assessment and program evaluation with staff and students.
- Designed a survey for students and teachers to evaluate the guidance program.

Continued

SCHOOL COUNSELOR continued

- Participated as a team member for the School Improvement Team (SCIT).

Performed Title I coordinator duties, planning and organizing initial structure mailings, assigning students to teachers, adhering to budgets, and scheduling classes.

NOVI COMMUNITY SCHOOLS, Novi, MI   2002 - 2007
GUEST TEACHER

Substituted in the middle school and high school, teaching most subjects, including special ed. Immediately tried to develop a rapport with students and engage in discussion of relevant topics. Facilitated the discussion to steer towards daily lesson plan. Discussion and debate kept students centered, entertained, and open to learning.

- Given long-term teaching assignment for students with disabilities. Taught math, science, and social studies in grades 6–8 for a full semester. There were 5–10 students in each of four classes, ages 11–13 - many students had ADHD. Wrote lesson plans, graded assignments, and consulted with parents.

DETROIT PUBLIC SCHOOLS, Detroit, MI   1993 - 2002
FRENCH & SOCIAL STUDIES TEACHER

Taught five classes each day, with each class having 30–35 students, engaging their curiosity and research abilities in structured classroom activities. Provided lectures, notes, study guides, and projects for courses in American History, Government, Economics, World Geography, Global Issues, and French.

- Devised an effective structure for parent communication.
- Gathered resources as supplemental materials to be used in conjunction with assigned texts to give students a richer experience.
- Assigned different subjects each year, showed flexibility in providing first-rate learning experience for each subject.
- Developed a system to track work and assignments while moving to different rooms for each class period.
- Provided students with practical experience, such as making menus and calendars in French.
- Member of School Improvement team and on the committee to improve student self-esteem.

Professional Commitment

Association Involvement
- American Counseling Association
- American School Counselor Association
- Michigan Counseling Association
- Michigan School Counselor Association

Recent Conference Participation
Launching Career Awareness - Oakland Education Service Agency
Legal Issues for School Counselors - Washtinaw County Counselors Association
Counseling Groups in Crisis - Michigan Association of Specialists in Group Work
A.D.H.D. in the New Millennium - Oakland Schools
Bully-Proofing Your School - Oakland Schools
The Human Spirit & Technology - Michigan Counseling Association
Understanding Attachment Disorders - Medical Educational Service
Grief Counseling Skills - Cross Country University

"My work brings meaning to my life."

Nancy Scott

17 Yellow Rose Circle
Lamesa, TX 79331-5813

(806) 555-1079
n.scott@gmail.com

Environmental, Health, & Safety
Performance Summary

Environmental, Health, & Safety specialist experienced with program development that profitably promotes occupational health and safety. Encourages a culture of safety that minimizes workplace incidents, resulting in cost savings associated with accidents and fines from state and federal non-compliance issues. Solid interpersonal skills and cross-functional team diplomacy coupled with effective leadership abilities. Experience with emergency preparedness and response.

Professional Skills

* EH&S Management
* Regulatory Compliance
* EH&S Task Coordination
* SPCC Plans
* Environmental Assessments
* Data Collection & Analysis
* Workplace Hazard Reduction

* Worksite Safety Practices
* Accident Investigation
* Facility Inspections
* Environmental Permits
* EH&S Internal Audits

Professional Experience

Black Gold Energy, LLC, Odessa, TX   2010–Present
O&G exploration and production company with nine drilling rigs and PHMSA-regulated pipelines.
EH&S Manager   2012-Present
2nd hire in EH&S Department, promoted to manager in 24 months. Well, facility, and equipment inspections, SPCC Plans, and train personnel. Advise corporate departments on environmental and safety issues. Conduct Environmental, Health, & Safety training programs for all departments and employees.

- Prevent regulatory fines and shutdowns with oversight of proper state and federal filings.
- Reduce fines due to improper driver training, logs, files, and documentation of vehicle maintenance.
- Significant savings in fines for failure to comply with state and federal regulations with pipeline regulation and inventory control.
- Initiated system for investigating potential purchases for environmental and safety issues, saving the company money by detecting problems that either canceled sale or led to a substantial price deduction.
- Controlled fines by evaluating air pollution control permit applications, inspected facilities to ensure compliance, and worked with departments to minimize air emissions and pollution.

Education

Texas A&M BS Science, Energy, and Environmental Resource Management   2009

Professional Certifications

Registered Environmental Manager	REM #8226	NREP
Certified Environmental Auditor	CEA #5400	NREP
Certified Environmental and Safety Compliance Officer	CESCO #972214080	NREP

Professional Organizations

National Registry of Environmental Professionals
Texas Petroleum Association

Superior references available

196

Brooke Epstein

1966 W. Main Street
Fairfield, IL 62842

(618) 555-1951
consultant.lifesci@earthlink.net

Life Sciences Consultant

PERFORMANCE SUMMARY

Eight years' experience in Life Sciences working at the intersection of medical science and business. B.S. in Engineering (Bio-engineering major) and an MBA. Fluent Mandarin & Spanish. Experienced in research and development, discovery, business process re-engineering, product development, due diligence, technical writing, and presentations.

✓ Successfully develops & brings products to market, meets regulatory compliance, and streamlines internal processes.
✓ Ability to drive organic revenue growth, reduce working capital and risk, and enhance margins and efficiency.
✓ Effectively communicates with all levels of the organization, vendors, and clients.
✓ Manages projects within scope, schedule, and budget while satisfying project requirements for clients.
✓ Excellent interpersonal and cross-functional team leadership abilities.

PROFESSIONAL SKILLS

Research & Development	Technical Writing/Reports	Process Improvement
Life Sciences & Health Care	Product/Business Recommendations	Process Design
Project Management	Client/Vendor	Risk
Statistical Analysis	Negotiations	Margin Enhancement
Data Collection & Analysis	Forecasting/Budget Planning	Business Development Strategies
Market Analysis	New Product	Regulatory
Technology Evaluation	Development &	Compliance
Financial Analysis	Launch	

PROFESSIONAL EXPERIENCE

The Cyrn Clinic, Johnsonville IL   2012–Present
Research Supervisor
Responsible for lab and research operations; supervises related staff, including on-boarding and off-boarding, plus training residents and scientists in experimental methods, safety procedures, and institutional protocols, leading to fewer compliance issues.

• Increased employee satisfaction to an all-time high of 97%, resulting in improved productivity and lower turnover.
• Managed relationships with regional teaching university scientists and physicians, resulting in a joint disease-specific center.
• Introduced new policies and procedures for security, IT, administration, and Human Resources to increase efficiency.

Warp-Speed Bio Sciences, Cincinnati OH   2009–2012
Research Associate
Due Diligence associate. Performed technology and commercialization assessments, gathering competitive intelligence, providing summary reports, and making recommendations to CSO and CEO regarding funding for startup medical device companies.

• Built relationships with physicians and inventors, resulting in the formation of two new medical device companies.

- Conscientious research allowed company to avoid potential legal issues regarding patent attributions.

MIcroRNA, Boston MA   2003–2009
Engineer
Oversaw development and manufacture of all products. Interfaced with clients, vendors, and the scientific community.

- Identified a need for and implemented a class 100 clean room, reducing production errors and costs by 15%.
- Increased sales by 10% by persuading scientists and clinicians to try products in new areas of use.

EDUCATION/CERTIFICATIONS/AWARDS

Master of Business Administration, Northwestern University   2009

Bachelor of Science in Engineering, Ohio State University   2003
Major: Bioengineering
Awarded Whitaker Foundation Industry Internship

Certifications
Bronze Quality Fellow Certification   2010
Mayo Quality Fellows Program
Sponsoring Organization: Mayo Clinic College of Medicine

PUBLICATIONS & PRESENTATIONS

Molecular ███████████████████████████████ / Journal of Investigative Dermatology / A. Crane, K. Carole, Y. Blangham, K. Lilstakicz. 2011.

███████████████████████ Expression is Associated with Increased Differentiation and Decreased Proliferative Capacity of ███████████ / Society for Investigative Dermatology / A. Crane, K. Lilstakicz, J. Petigrew, M. Lisetz, M. Swittnetcz, J. Corbiss. 2010.

████████ Profiling and Normalization on █████████ / BioExpo, AZ/ M. Lisetz, M. Swittnetcz. Phoenix, AZ / 2009.

RESEARCH STUDIES

A Tissue ████████████████████████████████ Malignancies / AK. Carole, Y. Blangham, K. Lilstakicz, K. Tate. 2011–Present.
A Pilot study of ████████████████ / K. Lilstakicz, J. Petigrew, M. Lisetz, J. Corbiss. 2010–2012.

Role ██████████████████ Carcinoma / F. Frankel, J. Landy, P. Purim, D. Homeforr. 2010–2012.

AFFILIATIONS & VOLUNTEER ACTIVITIES

Biomedical Engineering Society, Member   Current

Illinois Management Society, Member   Current

Licensing Executives Society, Illinois Chapter, Member   Current

Superior references available

Emerson Smith

1400 King George Boulevard
Savannah, Georgia 31419

(912) 555-0660
guyfriday@yahoo.com

HR Admin Assistant

Performance Summary

4 years' experience as Human Resource Administrative Assistant in a large retail environment. Provides administrative services as needed to assist in smooth functioning of HR department. Experienced in employee relations, benefits administration, recruitment, staff development, and employment laws, employee retention, and succession planning. Knowledgeable in employment laws, including ADA, OSHA, and FMLA.

- Ability to deal with ambiguous situations using diplomacy and tact.
- Researches and resolves issues for all levels of employees, executives, and customers.
- Schedules meetings, travel arrangements, and other tasks as needed.
- Organized and detail oriented, with the ability to work in fast-paced, deadline-driven environments.

Professional Skills

* Employee Relations	* Onboarding	* FMLA
* Employee Counseling	* Employee Records	* Project Management
* Recruiting & Staffing	* Benefits Administration	* Calendar Management
* Payroll	* Employee Scheduling	* OSHA
* ADA	* Training & Development	* Exit Processing

Professional Experience

Penney's Department Store, Hilton Head, SC   2012–Present
HR/Administrative Assistant

Processes and maintains employee documentation, including staffing, recruitment, training, grievances, performance evaluations, classifications, employee leave of absence, and unemployment claims. Manages work schedules, budgets, and labor hours, and prepares payroll information and reporting of total store payroll.

- Achieved highest employee retention in the district.
- Reached highest ranking for merit raise in store location for 3 years based on exceptional performance.
- Aided in increasing Best Practice HR scorecard to consistent rating of "Highly Effective" (90% +).
- Successful onboarding and training of 60+ employees during holiday seasons.
- Implemented tracking procedures for corporate audits, resulting in above industry standard of 75%.

Professional Development

HR Annual Class: Ethics, Harassment, and Respect Training   2012–Present
HR Learning ADA & FMLA   2013

Education

Texas Christian University, BS Psychology   2011

Professional Affiliations

SPHR Hilton Head SC Chapter

MICHAEL SHARPTON

8745 Country Club Drive South • Southtown, Ohio 43050

Home (614) 555-4552 • Mobile (614) 555-0953 • sharp_on_hr@sbcglobal.net

---

WORKFORCE DEVELOPMENT SPECIALIST

Performance Profile/Performance Summary

Organized and goal-oriented professional, committed to contributing to organizational objectives as a member of a committed team. Works well independently as well as collaboratively. Skilled communicator adept in coaching, training, and mentoring groups and individuals. Possesses outstanding organizational skills with focus on quality and detail.

→ Earned Certificate of Achievement from City of Columbus, Department of Human Resources: Citywide Training & Development Center of Excellence (12/2009)

→ Completed National Professional Certification in Customer Service from NRF Foundation Research & Education (10/2009)

→ Experienced youth outreach worker with success organizing and facilitating programs that reduced school truancy and gang participation.

→ Identified need, launched and facilitated youth peer discussion groups.

→ Developed workshops, seminars, and other activities to motivate youth.

Core Skills—

Training ~ Counseling & Coaching ~ Community Outreach ~ Program Coordination ~ Managing & Organizing
Persuasive Skills ~ Quality & Detail Oriented ~ Time & Task Management ~ Prioritizing
Multitasking ~ Problem Solving ~ Consensus Building

PROFESSIONAL EXPERIENCE

HONDA OF AMERICA MFG, INC., Marysville, OH • 1989 to 2009
Production Associate

Inspected vehicles to ensure quality; identified and remedied defects. Demonstrated versatility in handling wide range of functions including welding, painting, assembling, installing, quality inspecting, and test-driving.

Selected Accomplishments

- Consistently met "impossible" deadlines to attain company goals.
- Participated in various special projects including identifying and correcting safety hazards, testing noise levels, etc.
- Ensured compliance with OSHA guidelines.

PROFESSIONAL EXPERIENCE CONTINUED

PRIMERICA FINANCIAL SERVICES, Columbus, OH • 1990 to 1996
Financial Service Advisor

Built and managed business selling insurance and investment products to individuals and businesses.

Selected Accomplishments

- Acquired NASD Series 6 and 63 licenses
- Marketed company products; recruited and trained new agents.
- Educated prospects and clients on products, and importance of planning for the future and making sound financial decisions.
- Organized and led meetings; taught budgeting and importance of planning; recommended options.

EDUCATION/ADDITIONAL INFORMATION

UNIVERSITY OF CINCINNATI, Cincinnati, Ohio
Bachelor of Science in Criminal Justice
Associate of Applied Science in Law Enforcement Technology

PROFESSIONAL DEVELOPMENT

- Preparation for Series 6 & 63 Licensing Examination: Primerica Financial Services
- Henkels & McCoy Computer Training & Job Readiness Training in Customer Service
- City of Columbus, Department of Human Resources—Citywide Training & Development Center of Excellence: Certificate of Achievement; 2009.
- NRF Foundation Research & Education
- National Professional Certification Customer Service; 2009.

PROFESSIONAL LICENSES

- NASD Series 6 & Series 63
- Health, Life & Accident Insurance License

COMMUNITY/VOLUNTEER ACTIVITIES

- Youth Outreach Worker—Central Community House/Youth Outreach Project, Columbus, OH
- Group Worker—St. Stephen's Community House, Columbus, OH
- Volunteer—Dress for Success

Robert Rauschenberg

Encino, CA 91436   818.555. 6832   publicist@sbcglodal.com

Entry-Level in Publishing/Marketing

"Worked my way through school and interned every summer; I'm energized, focused, hard-working, and professional."

Performance Profile/Performance Summary

➤ Professional work experience in Public Relations, Publishing, TV Production. Hard working and energetic, with a proven ability to produce results in a fast-paced environment with critical deadlines. Outgoing and articulate communicator who works well with public and coworkers at all levels. Equally effective collaborating in a team setting and working independently. Fluent *English, Spanish, Yiddish*.

Professional Skills

➤ Critical Deadlines	➤ Microsoft Office	➤ Bilingual English/Spanish
➤ Public Speaking	➤ Research & Analysis	➤ Press Kits
➤ Team Player	➤ Content Copy	➤ Merchandise Sourcing
➤ Enjoys Challenge	➤ Works Independently	➤ Client Hosting
➤ Writing	➤ Location Scout	➤ Styling Assistant
➤ Problem Solving	➤ Presentations	➤ Multi-task
➤ Transcriptions	➤ Shoot Assistant	➤ Wardrobe
➤ Captions/Headlines	➤ Accommodation	➤ Word, Excel, PowerPoint

Education

BA in Mass Communications; Minor in Journalism   May 2012
UCLA

Professional Experience

Dynamic Publications/Sports Today Magazine, Hollywood, CA   Summers 2006–2007
Assistant/Intern (for Editor-in-Chief)

Worked closely with Editor-in-Chief and Fashion Editor of teen magazine. Prioritized and coordinated multiple assignments including transcriptions, research, and follow up. Contributed story ideas that resulted in publication.

- Provided hands-on assistance to Fashion Editor at photo shoots. Contacted leading manufacturers to obtain sample merchandise; organized clothing for shoots; assisted with overall styling.
- Wrote articles for fashion feature of magazine. Arranged photo shoots for article including selecting locations and arranging staff housing. Attended editorial staff meetings, providing input on story.
- Contributed ideas for fitness feature. Wrote captions, explaining new trends in fitness training.

Continued

Hollywood Marketing Associates, LA, CA   Summers 2005–2006
Assistant to Executive Vice President—Southern California Office

Assistant to EVP Hollywood office of national marketing and public relations organization.
- Whatever the EVP needed, I made happen, taking gofering to new heights.
- Performed computer work, hosted clients, scheduled appointments, etc.
- Assembled press kits and EPK's.

Media Management Productions, LA, CA   Summers 2004–2005
Assistant to Executive Vice President—Southern California Office
Assisted in coordinating makeup and wardrobe for television commercial productions.
- Coordinated wardrobe selections with set decorators.
- Arranged specific selections and appropriate sizes for individual models.
- Assisted location scout with identifying locations and negotiating fees.

Additional Skills

Foreign Languages
Tri-lingual English, Spanish, Yiddish

Computer Skills
Microsoft Office: Word, Excel, PowerPoint
Social Networking

"I will start at the bottom and earn my way up.
I will get things done, and done right."

Charles Chalmers

Manhattan, NY 11658   gallery_director@earthlink.net   (212) 555-1432

Gallery Director/Curator

Performance Profile/Performance Summary

My professional life is focused on art in all it embraces: drawing, painting, sculpture, photography, cinema, video, audio, performance and digital art, art history and criticism; my personal life is similarly committed. Recently relocated to Manhattan, I intend to make a contribution to the NY Arts community that requires my knowledge, enthusiasm, and sensibilities.

Core Competencies

✓ Art History	✓ Installation of Art	✓ Recruitment & Selection
✓ Art Theory	✓ Space Fluidity	✓ Private Collectors
✓ Art Research	✓ Hang/Light/Label	✓ Catering
✓ Art Communities	✓ Themed/Sequenced	✓ Graphics
✓ Alumni Networks	✓ Space Reconfiguration	✓ Photoshop
✓ Artist Networks	✓ Dynamic Dialogue	✓ PR
✓ Art Handlers	✓ Social Networking	✓ Intercultural Exchanges

Art History

Thorough knowledge of art history from caves of Lascaux through current artists such as Bruce Nauman, Jessica Stockholder, and Luc Tuymans. Film history from Lumiere Brothers to Almodovar. Current with key critical art and film theory. Ongoing workshops and lectures with the likes of Matthew Barney, Louise Bourgeoise, and Andy Goldsworthy.

Research New Artists

Connected to cutting-edge art and artists through involvement with the art communities and galleries of New York and Boston and the faculty, student, and alumni networks of RISD, Columbia, Boston Museum School, New England School of Art & Design, and now Mass Art. Twenty years of Manhattan gallery openings and networking with artists at MOMA, PS1, Guggenheim, Whitney, Metropolitan, Film Forum. Attend International Center for Photography workshops and lectures.

Gathering Artwork

Through local artists, regional and global artist networks, intercultural artist exchanges, alumni groups, first rank private collectors, personal and family networks, and Internet calls for submissions.

Art and the Community

Conception and launch of themed, resourced, and sequenced shows that invigorate campus and community involvement. Reconfigure existing art spaces to create dynamic dialogue with visitors. Education and outreach programs.

Installation of Art

Maintain fluidity of gallery space in preparing exhibitions with recognition of size/time considerations for the art, to insure a sympathetic environment for the presented works. Hang, light, and label shows in sequences that create dialogue between the works.

Continued

PR Materials

Energizing invitations, comprehensive press kits, illustrated press releases, and artist binder materials. Sensitive to placing art in historical/cultural context. Photoshop.

Management Experience

Fourteen years' art staff management experience, including curriculum development. Responsible for art instructors, art handlers, and maintenance crews, as well as working with printers, catering, and graphic arts staff.

Employment

1994-2005 Chair of Visual Arts, The Green Briar School

Duties: Curriculum development, portfolio preparation, internal and external monthly shows, theater sets, monthly video news show. Taught art history and all the studio arts, managed staff of three.

1989-2004 President Art Workshops

Duties: Private art studio and art history curriculum, staff of four. Private groups to Manhattan museums and gallery tours.

1980-1989 Freelance artist, photographer, and editor

Highlights from the *sublime* to the *ridiculous* include: Taught photography at Trinity School, Manhattan; photographer for the Ramones; editor of *Pioneer*, insurance industry trade magazine; assistant to Claudia Weill, documentary filmmaker, director of "Girlfriends."

Education

MFA. Magna cum laude. Columbia University, 1983
Awards: ****** ***** Prize for film criticism
Taught undergraduate Intro to Film, under Milos Forman and Andre Bazin.

Subscriptions

Art in America, *Art News*, *Art Forum*, *New York Times*, *Parkett*, *Sight & Sound*, *Film Comment*, *Modern Painters*.

Memberships

MOMA/PS1, Whitney Museum of American Art, Guggenheim, Metropolitan Museum of Art, DIA.

Nora Cho

11 Spruce St.
New York, NY 11509

(212) 555-6745
Email@gmail.com

ILLUSTRATOR ✍ GRAPHIC DESIGNER ✍ VISUAL ARTIST

CORE SKILLS

Textbook Illustration

❖❖❖

Scientific Drawings

❖❖❖

Museum Exhibits
Illustration

❖❖❖

Storybook Illustration

❖❖❖

Cartoon Image Design

❖❖❖

Greeting Card Design/
Illustration

❖❖❖

Artifact Replications

❖❖❖

Surface Coloration
Restoration

❖❖❖

Original & Production
Artwork

❖❖❖

Visual Aid Preparation

❖❖❖

Photo-Realistic
Illustration

❖❖❖

Logo Design

❖❖❖

Full-Figure Drawing

❖❖❖

PERFORMANCE PROFILE/PERFORMANCE SUMMARY

Creative, diverse illustrator and artist with extensive experience in designing and developing a broad range of visual pieces to meet business and program objectives of both employers and their clients. Particularly adept in creating original, vibrant artwork that captures attention from serious and casual viewers. Additional skills:

- *Developing Products* — Able to translate concepts into well-designed products by integrating various elements, including illustration, formatting, photography, and typography. Combine innovative thinking with logical design elements.
- *Conveying Messages* — Create illustrations that articulate key ideas and earn recognition for aesthetic quality. Excel in reinforcing positive messages.
- *Meeting Expectations* — Maintain consistent track record of fulfilling organizational goals. Highly adaptable to changing needs and requirements.

SELECTED WORKS *(a full portfolio is available for immediate review)*

Marketing Material & Product Design

- International Colloquium for Biology of Soricidae — **Logo, image, and product development** for line of merchandise used in international conference.
- Carnegie Museum of Natural History — **Sweatshirt** *The American Mastodon* for the museum's gift shop. Designed and produced original artwork for full line of products sold in association with The Walton Hall of Ancient Egypt. Created full-sized, full-color paintings for children's area, The Discovery Room.
- H.J. Heinz Pittsburgh Historical Center — **Photo-mural retouching** activities to enhance key display areas.
- Tucson Children's Museum — Initial design and development of cartoon images for outside banner/T-shirt image and other museum merchandise.

Book & Magazine Illustrations

- *The Carnegie Magazine, Pittsburgh Magazine* Miscellaneous illustrations and graphics.
- *The New York Times, Time, Johns Hopkins Magazine, others* Widely published illustrations through the United Press International.
- Dr. L.E. McCullough Instructional drawings for *The Making and Playing of Ullean Pipes*, including musical notation.
- Dr. Sandra Olson Reconstruction illustration of Paleolithic horse fetish for *Horses Through Time.*

Scientific Illustrations

- *National Geographic* 11"x14" acrylic reconstruction of *Eosimias sinesis.*
- Cultural & Environmental Systems Artifacts for Technical Series #56.
- *Walton Hall of Ancient Egypt* Scientifically accurate recreation of 18th dynasty tomb walls and entire hall as graphics artwork. Built complete scale models, coordinated all illustration production with various collaborators, and earned commendation from Egyptologists for accuracy of reconstruction.

CAREER PROFILE

Creative, diverse illustrator and artist with extensive experience in designing and developing broad range of visual pieces to meet business and program objectives of both employers and their clients. Particularly adept in creating original, vibrant artwork that captures attention from serious and casual viewers. Additional skills:

- _Developing Products_ — Able to translate concepts into well-designed products by integrating various elements, including illustration, formatting, photography, and typography. Combine innovative thinking with logical design elements.
- _Conveying Messages_ — Create illustrations that articulate key ideas and earn recognition for aesthetic quality. Excel in reinforcing positive messages.
- _Meeting Expectations_ — Maintain consistent track record of fulfilling organizational goals. Highly adaptable to changing needs and requirements.

SELECTED WORKS _(a full portfolio is available for immediate review)_

Marketing Material & Product Design

- International Colloquium for Biology of Soricidae — **Logo, image, and product development** for line of merchandise used in international conference.
- Carnegie Museum of Natural History — **Sweatshirt** _The American Mastodon_ for the museum's gift shop. Designed and produced original artwork for full line of products sold in association with The Walton Hall of Ancient Egypt. Created full-sized, full-color paintings for children's area The Discovery Room.
- H.J. Heinz Pittsburgh Historical Center — **Photo-mural retouching** activities to enhance key display areas.
- Tucson Children's Museum — Initial design and development of cartoon images for outside banner/T-shirt image and other museum merchandise.

Book & Magazine Illustrations

- _The Carnegie Magazine, Pittsburgh Magazine_ Miscellaneous illustrations and graphics.
- _The New York Times, Time, Johns Hopkins Magazine, others_ Widely published illustrations through the United Press International.
- Dr. L.E. McCullough Instructional drawings for _The Making and Playing of Ullean Pipes_, including musical notation.
- Dr. Sandra Olson Reconstruction illustration of Paleolithic horse fetish for _Horses Through Time_.

Scientific Illustrations

- _National Geographic_ 11"x14" acrylic reconstruction of _Eosimias sinesis_.
- _Cultural & Environmental Systems_ Artifacts for Technical Series #56.
- _Walton Hall of Ancient Egypt_ Scientifically accurate recreation of 18th dynasty tomb walls and entire hall as graphics artwork. Built complete scale models, coordinated all illustration production with various collaborators, and earned commendation from Egyptologists for accuracy of reconstruction

Tina Turner

Middleburg, VA 20118   540-555-5470   eventwizard@comcast.net

Meeting Planner
Conferences · Events · Fundraising · Golf Tournaments

"Successful events look effortless. I take care of business with quiet efficiency."

PERFORMANCE PROFILE/PERFORMANCE SUMMARY

14 years' experience in all aspects of event planning, development, and management. Multitask with strong detail, problem-solving, and follow-through capabilities. Demonstrated ability to manage, motivate, and build cohesive teams that achieve results.

PROFESSIONAL COMPETENCIES

• Government	• PACs	• Associations
• Conferences & Meetings	• Special Events	• Fundraisers
• Logistics	• Meetings & Workshops	• Tours & Competitions
• Database Management	• High-net Donors	• Vendor management
• Team Management	• Planning/Organization	• Contracts
• Budgets	• Negotiations	• Access
• Excel	• PowerPoint	• Outlook
• MS Project	• Publisher	• MeetingTrak

PERFORMANCE HIGHLIGHTS

Planned and coordinated government, association, and private conferences, meetings, events, and fundraisers: all conference activities, workshops, meetings, tours, and special events. **Saved $72,000 on most recent meeting.**

Meeting Coordination

Negotiated hotel and vendor contracts. Prepared and administered budgets. Arranged all on-site logistics, including transportation, accommodations, meals, guest speakers, and audiovisual support.

- Coordinated 10-26 annual workshops for Centers for Disease Control and Prevention.
- Coordinated 2004 National Conference on Smoking and Health (2,000 participants).
- Organized 6,000-participant national annual conferences.
- Coordinated Global Scholarship Pre-Conference Training.
- Developed and supervised education sessions at CSI's 2001 National Convention.
- Directed CSI's National Seminar Series.
- Developed, promoted, and implemented CSI's National Certification Program.
- Managed logistics for Regional Pacific Training in Guam.

Fundraising

Coordinated PAC fundraising events. Supervised high-donor club fulfillment benefits. Team player in the development and implementation of membership and retention programs for BUILD-PAC.

- Coordinated 2 PAC golf tournaments
- Spouse programs
- Parties

Continued

EVENTS MANAGEMENT HIGHLIGHTS

- Centers for Disease Control and Prevention/Office on Smoking & Health
- Tobacco Control Training & Technical Assistance Project
- Health & Human Services Department's Administration on Children, Youth, and Families Grant Review Contract
- Food and Drug Administration
- Centers for Disease Control and Prevention/National Center for Health Statistics
- National Library of Medicine
- Housing & Urban Development Grant Review Contract
- CSI National Seminar Series
- CSI 1998 & 1999 National Conventions and Exhibits

PROFESSIONAL EXPERIENCE

CORPORATE SCIENCES □ Rockville, Maryland   2008-Present
Senior Conference Specialist
ROCKVILLE CONSULTING GROUP □ Arlington, Virginia   2003-2008
Logistics Manager
Senior Conference Coordinator   1997-2003
CONSTRUCTION SPECIALISTS ASSOCIATION □ Arlington, Virginia
Assistant Coordinator of Education Programs
NATIONAL ASSOCIATION OF PIPE WELDERS □ Washington, D.C.   1997
Assistant Director, Fundraising

EDUCATION, CERTIFICATION & AFFILIATIONS

VIRGINIA POLYTECHNIC INSTITUTE □ Blacksburg, VA
B.S. Exercise Physiology, Minor Psychology   1996

Certifications
Go Members Inc. MeetingTrak Certification □ 2009
Certified Meeting Professional (CMP) – 2007

Professional Affiliations
- Meeting Professionals International – Annandale Chapter (AMPI)
- Logistical Committee
- Educational Retreat Committee
- Member Services Committee
- Community Outreach Committee
- Connected International Meeting Professionals Association (CIMPA)
- DC Special Olympics – Volunteer
- Hands On DC – Volunteer
- SPCA of Northern Virginia – Volunteer

"I take care of the details, always."

123 Main Street
Fredericksburg, VA 22408

Nancy Wright

Home (540) 555-2396
Mobile (540) 555-5743
nancywright@yahoo.com

Group Manager • Account Director • PR Manager

Performance Profile

High-tech public relations professional with 13 years' experience, including nine in Silicon Valley, in the software, Internet, networking, consumer electronics, and wireless industries. Substantial experience in PR and strategic communications campaigns that lead to company acquisitions. Experienced in all aspects of strategic and tactical communications from developing and managing multiple campaigns, accounts, and results-oriented teams to developing and placing stories. Seasoned motivational speaker and freelance TV color commentator. Two-time Olympic gold medalist.

Core Competencies

High Tech Public Relations	Media Relations	New Business Development Team Management	Market Research
Strategic Communications	Craft & Place Stories		Build & Lead Teams
Executive Communications	Strong Writing Skills		Mentor
PR Messaging & Tactics	Media Training	Budget Management	Client Satisfaction
Story Telling	Multiple Projects	Account Management	Organizational Skills
Collateral Materials	Story Placement	Project Management	Thought Leadership
Leadership Branding	Counsel Executives	Detail Oriented	PR Counsel
Analyst Relations	Strong Editing Skills	Acquisition Positioning	Social Media
		Pitch Media	

Strategic Public Relations Leadership

Orchestrated PR campaigns that positioned companies as both industry leaders and sound investments. Developed and directed PR campaigns for four companies that were subsequently acquired within two years of the campaigns: *InfoGame Technologies* (creator of the first iProduct®, acquired by *ABC Network*), *Triiliux Digital Systems* (acquired by *Intel*), *LinkExchange* (acquired by *Microsoft*), and *The Internet Mall* (acquired by *TechWave*). Proven client satisfaction demonstrated in repeat business and account growth: over a span of ten years, contracted by former *InfoGame* execs to serve as communications counsel for *NextLink Technologies, ABC Network Systems,* and *AirPlay Networks*.

Executive Communications Management

Executive Communications Manager for iconic executive and public speaker, *Charles Smith, Group VP, Service Provider Sales, ABC Network Systems* (currently *senior VP* and *technology evangelist* for *ABC Network*). Developed communication messaging, strategy, and platform skills for VP, Group VP, and C-level executives.

Media Coverage

ABC World News Tonight, CNN, The Today Show, Associated Press, Baltimore Sun, Boston Globe, Business Times, Business Week, CNN.com, Fast Company, Financial Times, Forbes, Fortune Magazine, Inc., MSNBC.com, New York Times, Parade, San Jose Mercury News, SF Chronicle, USA Today, Wired, Wall Street Journal, AdWeek, CommsDesign, Computer Reseller News, Computer Retail Week, Computer Shopper, Computer World, CRN, CNET, EE Times, Embedded Systems Design, Internet.com, InfoWorld, InformationWeek, Internet.com, Internet Telephony, LightReading, Network World, Phone+, PC Magazine, Red Herring, TMCnet, VoIP News, VON and ZDNet, Dataquest, Forrester Research, Frost and Sullivan, Jupiter Communications, Yankee Group.

——Professional Experience——

Principal   **2003 to Present**
Wright & Associates Public Relations, Anywhere, VA

Develop and deliver strategic communications. Drive all PR strategy and tactics, messaging, media training, media relations, budget management, story creation, and placement for technology clients.

- Representative clients include *AirPlay Networks* (former *InfoGame* and *NextLink client*), *ReligiousSite.com* (founded by *eCompany.com* founder), and *PanJet Aviation*.

Principal   **2001 to 2003**
Three Kids Public Relations, Redwood City, CA
Developed and implemented all strategic and tactical aspects of public relations for Silicon Valley clients, including thought leadership, leadership branding, story creation and telling, media materials, stories, media relations, and publicity.

- *ABC Network Systems*—Executive Communications Manager to Charles Smith, Group VP at *ABC Network*, a highly pursued public speaker.
- *NextLink Technologies*—Company's first PR counsel. Repositioned obscure company, impaired by trademark dilution, into an industry leader by leveraging market's widespread knowledge and use of *NextLink's* industry-standard *GreatD* networking software.

Marketing Manager   **2000 to 2001**
ABC Network Systems, San Jose, CA
Directed internal, cross-functional marketing for *iProduct*, following ABC Network acquisition of *InfoGame* and its technology.

- Shortly after acquisition, ABC Network dissolved *InfoGame/Managed Appliances Business Unit (MASBU)*.

Public Relations Manager   **1998 to 2000**
InfoGame Technology Corporation, Redwood City, CA
Advised CEO and VP of Marketing on all aspects of PR. Developed and implemented all strategies, tactics, and stories.

- Revamped the startup's teetering image, which was ruining *iProduct* sales. After two press tours, garnered hundreds of additional stories in all top trade and consumer media with the *iProduct Reviews* program. Catapulted company into a leadership position in the Internet appliance industry, setting it up for acquisition. *iProduct* is now a household name.
- Managed and inspired cross-functional teams of marketing, operations, and customer service to work outside their job responsibilities to deliver excellent service to hundreds of editors beta-testing the *iProduct 2.0*.

Account Supervisor; Senior Account Executive; Account Executive   **1996 to 1998**
XYZ Advertising & Public Relations (Acquired by FLEISHMAN-HILLARD in 2000), Mountain View, CA
Promoted annually for successful track record of positioning unknown companies as both industry leaders and solid investments/acquisitions. Designed and managed all PR strategy and activities for start-up, software, Internet, and networking companies. Managed teams of up to ten PR professionals.

- Repositioned, rebranded, relaunched, and reintroduced *InfoGame*, the *iProduct 1.0* and *2.0*, positioning them collectively as leading the nascent Internet appliance space.
- Accelerated *Triiliux* and its CEO out of obscurity and into undisputed leadership through media placement and top speaking engagements.
- Transformed unknown *LinkExchange* into a highly publicized leader in the Internet advertising arena. Placed hundreds of stories in both business and industry media.
- Launched *The Internet Mall*, landing continual coverage in all top Internet and business publications.

——**Complementary Experience**——

Motivational Speaker/Guest Celebrity   **1989 to Present**
Coach audiences on how to use the Olympic model to set and achieve goals, and succeed in business and life. Representative clients: *IBM, Hardees, Speedo America, Busch Gardens, Alamo Rent-A-Car*.

Television Sports Commentator   **1987 to 2000**

Swimming analyst for *NBC, ESPN, FoxSports, SportsChannel, Turner Sports,* and others. Covered the *Olympics*.

Awards & Achievements

Winner—Two Olympic swimming gold medals plus one silver and one bronze.

Recipient Southland Corporation's *Olympia Award* for academic and athletic leadership.

NCAA, USA, Southeastern Conference swimming champion and *26-time NCAA All American.*

Hall of Fame Inductee: *International Swimming Hall of Fame, University of Florida, Pacific Northwest Swimming, Washington State Swimming Coaches Association, Mercer Island High School.*

EDUCATION—University of Florida, Gainesville, FL; BS in Journalism, Minor in Speech.

Terry Riley

945 Main St.   Lubbock, TX 79400   806-555-2304   account_manager@*yahoo.com*

ACCOUNT MANAGEMENT
Business Development • Client Retention • Territory Development

Performance Overview

Determined, customer-driven sales professional with extensive experience and track record of success in B2B sales account management within the vending product industry.

Demonstrates ability to gain customer trust and secure win-win results. Builds strong partnerships with small business owners and decision-makers within high-profile businesses: **WalMart**, **McLane** and business partners **Coca-Cola, Pepsi**.

Core Competencies

➢ Consumer Product Sales	➢ Prospecting	➢ Account Management
➢ Customer Relationships	➢ Order Fulfillment	➢ Inventory Management
➢ Merchandising	➢ POS Advertising	➢ Needs Fulfillment
➢ B2B	➢ Installation	➢ Product Maintenance
➢ Field Research	➢ Presentations	➢ Negotiate Contracts
➢ Training	➢ Closing	➢ Product Placement
➢ Market Share	➢ Key Accounts	

Revenue Growth – Maintained consistent, year-over-year pattern of increasing revenues through robust and downturn economies, from $50,000 to $1.2 million as illustrated below:

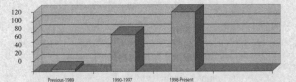

PROFESSIONAL EXPERIENCE

VENDING, INC., Lubbock/Amarillo, TX   1989 – Present
Specializing in sales, installation, and maintenance of vending machines throughout Texas.

Sales Representative/Account Executive

Gained increase in responsibilities as business grew from wholesale liquor distributor to include sales and service of vending machines. Conduct extensive field research to determine optimal locations for machines; develop and deliver presentations to prospective customers detailing how merchandise will add to their bottom line.

Negotiate contract terms and handle all closing and follow-up service activities. Additionally serve as Acting Manager in overseeing performance of 12 team members.

Key Contributions & Accomplishments:

- *Product Placement & Market Share* – Grew number of machines from **1** to **450** from 1989 to 1998 prior to Lubbock opening; expanded inventory from **89** machines in 1998 to **780** by 2004, buying out some of the largest vendors in the area. Earned position as one of top vendors market-wide.
- *Key Account Management* – Built strong, sustainable relationships with broad range of accounts, including: **X-Fab of Texas, Industrial Molding, McLane, Owens-Corning, Wal-Mart**.
- *Customer Service* – Provided excellent service for customer companies throughout tenure, characterized by immediate, thorough resolution of problems with equipment and friendly service.

PROFESSIONAL DEVELOPMENT

Sales Training
Multiple workshops featuring highly-recognized speakers, including:

Zig Ziglar • Paul Tracy • Anthony Robbins

Technical Skills
Skilled in MS Office and Internet tools. Able to operate forklift, pallet jack, and other equipment.

MARY ANN BURROWS

123 Randolph St.   Wilmington, Delaware 19801   806-555-2947   closing-queen@yahoo.com

---

Outside Sales/Account Manager

Performance Profile/Performance Summary

Energetic and goal-focused sales professional with solid qualifications in large account management and customer relationship building/maintenance. Proven ability to develop new business and increase sales within established accounts and mature territories.

Self-confident and poised in interactions across all business hierarchies; a persuasive communicator and assertive negotiator with strong deal-closing abilities. Excellent time-management skills; computer literate.

Core Sales Skills

✓ Closing	✓ Account Development	✓ Account Management
✓ Prospecting	✓ Business Development	✓ Market Turnaround
✓ Cold calling	✓ Customer Relations	✓ Consultative Sales
✓ Advertising	✓ Commercial accounts	✓ Territory Management

Professional Experience

Morris Mfr. Co., Wilmington, DE	1998 – Present
SALES EXECUTIVE	2004 – Present
MANAGER, Harrisburg Store	2000 – 2004
MANAGER TRAINEE, Wilmington Store	1998

Promoted and challenged to revitalize a large metropolitan territory plagued by poor performance. Manage, service, and build existing accounts; develop new business, establishing both regional and national accounts. Serve as key liaison for all customers and work as the only outside sales representative in the company. Produce monthly reports for major national accounts.

- Reversed a history of stagnant sales; delivered consistent growth and built territory sales 22%, to $4.75 million annually, in less than 2 years.
- Surpassed quota by a minimum of 20% for 14 consecutive months.
- Personally deliver 95% of all sales generated for the company's main site.
- Prospected aggressively and opened more than 60 new commercial accounts.
- Improved account service and applied consultative sales techniques; grew sales in every established account a minimum of 15%.

MANAGER, Harrisburg Store
Initially recruited as a management trainee and rapidly advanced to management of a retail location generating $1 million annually. Supervised and scheduled 12 employees. Budgeted and produced advertising, oversaw bookkeeping, and set/managed sales projections and growth objectives.

Education, Training & Associations

B.S., BUSINESS MANAGEMENT	1998
Wilmington College, New Castle, DE	

Additional Training

Building Sales Relationships
Problem Solving Skills

Professional & Community Associations

Member, Chamber of Commerce
Member, Country Club and Women's Golf Association
Youth Soccer Coach and FIFA Certified Referee

Tab Forman

New York, NY 11509   (212) 555-3853   Tforman69@gmail.com

Brand/Product Manager, Gaming Industry

You seek:

Brand/Product Manager, WizKids.com

"Experienced Brand Manager to direct product lines, develop strategic marketing promotions, product research & positioning, and cross-departmental interfacing. 3+ years' management/marketing experience. A+ with game marketing experience." Wizkids.com job Posting at Monster

I deliver:

Performance Profile

15 years' experience in sales and marketing leadership positions. Proven track record in strategic marketing promotions and brand development. Strong commitment to maintaining highest level of product quality while driving revenue growth through coordinated brand management strategies.

Product research and positioning: Coordination of Unique Selling Proposition (USP) with sales/customers/business partners. All core marketing and business development disciplines, with particular strength in product evangelism. Hold deep passion and interest in gaining market share for gaming company. Certified HeroClix Facilitator; run authorized demos of CreepyFreaks and promote Pirates of the Spanish Main, both WizKids products.

Gaming Highlights

- Lifelong participant in the field of gaming, worked for gaming pioneer Chaosium.
- Worked for renowned game designers Sandy Petersen and Greg Stafford.
- All editing, mapping, layouts, and writing for SuperWorld and Companion of SuperWorld.
- Supplemental modules for Cthulhu.
- Gaming store owner, sold business that remains profitable two decades later.

Professional Skills

Product Research & Analysis	Strategic Promotional	Editing, Mapping, Layouts,
Competitive Positioning	Campaigns	Writing
Presentations, Negotiations,	Collateral Material	Vendor Relations
& Closing	Development	Recruitment, Selection
Product Line Management	Strategic Game Marketing	Performance Review
Team Building & Leadership	Point-of-Sale Displays	Advertising Performance
Customer Relationship	Prospecting & Lead	Metrics
Building	Generation	Profile Assessments
		Presentation Skills

Professional Experience

ANVIL BUSINESS DEVELOPMENT, Seattle, WA   2004 – Present
Marketing Manager
Responsible for all marketing strategies, vendor relationships, hiring/training sales staff, evaluating team performance, and completing sales in hands-on account executive role. Contract with companies to develop market presence for telecommunications products and services, working with broad range of clients that includes retailers, software development firms, and real estate developers.

- Redeveloped website and all marketing materials for key client Pacific Rich Homes. Tracked results of advertising placements, created sales/marketing plan, and secured exposure in Everett Business Journal.
- *Results: Increased sales and established pre-selling pattern affecting every community.*

- Improved management of product line (profile assessments) by writing brochure for customization to 5 industries, including health care and nonprofit organizations.

ESCHELON/ICM COMMUNICATIONS, Seattle, WA   2000–2004
Account Executive
Oversaw all aspects of sales, with focus on medium-sized companies. Scope of responsibility included making cold calls, conducting fact-finding research, delivering presentations, securing new accounts, and creating referral partner network.
- Introduced sales and marketing strategies that contributed to product improvement and revenue growth in downturn, heavily competitive market.

NORTHWEST WIRELESS, Seattle, WA   1996–2000
Account Executive
Directed sales and marketing initiatives for business clients. Managed all phases of sales cycle, transitioning to consultative selling approach as company increased lines to accommodate customers.
- Played key role in driving company from startup to Nextel New Dealer of the Year recognition in 1998. Assisted in migrating company from one to multiple carriers.

AFLAC, Seattle, WA   1994–1996
Broker
Represented supplemental insurance programs to companies and their employees.
- Created "package" approach to sell multiple insurance lines simultaneously, resulting in 228% revenue increase and average sale growth from $360 to $820 annual premium.
- Earned formal recognition as Number One Producer for largest supplemental insurance company worldwide; received commendations for opening most new groups in WA/OR region in 1995.

RESOURCE MANAGEMENT CENTER, Seattle, WA   1985–1993
Senior Partner
Hired as Sales Manager and earned subsequent promotions to GM and Senior Partner, respectively. Delivered consulting and training seminars in all areas of business management, including finance and accounting, business growth, personnel law and management, taxes and reporting, and personal development.
- Spearheaded company's expansion into computer market to offer high-end accounting systems, wide area networks, centralized processing solutions, and ISDN to customers.

Professional Training Courses

Dale Carnegie Sales Training ¡ Brian Tracy-Strategic Sales Training ¡ Tom Hopkins Sales Training ¡ Nextel Basic, Advanced, and Consultative Selling Training ¡ Certified PSI Disk Cashing Controllers ¡ Certified PC Multi-User Operating System ¡ Certified Novell Netware ¡ License in Insurance for Health, Life, and Disability ¡ Certified & Certified Trainer in Cafeteria Plans/Section 125 ¡ Telecommunications Training Courses: PBX Trunks, Digital Switched Service, Digital Data Service, ISDN, Frame Relay Service, Self-Healing Network Service, DS1 (includes SHARP/ SHARP+), DS3, Analog Private Line

Computer Skills: Skilled in Excel, Word, and PowerPoint; experienced with sales programs Onyx, Gold Mine & ACT
Community Involvement: Community Advocate, Role Playing Game Association (RPGA). Work with at-risk youths, providing fun, appealing alternative to prohibited activities.

Stellar references available.

47 Rue des Reves

75013 Paris, France

Margot Lemieux

Mobile: +11.33.1.234-1234

margot.lemieux@gmail.com

CHANNEL SALES EMEA, US & APAC MARKETS

Performance Summary

7 years' experience in EMEA, US and APAC sales in SaaS, IT solutions, software, and communications. Strong strategic and analytical skills. Able to create solutions that consistently achieve rapid growth and international expansion. Expert in establishing multichannel routes to market, including direct, inside, and online sales. Fluent in French, English, Spanish, Basic Mandarin.

Professional Skills

Sales Growth	Partner Eco-System Recruitment	Territory Development
Marketing	Initial Public Offering (IPO)	Strategic Sales Planning
Business Development	Team Development	Project Management
Mergers & Acquisitions	Financial Analysis & Budgeting	Performance Metrics
SaaS – Cloud Computing Sales		Channel Partner Program

Career Highlights

➢ Recognized as the *Top Talent* within Global Sales for two consecutive years.
➢ Expanded Go-to-Market model, resulting in onboarding software-centric business partners.
➢ Led turnaround of key products and services from a $3 million loss to $12 million profit.
➢ Top 10 sales worldwide, four of last six years.
➢ Contributed to the integration of two business lines after $225 million merger and acquisitions.

Professional Experience

Dassault Group. Paris, France   2007–Present
Regional Sales Director, Key Accounts, Emerging Markets, EMEA, APAC   2012–Present
Promoted to lead transformation and drive growth of Global Accounts within EMEA & APAC countries. Directs team of four sales managers with $8 million in hardware, software, and professional services revenue.
• Increased client base 18% and tripled revenue of EMREA/APAC accounts in less than two years.
• Reduced sales E:R to 5% by developing new business model that focused on key client services.
• Recognized for winning a $1.4 million client, ▇▇▇▇▇▇▇▇, the largest single deal in the region.

Sales Manager, Key Accounts, Emerging Markets, EMEA, APAC   2009–2012
Established a new line of business within the EMEA, APAC region. Developed new sales strategies and Go-to-Market plans. Recruited, hired, and managed three staff members. Led the successful launch of three new products.
• Established and grew a world-class team of 12 sales staff to launch three new product lines.
• Generated new net revenues of $2.5 million and $1.3 million net profit within the first year and grew by 300% in second year.

Sales Associate EMEA & APAC Accounts   2007–2009
Serviced existing accounts within region; brought in three new Global 1000 clients.
• Part of team introducing four product lines to region.
• Grew sales by 225% over three years.

Education

MS Political Science, Sorbonne, Paris   2011
BS Engineering, Worcester Polytechnic Institute, U.S.A.   2007

JENNIFER HOLLIS

239D Sigourney Street • Hartford CT 06102
Home: 860-526-9606 • Cell: 480-345-9885 • jhollis.success@comcast.net

SALES MANAGEMENT

Performance Summary

12 years' experience in recruitment, selection, training, & development of sales teams & sales managers. Full P&L and strategic planning responsibilities for widely dispersed teams of 125+ members and building of management structure. Verifiable record of success in leading teams and operations to multimillion-dollar growth, market share gains, and profit increases.

➢ <u>Leadership</u> – Ability to build sales teams and sales managers that exceed their own expectations, creating a culture that empowers success.

➢ <u>Operations Growth</u> – History of implementing winning strategies for immediate and sustainable success in start-up, growth, maturity, and turnaround environments.

➢ <u>Cross-Functional Communication</u> - Organizational communication skills that foster superior abilities in cross-functional teams. Ability to align strategic lead products with clients' strategic initiatives.

Sales Management & Training Skills

Selection, development, motivation and discipline of sales staff in all aspects of account planning and sales execution, including management of sales cycles and sales events. Oversee accounts and manage and direct resources to win department / clinical and C-Suite–level buy-in.

Technical presentations	Conceptual selling	Consultative sales
Performance evaluation	Contract negotiations	Motivation
Performance improvement	Discipline	Recruitment with high retention
Conflict management	Relationship building	Sales forecasting
Organizational communication	Account management	Extended sales cycles
Territory management	Closing consistency	Customer service

Sales Process & Productivity Skills

Statistical analysis	Quantative analysis	Cost modeling
Customer research	SaaS familiarity	Customer research
Customer targeting	Market analysis	Report formatting
Workflow design analysis	Project management	Profit & Loss

PROFESSIONAL EXPERIENCE

Green World Services   2012-Present
Director, Bio Science Services
Responsible for launch of backend supply chain management services for waste reduction /disposal in health care environments. Generated agreements with pharmaceutical distributors and health care service organizations, as well as IDN and GPO organizations.

■ Selected, trained, and coached a health care–focused team, including Regional Sales Managers, Program Managers, and Regulators Affairs professionals.

■ Led sales and operations to revenues of $7 million and EBITDA margin of 27%.

■ Created e-commerce formulary classification database and pharmaceutical waste management programs.

■ Launched go-to-market sales & operational strategy for pharmaceutical waste management solutions.

■ All programs meet regulatory compliance with Joint Commission, EPA, & State regulatory agencies.

■ Established partnerships with pharmaceutical distributors | H/C service organizations | medical waste services, including DEA Controlled Substance management programs.

■ Established regulatory training protocols and documentation for internal/external clients addressing EPA and Environment of Care standards.

continued

Renew Environmental Services   2007-2012
Technical Services Manager

Recruited to plan and execute strategic sales and marketing initiatives to generate profitable operations in Life Science market. Full P&L responsibility, including 6 logistic center locations responsible for 14 states. Business unit consisted of 52 employees, including Profit Center Management, Logistics Coordinators, Field Techs, and Sales Reps.

- Implemented performance-based standards for multi-location organization to drive revenue and create cost performance improvements, resulting in increased revenue by 25% to $47M in first year, EBITDA improved to 29%.
- Improved EPA and OSHA compliance and decreased staffing costs by 7%.

Climate Controls   2003-2007
National Manager, Power – Climate Control Services

Full P&L accountability to create and implement nationwide sales/marketing strategy to penetrate specialized temporary power generation and temperature control solutions market. Managed 3 districts with total of 105 employees, including 42 sales professionals in 14 offices nationwide.

- Grew the company from zero to $50 million-plus in annual revenues, including $10 million in first year revenues, achieving breakthrough growth of 36% revenue and 33% PBT over a 5-year period.
- Spearheaded Health Care Emergency Management market penetration strategies and executed partnership agreement with FEMA and American Red Cross to provide support for disaster situations.

Enterprise Commercial Rentals   1996-2002
Manager - Pump & Power Services   1999 – 2002
Assistant Manager - Pump & Power Services   1996- 1999

Full P&L accountability for Technical Services division with a focus on turnkey engineered temporary power, pumping and trench safety applications. Established organizational structure, budgets, and salary levels for team of 100 employees; recruited and led team of 15 Profit Center Managers.

- Drove revenue growth for the division to over $40 million, including $5 million in incremental revenues within the first year by organizing sales functions into vertical market responsibilities.
- Increased revenues by 200% and achieved PBT margin of 30% through researching, analyzing, and opening 6 green field locations within an 18-month period.

EDUCATION & CREDENTIALS

Bachelor of Science in Chemical Engineering
Texas A&M

Executive Education Program
Texas A&M

Healthcare Environmental Management (HEM)
ECRI Institute

Superior references available on request

Marisol Lopez

259 Prentice Lane
Ridgewood, NJ 07450

(214) 555-4006
medsalespro@gmail.com

Medical Device Sales

PERFORMANCE PROFILE

11 years' experience as a bioscience and pharmaceutical sales professional knowledgeable in promoting products to physicians in teaching community hospitals, psychiatric institutions, Veterans Administration hospitals, and long-term care institutions. Provides technical product knowledge and associated benefits to health care providers. Solid background in account development, territory growth, profit enhancement, new product launches, and marketing strategy development. Proven sales track record backed by multiple awards and recognitions.

- Manages target industry segments, prepares forecasts, develops growth strategies, and identifies industry regulations, market trends, customer needs, competitive products, and pricing.
- Develops and nurtures relationships with advocates for customer relationship management.
- Easily develops rapport with physicians, clinical staff, management, and peers.

PROFESSIONAL SKILLS

*Creative Sales Strategies
*Territory Management
*Pharmaceutical Sales
*Leadership Skills
*Consultative Selling
*Clinical Knowledge

*Negotiation Skills
*In-Service Training
*Exceeds Sales Quotas
*Sales Objectives & Strategies
*Project Management
*Presentation Skills

*Industry Trends & Territory Analysis
*CRM
*Managed Care

PROFESSIONAL EXPERIENCE

Bard – Medical Devices NJ
Hospital Sales Representative, OH   2007–Present
Serving key city-based hospitals in Ohio, including key teaching institutions such as University of Ohio School of Medicine, OSU, and V.A. Hospitals. Responsible for all product launch and revenue-generating initiatives.

- Developed relationships with key thought leaders, speakers, and health care advocates to get products added to formulary for patients' use and benefit.
- Trained primary care, internal medicine, and OB/GYN interns and their preceptors on benefits and uses of Urology, Vascular, & Oncology products.
- Conducted presentations on new procedures and devices.

Sales Awards

- 2012 #1 Salesman in the Nation for the Primary Care Hospital Division.

Becton Dickinson Medical and Pharmaceuticals Company, Franklin Lakes, NJ   2003–2007
Hospital Intravenous Catheter Sales Representative, Long Island
Sold specialized intravenous vascular disposable products to doctors and nurses throughout Long Island.
- Identified key hospital accounts for conversion to Becton products.
- Identified key physicians of P&T Committee for presentation of products.
- Maintained account follow-up and identified new areas for growth.

EDUCATION

University of Texas, Arlington, TX   2002
Bachelor of Business Administration. Major: Marketing

Superior references available

Jalen Gilliard

26 Peridot Lane   (816) 433-9625
Independence, MO 64054   sports.pro@jalengilliard.com

Account Sales – College and Professional Sports

Performance Summary

Former professional athlete and sports management graduate with 5 years' experience exceeding sales quotas. Able to nurture relationships with business and sports professionals at all levels. Hands-on experience and passion for sports industry, with BS degree in Sports and Entertainment Management. Dedicated to accepting challenges. Excels in fast-paced environments. Career history of target market development and exceeding sales goals. Strong organization and multitasking skills.

- ✓ Excels in prospecting, qualifying, developing, and closing sales opportunities.
- ✓ Research and competitive analysis skills.
- ✓ Strong presentation and CRM skills.
- ✓ Strong written and verbal communication skills.
- ✓ Coachable and dedicated, with strong team-building and leadership skills.
- ✓ Technology: Microsoft Office 2007 and 2010 (Word, Excel, PowerPoint); Internet savvy.

Professional Skills

Prospecting & Closing	Negotiation	Package Development
Exceeding Quotas	Cold Calling	Account Retention
Consultative Sales	Relationship Building	Networking
Package Pricing	Competitive Analysis	Lead Generation
Market Development	Industry Research	
Client Acquisition	Promotions	

Professional Experience

TicketHub, Kansas City, MO   2010–Present
Corporate Ticket Sales

Responsible for Sports Events ticket sales to corporations, associations, and advertising incentive agencies. Consistently exceeds sales quota, builds lasting corporate relationships, and manages new sales staff selection and training. Designated turnaround coach for struggling hires.

- Ranked #3 national Sports Events ticket sales 2014
- Ranked #5 national Sports Events ticket sales 2013
- Ranked #6 national Sports Events ticket sales 2012
- Ranked #8 national Sports Events ticket sales 2011

Education & Professional Development

Fontbonne University, St. Louis, MO   2010
Bachelor of Science in Sports and Entertainment Management

Professional Tight End – Bengals   2007
                    (Severe rotator cuff injuries)

Superior References Available

MALIK JOHNSON

804-555-0492   Washington, DC   mj.topseller@gmail.com

Internet Sales

Performance Summary

Top-producing Internet Sales Professional with history of delivering business solutions that align client objectives with available technical resources. Strong technical background and in-depth product knowledge help identify customer needs, allay concerns, and become trusted customer resource and advisor. Proven ability to resolve complex problems, open new markets, and close multimillion-dollar sales.

♦ Solid understanding of key account management, with a highly accessible service orientation and rigorous follow-up.

♦ High energy, action oriented, and ready for challenges; seizes and acts upon opportunities that others often overlook.

♦ Expert in building and maintaining relationships with key corporate decision makers and establishing large-volume, high-profit accounts with excellent retention/renewal rates.

♦ Strong business and analytical acumen, adept at using data to uncover opportunities.

Professional Competencies

✓ Consultative Sales	✓ Account Development & Retention	✓ Problem Resolution
✓ Active Listening	✓ Presentation	✓ Negotiation
✓ Closing	✓ Project Management	✓ Financial Analysis/ROI
✓ Customer Service Mindset	✓ Collaboration	✓ Entrepreneurial
✓ Prioritizing	✓ Independent Action for Opportunities	✓ Brainstorming Ideas

Performance Highlights

♦ Retained $250K annual account and renewed for additional two years; client had been planning to change providers by leveraging resources and applications.

♦ Captured $240K in new sales and monthly revenue increase of $20K in usage fees by pinpointing lead management opportunity for outside field sales.

♦ Grew annual sales from $240K to $720K among group of related companies by securing introductions and building/nurturing division manager relationships.

♦ Secured more than $500K in revenue and opened new market by establishing MapQuest's presence in reseller market.

♦ Increased adoption rate of online bill pay by 44%, generating additional $3M in sales in first six months of promotion.

Professional Experience

Comcast, Washington, DC   2012–Present
Wireless Sales Executive, *Fortune* Client Group

New account generation, plus retention and growth for large enterprise customers as well as mid-market businesses and organizations (*Fortune* 500 to 5000). Billed revenues in excess of $3M.

♦ Captured $1.65M in new sales and increased usage fee revenues $20K per month with data analysis.

♦ Retained dissatisfied client & increased annual revenue from $250K to $350K.

♦ Saved departing client, raised revenue from $200K to $450K, and increased commitment from 2 to 3 years.

AOL/Time-Warner, Washington, DC   2007–2012
Sales Associate
Sold AOL MapQuest mapping software to major companies in the Mid-Atlantic Region. Accounts included Microsoft, Cisco, MetroQuest, TicketHub, and others.

- Captured over $30M in annual revenue by successfully managing development of AOL, CompuServe, and Netscape e-mail applications.
- Routinely exceeded quotas and increased sales from $650K to $1.7M over 5 years.
- Delivered approximately $3M in revenue by migrating thousands of e-mail users onto AOL mail platform over one year period.
- Closed MapQuest's first East Coast reseller deal, generating more than $600K in sales.

Application Sales Project Management
Sold AOL, CompuServe, and Netscape e-mail applications, generating over $90M in annual revenue.

- Successfully developed comprehensive project plans that included internal and external dependencies, schedules, risk analysis, and risk management plans.
- Proactively systemized and simplified chaotic data and vague requirements, which kept teams and projects productively focused.
- Meticulously tracked and monitored projects, communicating status to senior management, project teams, and key stakeholders.
- Negotiated $10M in annual agreements by selling unused network bandwidth.
- Increased adoption rate of online bill pay by 54%, generating additional $3M in sales in first six months.

Honors & Awards

- Honored with "Excellence to Sell" award for overall sales attainment in 2010, competing with 300 other Sales Executives
- Sales Achievement Excellence Award, four consecutive years
- National Accounts Sales Achievement Award from Engineering Team

Education

BA, Social Science, Emory University, Atlanta, GA

Superior references available

Laurie Anderson

Brunswick, Maine 04406   207.555.1234   insidesales@yahoo.com

INSIDE SALES MANAGER ~ OFFICE MANAGER

Performance Profile/Performance Summary

10+ years as Inside Sales and Office Manager, experienced with all phases of the sales cycle. Excellent problem-solving skills and systems expertise: conversions, upgrades, and training. Thrive in manufacturing and production arenas; detail-oriented, friendly, and personable, a self-starter and team player.
Consistently exceed objectives and increase bottom-line profits for employers. A quick learner and excellent communicator with an ability to perform well in a multitasking environment.

Professional Skills

☐ Office Management	☐ Credit and Collections
☐ Project Management	☐ Problem Identification/Solutions
☐ Customer Service	☐ Sales Management Support
☐ Customer Sales Profiles	☐ Commission Reporting
☐ Inventory Control	☐ Inside Sales

Professional Experience

AMERICAN BOUQUET COMPANY, INC. Edison, Maine   1990-2003
Inside Sales Account Manager   1998-2004

Responsible for maintaining $7 million of current business and coordinating all functions between the outside sales staff and internal departments.

- Directed and coordinated activities concerned with the sales organization including screening and evaluating new customers, performing credit authorizations, verifying client's sales history, and compiling monthly sales comparisons.
- Appointed as inside Sales Account Manager to handle a major supermarket chain buying $3 million of floral products, resulting in a 23% sales increase in the first year.
- Provided sales forecasts for holidays and special events that greatly increased the efficiency and accuracy of production schedules and purchasing requirements.
- Designed an innovative program to evaluate effectiveness of new marketing campaigns. Hired and supervised a merchandiser to track the program on a weekly basis.
- Assisted the marketing department in designing individual color layouts for major customers, as well as writing advertising copy and product-pricing bulletins.

Office Manager   1993-1998

Manage a multitude of tasks contributing to the daily operations of American Bouquet Company. Responsible for hiring, training, motivation, and supervision of telemarketing staff.

- Developed and implemented various systems for optimizing production resources and increasing efficiency. Designed Excel spreadsheets and standardized forms for use by all departments.
- Enhanced interdepartmental communications, resulting in reduced production and billing errors.

Administrative Assistant   1990-1993

Coordinated communications between sales and production. Performed credit checks, collections, and resolved price discrepancies. Responsible for inventory, price lists, and customer lists.

- Project Manager for developing, implementing, and maintaining an inventory control system that utilized coding to correlate new orders with production scheduling.

Education

BA in Political Science, *RUTGERS UNIVERSITY*, New Brunswick, New Jersey   1990

Jacqueline Alois

188-17 Greenway, Salt Lake City, UT 84101
801-555-3532
topmarcomm@alois.net

Marketing Communications
Database Management ❖ E-mail Template Design

Performance Profile/Performance Summary
Sales and Marketing Support Professional with more than 14 years of experience in time-sensitive, fast-paced environments. Highly developed skills in oral and written communications, multitasking, attention to detail, and perseverance to completion. Keen insight into clients' perspectives, goals and target audiences. Proficient with various software programs including Word, Excel, Access, and Goldmine.

Professional Competencies

➢ Database Administration	➢ Market Research	➢ Project coordination
➢ CRM	➢ Procedural Training	➢ Business development
➢ Copywriting	➢ Sales lead qualification	➢ Event management

Professional Experience

Grayrock Communications Inc., Bear Creek, UT   1999–Present

Trade show design

Database Marketing Coordinator

Assist the President, Creative Director, and sales force of 7 in developing targeted messages to promote company's services. Contribute ideas in brainstorming sessions and translate concepts into persuasive written materials (brochures, web pages, and e-mail templates).

- ❖ Generate leads through extensive phone contact, which has facilitated the closing of numerous sales by determining clients' interests and addressing their specific needs or concerns.
- ❖ Enter and update all pertinent information for up to 500 clients and prospects on Goldmine system; create profiles and periodically send electronically distributed promotional pieces to keep company in the forefront for future business.
- ❖ Initially train new sales consultants on data mining to their best advantage as well as empower them for success in prospecting and cold calling. Organize sales assignments to avoid duplication of efforts.
- ❖ Coordinate all pre- and post-sale details with various departments.
- ❖ Demonstrated versatility and talent in several areas; retained on staff despite 2 company downsizings.

QUIGLEY & VANCE, CARRINGTON, UT   1997–1999

Graphic arts

Inside Sales Representative

Performed duties of sales liaison, assistant purchasing agent, and customer service representative. Streamlined department by automating the quote process and systematizing sales literature.

Education
Westview County College, Randolph, UT — A.A.S., Marketing Communications   1997
Shelton Institute, Shelton, UT — Applied Writing and Database Administration courses   1998

James Marksmith

7645 Kiev Street • West Bloomfield, MI 48324 (248) 555-1047 • marketingmavin@sbcglobal.com

Marketing Management
Strategic Marketing/Public & Media Relations/Special Events/Event Management

Performance Profile/Performance Summary

Energetic and results-focused marketing manager who combines vision, creative talent, and strong business acumen to identify market trends and create high-impact marketing strategies and materials. Outgoing leader and team-builder able to forge key relationships and partnerships that drive brand and company awareness.

Core Expertise and Leadership

✓ Strategic Sales	✓ Promotions	✓ Marketing
✓ Branding	✓ Market Planning	✓ Event Coordination
✓ Media Relations	✓ Client Relations	✓ Strategic Partnerships
✓ Newsletters	✓ Public Speaking	✓ Project Management
✓ Strategic Alliances	✓ E-Marketing	✓ Website Management
✓ Website Development	✓ MarComm	✓ Business Development
✓ Social Networking	✓ Advertising	✓ Print & Online Marketing

PROFESSIONAL EXPERIENCE

THE DOWNTOWN DARLINGS, West Bloomfield, MI   2008-Present
Marketing & Public Relations Director

Participate in managing all aspects of company including market research, online advertising, administration, and finances. Evaluate demographics, establish relationships with trendy local restaurants, place advertisements in "young professional" condo complexes, build networking contacts. Orchestrate events—from conceiving idea and theme to promoting, handling logistics, and on-site hosting.

- Executed launch of first and only premiere for-profit social network for women focused on elevating Orlando's fashion and arts scene and offering unique events.
- Garnered immediate media attention, including article in *East Orlando Sun*, and generated public awareness of start-up organization.
- Generated "buzz" and positive feedback for quality of events that has increased attendance at events.
- Received invitation to partner with *City of West Bloomfield* and *Detroit Style* during "Fashion Week."
- Elicited quote from *Downtown Confidential*—*"The Downtown Darlings are always seeking ways to bring you the inside story on all things fashion with edge traditionally associated with downtown."*

KEYSTONE PARTNERS, Detroit MI   2007-2008
Licensed Brokerage Assistant/Marketing Assistant *(recent hires laid off due to economic downturn)*

Joined top-ten commercial real estate company to develop personal business as well as provide marketing support to team. Oversaw marketing efforts of three brokers. Created press releases and established relationships with key media contacts. Conducted market research; managed client and contact database, designed brochures and advertisements. Assisted brokerage team with contract preparation and notarizing documents, setting up conferences and business meetings, and coordinating schedules.

- Completed all assignments on time in extremely fast-paced, high-pressure environment.
- Collaborated as team member in securing major national and local corporations as clients.

SHERLOCK HOLMES REALTORS, Southfield, MI   2006-2007
Marketing Director & Sales Associate

Provided marketing and public relations support to team of five brokers in sales, leasing, and redevelopment of commercial properties (industrial, office, and retail). Designed and produced all online and print advertising, brochures, direct mail, presentation materials, etc. Created new concepts, maintained website, orchestrated events, and handled variety of special projects. Additionally, built personal business representing tenants and landlords.

- Represented company at retail conferences to elevate company profile and generate additional sales.
- Represented insurance company in relocation and opening of 7 offices within Michigan.
- Initially hired as intern; received promotion after only 30 days, after proactively designing new marketing materials, increasing online presence of listings, authoring bios, and improving effectiveness of software.
- Persuaded company to upgrade marketing efforts, directly impacting increased sales and bonuses.

KAPLAN TEST PREP AND ADMISSIONS, Detroit, MI   2004-2006
Marketing Manager—Graduate Programs

Marketed test preparation services and managed day-to-day office operations. Delivered product-related presentations to large groups, organized and administered campus events, and conducted informational seminars. Created local advertising and promotional programs; oversaw production and design of schedules, flyers, promotional letters, and mailings. Conducted class orientations, ensured facility and inventory maintenance, handled customer service requests, and processed enrollments. Trained and supervised student advisors through self-created training guides and workshops.

- Hired out of hundreds of applicants following delivery of one-hour sales presentation as part of interview process.
- Increased student enrollment 15%.
- Achieved recognition as one of the top "grad" marketers in the state.
- Competitive analysis and market repositioning result in move up to #1 local agency

---

EDUCATION/PROFESSIONAL DEVELOPMENT/RECOGNITION

ROLLINS COLLEGE, *Crummer Graduate School of Business*, Winter Park, FL
MBA in Progress, Major in Marketing and Entrepreneurship; Completion January 2011
Activities: Member, PMBA Association

WEST VIRGINIA UNIVERSITY, Morgantown, WV
BSBA in Business Management; 2004 (GPA 3.5/3.8)
Honors: Deans List, Presidents List, Recipient: Outstanding Leadership Award (*Top Management Student In Class*)
Activities: Delta Sigma Pi (Professional International Business Fraternity), Social Chair; *Society for Human Resource Management* (SHRM), President; Volunteer Coordinator, *Ronald McDonald House*

Professional Development/Licenses
Florida Real Estate License, Florida Licensed Notary

Computer Skills
Microsoft Office (Word, Excel, PowerPoint, Outlook, Access, Publisher)
Adobe Creative Suite, ACT!, Microbase Software, CCIM and STDB tools

Corporate Awards/Recognition
Received numerous presentation awards at Kaplan including plaque for successful presentations (2006), two spring training (2006) presentation certificates for presentations to the ASAP District III Conference in Orlando, FL

Community Activities
Ronald McDonald House 2003-2004

Carla Killstack

56 Pine Hill Road, Enfield, CT 06082   860-555-2348 ▪ maketingsavvy@juno.net

MARKETING   BRAND   PRODUCT MANAGEMENT

Performance Profile/Performance Summary

MBA in Marketing Management, 16 years' hands-on experience with the entire brand-development, sales, and product-management cycle. Proven track record in audio, wireless, software, and other technologies, with multi-industry applications.

From opportunity identification, competitive analysis, forecast, cost and price modeling through product commercialization, development, and positioning, brand-awareness development, pipeline, segment, and channel building, to market and customer segmentation, CRM and sales cycle (both B-to-B & B-to-C design-build and bid-awarded contracts).

Core Competencies

Brand Awareness/Development	New Product Development	Relationship Management
Competitive Product Positioning	Customer Targeting Strategies	Performance Metrics Evaluation
New Opportunity Identification	Pipeline & Channel Building	Customer Loyalty & Retention
Customer Segmentation	Data Evaluation	Price Modeling
Competitive Analysis	Consultative Selling	Product Commercialization
Vendor Training	Forecast, Cost & Pricing	Marketing Communications

Technology Competencies

Caliber RM	BSS London Architect	Pro Wireless Systems IAS
SAP	Smartsheet CRM	Harman System Architect
Stellnett	Middle Atlantic RackTools	Microsoft Office

Competitive Overview

⮑ **Market Research & Competitive Analysis** – Market research and competitive analysis for new opportunity identification and product development, including notable achievements in wireless product development with ******, Inc. resulting in changes and growth to product lines.

⮑ **Segment, Channel, Product, & Pricing Strategies** – Experienced in modeling, forecasting, and pricing for audio, wireless, and software product lines. Proficient in synthesizing marketing elements, including customer segmentation, channel development, and competitive analysis to achieve objectives.

⮑ **Sales Engineering background** builds rapport with Systems Engineering to quickly establish requirements and ensure customer fulfillment, loyalty, and retention.

⮑ **Interdepartmental Sales/Marketing Collaboration** – Extensive background working with Marketing Communications, Sales Management, and other interdisciplinary teams to execute segment strategies. *Supported by technical understanding of complex technology products.*

⮑ **Customer & Partner Relationship Management** – Reputation for strong, sustained relationships with customers, independent representatives, international distributors, and channel partners to facilitate sales growth. Provides exceptionally high level of support to accounts, perceived as a leader and contributor.

Professional Experience

International Audio – New York NY   2007-Present
Manufacturer's Representative/Sales Engineer

Primary liaison between 10 brands and account base including: 9 distributors, 38 direct dealers, and 18 consultant firms across a 3-state region. Executed marketing strategies to increase   *(continued)*

brand awareness and optimize revenues, including consultative selling and system design strategies for aligning solutions with client requirements. Teamed with key accounts to promote brands at regional trade shows and delivered on-site client training.

Key Contributions & Achievements

- **Established partnership with nationwide IT dealer CDW,** establishing multi-line support within new strategic segment and a 15% sales increase.

- **Increased dealership across brand base by 40%** through aggressive prospecting and presentation of hardware/software solutions to key decision-makers.

- **Drove 10% year-over-year growth at Illinois hub of AVAD** (major nationwide residential distributor) and helped location reach #1 ranking within 12 months, following implementation of new products.

- **Captured system upgrade with U.S. Cellular Field from major competitor** by providing value-added design and implementation support.

- **Strengthened company capability as a solution provider** and facilitated an increase in call frequency/prospecting as the point person for technical support to outside sales representatives. Provided continual strategies to vendors, including use of Smartsheet CRM software.

AKG International Incorporated – Mebane NC   1997-2007
Associate Product Manager, Commercial Audio Products, 2000-2007
Product Marketing Specialist, Commercial Audio Products, 1997-2000

Hired as Product Marketing Specialist, functioning as the "Voice of the Customer" on product development teams to define user requirements, forecasts, costs, and pricing for globally distributed audio hardware and software products.

Promoted to Associate Product Manager to lead team of 20 in addressing and resolving product commercialization issues. Initiated early contact with customers to pre-qualify product requirements. Negotiated balance between cost and performance to meet goals.

Key Contributions & Achievements

- **Led the 1st successful advance development effort** in the company's history. Introduced new technology tools to enhance the user experience.

- **Contributed to $20 million in new line sales revenue** through product commercialization of 6 product lines, including the professional-tier wireless microphone line (UHF-R) and complementary Wireless Workbench software.

- **Improved capabilities of domestic and international sales force** through training to position new audio products within their portfolio; trained independent representatives and global distributors on new products; and engaged partners in promoting products at trade shows.

- **Improved capabilities of domestic and international sales force** through training to position new audio products within their portfolio; trained independent representatives and global distributors on new products; and engaged partners in promoting products at trade shows.

- **Earned performance-based awards** that included the individual AKG Incorporated Associate of the Month and the shared AKG Incorporated Associate of the Month Team.

Bridgewater Custom Sound – Harvey, IL   1994-1997
Sales Engineer

Interacted with end-users across multiple industries, including Education, Government, and Hospitality, to assess and meet needs. Designed, proposed, and sold A/V system solutions, including both design-build and bid-awarded contracts. Provided technical support and training to accounts.

Continued

Key Contributions & Achievements

- **Contributed to the largest bid award in company history** by teaming with the company president to develop a key relationship with globally recognized Kirkegaard and Associates.

- **Managed subsequent renovation projects for Kirkegaard.** Valparaiso Performing Arts Center, in the Old St. Patrick's Church and a Municipal Conference Center.

Education & Professional Development

MBA in Marketing Management
Keller Graduate School of Management – Chicago, IL – 2002

BA in Audio Arts and Acoustics
Columbia College – Chicago, IL – 1994

Professional Development
Focus Group Moderator Training & Qualitative Market Research, The Burke Institute
Interpersonal Conflict Resolution, University of Wisconsin
Zehren Friedmen & Associate's Professional Presentation Skills
Orasi Software's In Search of Excellent Requirements
Microsoft Visio 2003
Certified Technology Specialist, International Communication Industry Association

Professional Affiliations
International Communications Industry Association (ICIA)
National Association of Broadcasters (NAB)
National Association of Music Merchants (NAMM)

Global Background
Trade show representative in:
Great Britain
Germany
The Netherlands
Canada

MEGHAN M. ENGLAND

300 Bristol Circle • New Fort, NY 12509 • (201) 555-2947 • email@email.com

Latin America
INTERNATIONAL SALES/MARKETING MANAGER
Strategic Planning/Recruitment, Selection & Training/Business Development/Bilingual

Performance Profile/Performance Summary

Innovative marketing professional with domestic and international credentials in new market identification and penetration. Skilled in strategic planning, competitive analysis, branding, regional advertising challenges, and client relations. Recruitment, selection, and training are key strengths. Polished communications, presentation, negotiation, and problem-solving skills all thrive in an intensely competitive, dynamic environment. *Fluent Spanish*.

Core Competencies

- Strategic Business Planning
- Budget Management
- Business Development/Planning
- Staff Training & Development
- Marketing Program Design

- Market Identification
- Team Building & Leadership
- Account Relationship Management
- International Client Relations
- Key Networking Skills

Professional Experience

SAP AMERICA/SAP CHILE/LATIN AMERICA   2004 to Present
Fast-track progression through the following key international marketing management positions:

Latin American Marketing Manager, TAPP LATIN AMERICA – Newton Square, NY

Direct and manage 360-degree company marketing programs throughout Argentina, Bolivia, Brazil, Chile, Colombia, Mexico, Paraguay, Peru, Puerto Rico, Venezuela, Uruguay, and the Caribbean Islands. Oversee all aspects of Latin American regional marketing operations with broad responsibility for strategic planning and the indirect supervision of a staff of four marketing managers and various partner PR/advertising agencies.

Initiate, develop, and nurture new leads to generate additional sales revenues; collaborate with sales representatives to turn over leads and establish key relationships. Accomplish marketing goals by launching comprehensive marketing, advertising, and branding plans. Manage PR marketing functions through press releases, C-level executive interviews, press conferences, professional networking, and by creating an educational focus to allow greater company exposure. Ensure top-level customer satisfaction; collaborate with various outside agencies to administer and analyze customer surveys.

Developed and manage a $3 million marketing budget encompassing strategic industries such as banks, the public sector, and utility companies, as well as strategic solutions involving customer relationship management, enterprise resource planning, supply chain management, and small/mid-sized businesses. Design and implement regional advertising/branding strategies, and analyze progress through brand tracking studies and competitive reports. Pioneer and manage key relationships with high-profile industry analyst firms. Interact with an outside global advertising agency to effectively leverage internationally syndicated relationship marketing campaigns. Serve as a company representative, liaison, and central point-of-contact for providing vital information, managing market research, and resolving issues at all levels.

Key Accomplishments:

- Spearheaded and manage a highly effective electronic quarterly newsletter, resulting in increased communications among Latin American employees.

- Directed an extensive 8-month regional team project in successfully training and educating all Latin American marketing personnel on the newly implemented CRM system in the areas of budgeting/planning, campaign planning, preparation, execution/analysis, lead management, and reporting.
- Developed and initiated the first regional budget with the global marketing team.
- Pioneered the centralization of advertising, resulting in greater discounts and significant savings.
- Accomplished greater recognition for the company, including the first and many additional publications on the company president in regional magazine articles.

Marketing Manager, TAPP CHILE – Santiago de Chile   2002 to 2004

Spearheaded, built, and launched the first marketing department for the company's Chilean subsidiary, with full responsibility for hiring, training, scheduling, supervising, mentoring, and evaluating marketing coordinator and marketing analyst staff members. Managed an $800,000 Enterprise Resource Planning marketing budget. Interacted directly with the sales team to implement marketing strategies and meet goals. Managed extensive market research and analysis functions by collaborating with a local agency to conduct focus group interviews in evaluating both company and competitor solutions. Involved in all aspects of production, public relations, sales, relationship building, and customer service.

Key Accomplishments:

- Created and implemented a lead-generation program, resulting in an increased amount of qualified leads for Account Executives and improved revenues due to shorter sales cycle.
- Built solid PR operations by developing and managing high-impact press strategies; concurrently continued to initiate key media relationships, conduct press conferences and executive interviews.

Latin American Coordinator, TAPP LATIN AMERICA – Wayne, NY   1998 to 2002

Managed the international rollout and training for the company's Sales and Marketing Information System. Traveled extensively to various international locations to oversee all implementation and training functions. Concentrated on providing a full range of support to Finance and Marketing Directors.

Spanish Teacher
CHASE CHEMICAL CORPORATION – Exton, NY   1995 to 1998
Taught Spanish to senior corporate executives.

────────────────── **Education & Credentials** ──────────────────

BS in International Studies
EDUCATIONAL UNIVERSITY – Ross, NY   1997

Language Studies
Seville/Segovia, Spain   1996

Comprehensive Spanish Language Studies
Adelaide, Australia   1995

Additional Professional Training in Business and Communications

Private Pilot License with instrument and commercial ratings

– Excellent Professional References Available on Request –

VAN MORRISON

1345 Duchess Street   stint_king@email.com
Poughkeepsie, NY 12601   845-555-4321

MEDICAL EQUIPMENT SALES

#2 in nation for sales, nominated for Representative of the Year,
anchors and trains new hires

Performance Profile

Top-producing sales professional with five years' experience, including three years in pharmaceutical sales. Strong closer who consistently exceeds targets in a consultative sales environment. Natural communicator with expertise in forging solid working relationships with professionals at all levels. Proven ability to identify and capture clients. Technical and motivational training skills, and public-speaking skills.

Professional Skills

✓ Problem Solving	✓ Account Development	✓ Account Retention
✓ Client Relations	✓ Business Development	✓ Consultative Sales
✓ Team Building	✓ Leadership	✓ Training & Educating
✓ Prospecting	✓ Closing	✓ Negotiations
✓ Consensus Building	✓ Multitasking	

Professional Experience

LEADING PHARMACEUTICAL CO., New York, NY   2011 to Present
Sales Representative
Consultative sales of select medications to MDs, Pharmacists, Pharmacy Technicians, and Pharmacy Managers throughout Metro New York area. Call on 250 accounts monthly, consistently exceed targets. Increased (product) *market share from 25%–46%.*

- Selected by District Manager to anchor and train new hires.

- *Placed #2 in nation* for sales of main product out of 2,500 reps.

- *Achieved #1 in district* two consecutive years, 2008, 2009.

- Nominated for *Representative of the Year* award, 2009.

- Nominated for company's most prestigious award, 2007.

COMPUTER MASTER, New York, NY   2005 to 2011
Account Executive
Gained valuable sales and client-relations experience with $5 million computer sales company.
- Serviced existing accounts and developed new business, including several major corporations.
- *Increased territory gross sales by 20%*

EDUCATION & PROFESSIONAL DEVELOPMENT

NEW YORK UNIVERSITY, New York, NY **B.S. in Communications**	2005
Team Train the Trainer (company sponsored)	2012
Sales Training (company sponsored)	2010, 2011, 2012

"Excellent references from employers, my clients, and peers are available at your request."

Toni Collette

Cleveland, OH   216.555.9364   100%plus@juno.com

Medical Sales Representative
"100% plus in sales and everything I do"

Professional Profile

17-year proven track record in prospecting, consultative sales, new business development, and account retention. Proficient in presentations, detailing products, conducting in-services with physicians and nursing staffs.

Strong customer assessment and well-developed closing skills for large capital purchases. Experienced sales trainer: platform and field training. Highly motivated, enthusiastic, and committed to professional excellence.

Sales Plan % by year

2010 - 103%	2007 - 105%	2004 - 90%	2001- 164%
2009 - 78%	2006 - 159%	2003 - 92%*	2000 - 110%
2008 - 100%	2005 - 138%	2002- 111%	*New territory*

Core Competencies

Medical Supplies	Capital Equipment	Instrumentation
Large Systems Deals	Large Capital Purchases	Prospecting
Consultative Sales	New Business Development	Account Retention
Sales Presentations	Introducing/Detailing	Physician/Nurse In-services
Needs Assessment	Sales Trainer	Field/Platform

Professional Experience

Experience includes the sales of medical supplies and capital equipment. As a Senior Monitoring Consultant, worked with sales representatives throughout the Western US to assist in the presentation and closing of large systems deals.

- Multiple orders for patient monitoring systems in excess of $1 million annually.
- Excellent product knowledge and fast learning curve.
- Excellent CRM evidenced by strong repeat business.

Career Progression

WelchAllyn Monitoring • Beaverton, Oregon	2000–Present
Senior Representative/Sales Trainer	2006–Present
Territory: Southern California, based in Orange County	
Sales Representative	2000–2004
Territory: Northwest, includes OR, WA, Idaho, Hawaii, and Alaska	
Simpatico-Medical • Seattle, Washington	1995–2000
Medical Sales Representative	

Education & Awards

Mt. Hood Community College	1994
Associate of Applied Science Degree • Medical Assistant Program	

Honors & Awards

National Accounts Award Winner *2009*	Monitoring Consultant of the Year *2006, 2008*
Multiple Sales Awards	Six Award Trips

Bilingual   **Sarah**   **MBA**
                                 Bernhardt

Perryville, VA 22033   703.555.3264   *multimediasales@juno.com*

ONLINE MULTIMEDIA SALES
Advertising, Communications, and Media

Performance Profile/Performance Summary

High-performing sales professional with a 20-year track record of success with high-profile clients for *best in class* companies. Consistently **exceeds sales quotas**. Deep expertise in brand management and product lines positioning. **Gifted sales strategist and tactician,** excels in channel development.

Sales Skills

- Sales
- Recruitment & Selection
- Performance Appraisals
- Overcoming Objections
- P & L
- Brand Management
- College Relations

- Telemarketing
- Training & Development
- Separations
- Contract Negotiations
- Cost Containment
- Strategic Alliance/Partners
- Employee Communications

- E-mail marketing
- Employee Retention
- Business Development
- Channel Development
- Relationship Management
- Diversity Strategies
- Sales Manuals

Excels in training and mentoring teams to outperform the competition. High level of personal and professional integrity, a passion for achieving organizational success, and a desire always to play on a winning team.

Professional Experience

POWER BUSINESS DEVELOPMENT – Ashburn, VA	7/1998 - 3/2007
Account Manager	3/2006 - 5/2007
National Ad Agency Channel Sales Representative	2/2005 - 5/2006
National Recruitment Sales Representative	7/1998 - 2/2005

Aggressively recruited to develop, revitalize, and nurture productive relationships with Fortune 1000 companies and government agencies such as *Inova Healthcare, BAE Systems, Lockheed Martin, FBI*, and *CIA*. Packaged and sold targeted multimedia-integrated talent solutions and services.

Key Accomplishments

- **Multi-Media Campaign Development.** Offered existing clients an opportunity to "fish in a different pond" by developing and recommending new and alternative multimedia account strategies targeted at niche and passive candidate markets. Packaged and sold non-traditional campaigns from non-print sources targeted to key audiences.
- **Product Development.** Credited for designing and spearheading the execution of a cutting-edge hotjobs.com product offering whereby keyword searches served up product-related ads along the margins of the website, generating more than $50k in incremental revenue per year.
- **Increased Advertiser Revenue.** Through a combination of face-to-face visits to 13-15 domestic markets, the creation of various telemarketing programs, and e-mail marketing campaigns, grew Easterner JOBS Advertising Unit by $10 million, an increase of 25%, representing one-third of all sales for the unit.
- **Sales Performance.** Consistently met and exceeded quarterly and annual sales revenue goals, up to 131% above quota.
- **Awards & Recognition.** Recipient of Presidents Club Year End Award for demonstrating a commitment to customers that is reflected in business performance, a high level of sales achievement and customer satisfaction. Recipient of several prestigious awards including two Vice Presidents Club Awards, three Sales Achievement Awards, two Sales Excellence Awards and a Publishers Award for Sales Excellence.

HOTJOBS.COM - Annandale, VA   1991 - 1998
Vice President/General Manager   1997 - 1998
Director of Client Services   1996 - 1997
Account Executive   1991 - 1996

Promoted and progressed rapidly through positions with increasing responsibility. Directed all aspects of sales, marketing, and operations functions, and managed full P & L ($10 million in revenue) for Washington, D.C. office. Generated significant new client business and produced employer-branded recruitment and retention advertising campaign and execution strategies.

Key Accomplishments

- **Cost Containment.** Spearheaded key cost-containment initiatives, saving thousands of dollars, resulting in a Top 10 (out of 35) "managerial profitability" ranking for the Washington, D.C. office.
- **New Business Development.** Partnered with the HotJobs sales channel in the design and implementation of a "business case building" sales contest, increasing HotJobs revenue by $2 million.
- **Sales Productivity.** Noted for driving $1 million in new business development in one year.
- **Process Improvement.** Spearheaded from conception to implementation an employee retention initiative. Launched monthly new hire performance appraisals (30/30's), which fostered a welcoming new hire experience and drastically improved retention. Hired, trained, and supervised a staff of 12 account managers, and provided ongoing staff mentoring and support, enabling them to grow company's client base.
- **High-Expectation Client Relations.** Painstakingly researched and subsequently instituted the recommended solutions outlined in the business book classic *"The Nordstrom Way: The Inside Story of America's #1 Customer Service Company"* to maximize HotJob's customer satisfaction.
- **Employer Branding.** Partnered with senior-level Human Resources clients in the design and development of uniquely branded corporate recruitment advertising strategies. Recommended tactical approaches for campaign execution.
- **Marketing Solutions.** Presented competitively positioned employee communication solutions and executed delivery of solutions such as collateral development, diversity strategies, university/college relations, and creative ad design to maximize employee communication programs.

Education

Masters of Business Administration
The Kogod School of Business – American University
Fully financed way through Business School

Bachelor of Science in Marketing
Michigan State University – East Lansing, MI

Professional Affiliation

Member - National Society of Hispanic MBAs

Robert Caro

#1 Vintage Court • Alexandria VA 20190 • cell: (703) 555-2937 • *revenuedriver@ameritech.com*

NATIONAL SALES MANAGER/KEY ACCOUNT MANAGER
Technology Services

Performance Summary

Award-winning and dedicated technology sales manager with 10+ years of success generating revenue and securing high-profile clients for industry leaders, such as *AOL/Time Warne*r, *Nutrisystem, Mediacharge, Safeway, Wal-Mart,* and *Monster,* with excellent client retention.

Proficient in entire sales cycle from lead generation through presentation to negotiation, closing, and follow-up. Excel in training and mentoring teams to outperform the competition. Numerous sales awards. High level of discipline, professional integrity, a passion for achieving organizational success, and a desire to always play on a "winning team."

Professional Skills

- Business Development
- Recruitment & Selection
- Strategic Alliances
- Cold Call Training
- Telemarketing
- Sales Meetings
- Distance Learning
- Direct Mail/E-mail
- Solution Sales
- Needs Assessment
- Performance Reviews
- Key Account Management
- Targeted Seminars
- National Training
- Post Sales
- Ad Agencies
- Contract Negotiations
- Proposals
- Relationship Management
- Vertical Channel Sales
- New Business Development
- Platform Skills
- Training Course Development
- Trade Shows

Numerous awards for consistently exceeding sales goals and forecasts. Utilize a consultative approach to assess client needs and provide solutions that meet client's strategic goals.

PROFESSIONAL EXPERIENCE

TELCORDIA TECHNOLOGIES - Sterling, VA   3/2005-Present

Telcordia Technologies provides trusted, neutral, and essential addressing, interoperability, infrastructure, and other clearinghouse services for communication service providers and enterprises worldwide.

National Sales Manager   3/2006-Present

Promoted from Account Executive to National Sales Manager in 8 months due to breakthrough sales results. Manage national sales programs and supervise 15 sales representatives. Recruit, interview, hire, and train staff and evaluate performance for regional placements. Conduct quarterly sales meetings, develop goals, and coordinate all local, regional, and national training efforts.

- **Sales Performance. Achieved 100% of sales quota despite a 60% reduction in staff.**
- **Awards & Recognition. Received 2005 Polaris Award, Neustar's most prestigious distinction,** which rewards superior performance and strong commitment to operational excellence. Nominees undergo a rigorous nomination and selection process, and awards are granted to the "top-talent" (less than 5%) of the company.
- Leadership. Empowered staff and built a focused and loyal national sales team that consistently generated higher-than-budget sales.
- New Business Development. Key player in cultivating relationships with national clients including *Nutrisystem*, *Expedia*, and *Mediacharge*. Personally conducted assessment interviews with prospective clients to identify needs and formulate appropriate solutions.

Account Executive   10/2005-3/2006

- Vertical Sales Campaign Management. Through rigorous cold calling and prospecting, launched company into the online advertising vertical, setting the stage for colleagues to follow. As a result, an impressive 65% of all online advertising currently comes through Neustar, and recurring monthly revenue exceeds $150,000.

HOTJOBS.COM – Annandale, VA   6/2004-9/2005

Yahoo! HotJobs has revolutionized the way people manage their careers and the way companies hire talent, and puts job seekers in control of their careers, making it easier for employers and staffing firms to find qualified candidates.

Southeast Account Executive

Aggressively sold recruitment business solutions including database, web job hosting, and job posting packages within the Mid-Atlantic and Southeast Regions. Applied a solutions selling methodology to the sales cycle, promptly completing proposals and sales activities, closing sales opportunities quickly and efficiently, and completing necessary paperwork steps to successfully set projects in motion.

- Revenue Generation. Consistently exceeded monthly revenue target of $15,000. Cold called and closed new business with major retail clients including *Safeway* and *Wal-Mart.*

TNS SOLUTIONS – Herndon, VA   1/2004-6/2004

TNS is the trusted source for the complete Oracle suite of data-centric solutions, including database, Oracle Fusion Middleware, and packaged applications.

Account Executive

Managed Sales for Oracle's 9iAS and Collaboration Suite, and developed new territory in district, including several key accounts such as RSA and Comstore. Managed a staff of 25 sales representatives.

- **Marketing.** Generated $1 million in new business development by creating local and statewide marketing programs to generate buzz around Symantec products and DLT's Commonwealth of Virginia contract.
- **Campaign Management.** Prospected for new business through various marketing campaigns, including telemarketing, direct mail, targeted seminars and partnerships with leading software firms.
- **New Business Development.** First to sell the hosted Collaboration Suite product to the Armed Forces Retirement Home, and secured the RSA relationship at DLT.
- **Trade Show Participation.** Networked extensively throughout the business community at industry trade shows, obtaining over 7,000 leads on average per event.
- **Awards and Recognition.** Generated the highest volume of accounts company-wide, and was recognized with the DTL's prestigious "Sales Leader Award."
- **Partner Development.** Liaised with DLT staff and *Oracle* team to successfully manage the *Symantec* relationship.

AOL TIME WARNER – New York, NY   3/1998-10/2003

Interactive services, cable systems, filmed entertainment, television networks, and publishing.

National Account Sales Manager

Sold print and online advertising across all *AOL/Time Warner* properties (159 websites and publications) including *People, Time Inc, Fortune, Netscape, and CompuServe.* Interfaced directly with C-Suite executives, negotiated high-dollar contracts, and coordinated implementation. Managed accounts in three major verticals (retail, travel and tourism, and online gaming) and orchestrated post-sale professional services and resources. Recognized market needs and provided clients with new solutions, ultimately expanding their customer base.

- **Revenue Generation.** Booked $2.3 million in new revenue from a previously dormant category, exceeding $1.8 million revenue quota within eight months.
- **New Business Development.** Created $1.5 million in new business opportunities through presentations, cold calling, and successful final negotiations.
- **Training Course Development.** Designed and implemented a live prospecting training class focused on topics such as utilizing unique online tools (ad relevance and niche online sites, etc.) and capturing contact information from prospects and leads.
- **Customer Relations and Retention.** Forged strong partnerships with both clients and ad agencies, and increased advertisers' retention rates by encouraging collaboration between both groups.
- **Sales Presentations.** Completed intensive national sales and presentation training, and ranked #1 (out of 30) and #7 in the country in both 2000 and 2001, based on number of deals closed.

EDUCATION & TRAINING

Bachelor of Arts in Business Administration
George Mason University • Fairfax, VA

Telecordia Technologies • Sterling, VA • 2008
Advanced Leadership Program

"I am eager to exceed expectations as a member of a quality team."

References available on request.

Kwang Hartson

Novi, Michigan 48300   248.555.2937   I_knowsales@yahoo.com

PHARMACEUTICAL SALES

Performance Profile/Performance Summary

High-energy sales professional with experience developing product awareness through consultative sales. A proven performer with a track record of outperforming sales goals, delivering high levels of customer service, and achieving successful sales results built on key strengths of:

- **Consultative Sales Skills** — experience and education involving custom pharmaceutical and consumer products
- **New Business Development/Territory Management** — prospecting and building a territory; identifying and capitalizing on opportunities, knowledge of sales cycles
- **Customer Retention/Relationship Building** — excellent communication (listening, speaking) and interpersonal skills
- **Goal Setting** — experience in setting and achieving both independent and team-driven targets

Core Sales Competencies

➢ Consultative Sales	➢ New Business Development	➢ Territory Management
➢ Prospecting	➢ Market ID	➢ Sales Cycles
➢ Goal Setting	➢ Customer Retention	➢ Relationship Building
➢ Contractual Sales	➢ Customer Service	➢ Strategic Partners
➢ Product Launches	➢ Strategic Planning	➢ Market Share
➢ Sales Trainer	➢ Problem Solving	➢ Interpersonal Skills
➢ Product Presentation	➢ Corporate Liaison	➢ Collaborative Thinking
➢ Account Maintenance	➢ Cold Calls	➢ Formulary Status Promotion

PROFESSIONAL EXPERIENCE

QUALIFIED HEALTHCARE INCORPORATED; Grand Rapids, Michigan   2004-Present

Leading contractual sales and marketing partner providing solutions to pharmaceutical and health care industries.

Pharmaceutical Sales Specialist

Manage team-driven pharmaceutical sales responsibilities in southeast Michigan territory. Interact with physicians, nurses, physician assistants, and medical professionals to represent a premier product line. Interact with other sales reps to do strategic planning, problem solving, and collaborative thinking. Manage 35-40 weekly calls on physicians to increase market share in territory.

- Coordinated product launch for new acid reflux drug (AstraZeneca).
- Petitioned physicians to contact their HMOs and recommend formulary status; received formulary standing.
- Member of market-leading Prilosec sales team.
- Consistently exceed sales quota; won highest call activity contest. Regional sales leader for hypertensive drug.

OFFICE MAX: Columbus, Ohio   2000-2004
Global retailer of office supplies, furniture, and technology.

Business Development Specialist   2002-2004

Promoted to develop new business while maintaining current business in competitive Southeastern and central Michigan territories; focused on small to medium-size companies. Managed complete sales cycle from initial contact through presentation and consultation to close of sale. Acted as liaison between sales center rep team and corporate office in Boston.

- Consistently exceeded expected percentage in regional and corporate sales.
- Trained new reps in all areas of product presentation, solution selling, and customer service.

Sales Representative   2000-2002

Managed sales and account maintenance with companies. Independently maintained relationships with company personnel to increase visibility and credibility. Developed leads through cold calls; met with customers to identify needs.

- Developed new customers; maintained high goal percentages; recruited to higher position.

EDUCATION

UNIVERSITY OF MICHIGAN; Ann Arbor, Michigan   1999
Bachelor of Science degree in Interdisciplinary Studies/Social Science with a focus in Health & Humanities; Minor: Psychology
Seminars: Leadership Sales, Presentations Skills

References available on request.

Pauline Zamudio
6789 Starbright Lane
Seattle, Washington 98101

206.555.0937
techsales@ameritach.com

Software & Technology Sales

Performance Review

Strong background in sales, sales management, business development, and account management. Skilled in Enterprise Software Sales, Enterprise Content Management (ECM), Business Process Management (BPM), and Business Process Outsourcing (BPO). Increased sales by developing strong relationships with clients, staff, partners, and management from initial contact through implementation. Demonstrated talents in building name brand awareness.

- Exceptional ability to research, analyze, and present information to diverse audiences.
- Skilled in development and implementation of marketing strategies that increase sales.
- Consultative sales, strong communication, negotiation, and needs assessment skills.
- Extensive experience selling to C-suite of large organizations.

Core Proficiencies

* Sales & Marketing	* Strategic Accounts	* Technical Sales
* Business Development	* Order Management	* Contract Negotiations
* Client Development	* Vendor Relations	* Business Process Management
* ECM	* FileNet	* Enterprise Document Generation
* Strategic Alliances	* Events	* Open Standards
* Relationship Management	* Platform Skills	* Government Programs
* Systems Integration	* Training & Development	* Business Process Outsourcers
* Cost Containment	* Document Management	* Business Process Analysis

Performance Highlights

✓ Created a niche market at Pyramid Solutions, providing a repeatable business process management (BPM) solution for national financial services and mortgage industries, utilizing FileNet technologies. Project profit margin increased by 35%.
✓ Awarded FileNet's "Innovative Solution of the Year" at Pyramid Solutions for development of a repeatable Business Process Management Solution in financial services industry. (2002)
✓ Met and exceeded quota by 103% and added (4) New named Accounts in 2006 at Thunderhead Limited.
✓ Recognized as "Top Partner - Kofax Midwest Region" at Pyramid solutions. (2001 – 2004)
✓ FileNet Presidents Club Achiever 125% > of Quota. (1991 – 1996)

Professional Experience

THUNDERHEAD, LTD. – London, England   2005 - Present
SENIOR SALES EXECUTIVE/BUSINESS DEVELOPMENT DIRECTOR

Software sales for 100% Open Standards-based Enterprise Document Generation for financial services and government programs. Negotiate contracts with new vendors and partners. Cultivate relationships from initial contact through implementation with partners, clients, staff, and management.

- Hired as first direct sales staff member for start-up operations in North America, gaining four named accounts in first year.
- Organized "Lunch & Learn" program for FileNet System Consultants and integration partners to provide product education.
- Established strategic partnerships with *UNISYS, BearingPoint,* and *IBM Global Services,* as well as several other system integrators.

TECHNICAL SOLUTIONS, INC. – NEW YORK, NY   2001 - 2005
DIRECTOR OF SALES & MARKETING

Charged with providing sales and marketing for systems integration and professional services organization. Increased brand awareness through development of comprehensive marketing materials. Analyzed business needs and implemented solutions that drove business growth. Created new pricing model and product structure.

Provided sales and deployment of ECM and BPM solutions nationwide. Managed relationships with *FileNet, Captiva,* and *Kofax.* Implemented Business Process Analysis methodology: analyzed and documented customer's current processes, and how the technology could streamline these processes. Customers included: *Flagstar Bank, Sun Trust, PMI, Comerica, Washtenaw County, Muskegon County, Oakland County.*

- Awarded FileNet's "Innovative Solution of the Year" for development of Business Process Management Solution in financial services industry. (2002)
- Exceeded quota by over 100% two out of four years.
- Earned membership in FileNet's ValueNet Partner Million Dollar Club (2002 – 2004)
- Developed and implemented new change management marketing program, assisting companies with installation of complex technology.

NEW SYSTEMS, INC. – NEW YORK, NY   1997 - 2001
REGIONAL SALES DIRECTOR

Directed and managed sales staff throughout the United States. Oversaw and managed budget of $6.2M. Created and implemented new value-based sales process for rapid prototyping of technology. Developed and installed Rapid Manufacturing Application within the Aerospace industry. Provided global sales support for *Ford Motor Company, DaimlerChrysler,* and *GM.* Trained sales and engineering staff members. Oversaw all regional operations, including deals and resources on a national basis. Established and managed relationships with Business Process Outsourcers (BPO).

- Reduced operating costs for field operations by combining facilities.
- Facilitated professional sales training boot camps.
- Discovered highly complex application, resulting in creation of InVisiLine braces.
- Transformed 3D Solutions sales force from product focus to solutions-oriented focus, through process analysis, training, and ROI models.
- Grew annual sales 15% by focusing sales teams on solution sales.

ABC CORPORATION – NEW YORK, NY   1990 - 1997
DISTRICT MANAGER/SENIOR ACCOUNT EXECUTIVE

Promoted from Senior Account Executive in 1995. Provided direction and management to 14 staff members, charged with providing large enterprise document management and BPM solutions. Gained new channel partners with application providers and consulting vendors. Charged with selling $5M solutions to C-level executives at large organizations, including *GE Aircraft Engines, Medical Mutual of Ohio, Goodyear Tire and Rubber, Steelcase, Dow, Ford Motor Credit, U of M Health Systems, Comerica, Huntington Banks,* and *Key Banks.*

- Increased indirect sales channels by 100%.
- Awarded "Presidents Club" for exceeding quota by 125%, 1991 – 1996.
- Earned "Rookie of the Year," 1990.
- Received "Eastern Region Top Producer," 1993.

Education

Bachelor of Science, Business Administration • The Ohio State University

– Columbus, OH

Samuel Butler, CPA

216 Liberty Way
Montgomery, AL 36110

(334) 547-1786
topaccountant@earthlink.net

Certified Public Accountant

Performance Summary

CPA with 10 years' experience in delivering tax services for: sales and use tax, premium tax, surplus lines tax, estate tax, and income tax on behalf of corporations, partnerships, limited liability companies, individuals, and trusts. Reviews data to ensure accuracy and compliance with Generally Accepted Accounting Principles (GAAP) and Sarbanes-Oxley Act (SOX) policies and procedures. Income tax preparations and recommendations regarding tax reporting issues and compliance requirements.

Professional CPA Skills

Forecasting	GAAP	Tax Strategies
Financial Analysis	FASB	Income Tax Research
Account Reconciliation	Internal Controls	Sales and Use Tax
Accounts Payable (AP)	SOX Compliance	Accruals
Accounts Receivable (AR)	Risk Management	Strategic Planning & Execution

Professional Experience

First Choice CPA, Montgomery, AL   2010–Present
CPA
Tax return preparation and review of trusts, estates, individuals, partnerships, and corporations for various industries, including IRS audits. Expanded services for three existing clients and obtained six additional clients.

- Generated more than $28,000 net savings by resolving a sales tax audit that had remained unsettled for 10 years.
- Averted penalties and additional taxes imposed on a clergy tax paper by resolving complex tax audit.
- Researched GAAP procedures and utilized PPC Accounting and Auditing Guidance as a springboard to assist in the audit plan for an A-133 Single Audit to request federal funding.

Botex, Inc., Montgomery, AL   2005–2010
Tax Specialist
Prepared monthly/quarterly state sales and use tax returns. Compiled and reviewed information for federal, franchise, and state income tax returns. Completed pre-audits on past sales and used tax returns for parent company and newly merged company to prepare for state audits.

- Streamlined and decreased monthly sales/use tax compliance processing time by 66%, from 15 working days down to 5 working days.

Education & Certifications

Certified Public Accountant (AL), CPA Certificate #3675   2007

University of Kentucky, BS Accounting   2005

Professional Affiliation

Alabama Association of Certified Public Accounts (AACPA)   Current

Superior references available on request

153 Old Battlefield Trail
Arlington, VA 22203

Luis N. Hernandez

Home (702) 894-6238
Mobile (702) 924-7817
compliance.officer@aol.com

Compliance Officer

"Keeping profits within the company, and compliance problems without."

Performance Summary

Compliance Officer with 5 years' experience working for a leading financial institution. Minimizes risk by executing policies and processes that prevent fraud and loss of assets. Natural ability to analyze data, investigate transactions, and document findings. Additional knowledge of Treasury AML guidelines, Patriot Act, Securities Rules, OFAC, AML/KYC regulatory policies, and suspicious activity reporting requirements.

Professional Skills

Anti-Money Laundering Guidelines	Case Management	Code of Ethics	AML Investigations
Collection and Examination	Detection & Prevention	Document Review	Patriot Act
Fraud Investigations	Conduct Due Diligence	Risk Mitigation	Quality Control
Report Development	Monitoring	Policies & Procedures	High-Risk Jurisdiction
Identifying Terrorist Financing	Transactional Review	Customer Asset Movements	Information Security

Professional Experience

HSBC, Arlington, VA   **2011 to Present**
A multinational financial services corporation.
Compliance Analyst

Ensures employee compliance with Employee Code of Ethics policies and procedures. Analyzes and resolves inquiries on external trading accounts, investments, and general Code of Ethics policies and procedures. Served as subject matter expert for Markets and Banking employees, ensuring compliance with internal and external Code of Ethics.

- Reduced supervisory review time of employee brokerage accounts 35% by assisting in development and reconciliation of web-based New Hire Account Disclosure application.
- Completed training of 12 new staff members on policies and procedures in conducting reviews of Code of Ethics documentation 3 months ahead of schedule.
- Assists in implementation of employee annual certification process and implemented new processes for divisions, ensuring external activity requests are reported and current.
- Ensured that marketing and banking for Mid-Atlantic Division adheres to identical new employee outside activity documentation by leading coverage scope project.

Compliance Assistant   **2010–2011**
Provided administrative research and project management support for compliance officers.

Education & Affiliations

BBA, Finance. Pace University, NY   2009
National Association of Compliance Officers (DC Chapter)   Current

Excellent references available on request

35 Ivy Court
Squirrel Hill, PA 15232

Johanna Hendrickson
CPA, CIA

Cell (412) 348-3432
jhfinance@yahoo.com

Internal Auditor

Performance Summary

CPA and CIA with 10 years' experience in accounting and financial services for global corporations. Considered, decisive, and effective financial strategist with proven success ensuring compliance with federal, state, and internal corporate regulations and policies. Maintains the overall integrity of accounting and financial systems. Skilled in coordinating with regional finance teams on statement preparation. Prepares financial statements for management and key stakeholders. Impeccable integrity and work ethic.

Professional Skills

Financial Analysis	Variance Analysis	GAAP	SAP & PeopleSoft
Financial Close	Sarbanes-Oxley	FCPA	Staff Leadership
SOX/Non-SOX	Communication	Relationship	Report Development
Controls	Financial Statements	Development	Documentation
Account	Issue Resolution	Internal Controls	Compliance
Reconciliations		Financial Reports	
Microsoft Office Suite			

——Professional Experience——

Big Can Management (BCM Inc.), Pittsburgh, PA   2010 to Present
Provider of recycling and waste management services
Internal Auditor

Management support for internal audits: SOX and non-SOX controls for multiple business units. Performs comprehensive risk-based analysis of the control environment. Identifies findings for entry into audit reports. Leads closing meetings; discusses necessary action plans related to audit findings and coordinates with area management to resolve outstanding issues. Responsible for sending draft & final audit reports to management.

- Key contributor to integrated IT Audit, resulting in $165,000 reclassification of revenue.
- Identified $120,000 of unbilled revenue that current billing system was unable to accommodate.
- Performed testing of SOX-related controls on behalf of BCM's external auditors, resolving questions.

Gulf Marine, Mississippi   2009 to 2010
Offshore energy services
Internal Auditor

- Directed internal audits of both SOX and non-SOX controls at facilities in South America and EMEA. Ensured compliance with Foreign Corrupt Practices Act. Provided assistance in preparing annual risk assessment for use in development of internal audit plans. Spearheaded the development of audit programs for unaudited processes.

- Identified $75,000 in obsolete inventory by performing a review and analysis of the inventory accounts for tracking shipments to worldwide locations by contracted freight forwarder.
- Reduced liability to less than $2 million by facilitating tax audit conducted by government in Equatorial Guinea.
- Reversed $80,000 in accrued balance after review of Cameroon balance sheet reconciliations and Ghana labor laws, determining contingent severance liability was incorrectly recorded.
- Saved the company $14,000 over three months by coordinating with an in-house travel agent to reduce cost for tickets frequently booked to company operating locations.

Ciba Vision, Salt Lake, UT   2005 to 2009
Manufacturer of optical lenses
Internal Auditor

Responsible for internal audits of lens manufacturing facilities, including post-acquisition audits to assess local management compliance with corporate policies. Ensured compliance with LSF, the French equivalent of SOX. Managed closing engagements for newly acquired businesses, meeting with local area management to outline steps necessary to ensure accurate assertions.

- Selected to assist in a special project to analyze structure of pricing for North American operations, including coordination with corporate pricing staff to analyze pricing strategy.
- Identified non-compliance with standard accounting procedures, including failure to perform aged receivable analysis and record bad debt reserve and failure to record accruals for inventory purchases, SG&A expenditures, and expensing amounts that should have been established as pre-paids.

UPS, Kansas, MO   2000 to 2005
Global Logistics company
Accounting Research Analyst

Provided maintenance of the accounting data for long-term aircraft leases, ensuring all leases were accrued on straight-line basis and amortizing gain on sale-lease aircraft. Reviewed expense line items for leased property and equipment expense, as well as long-term aircraft lease expense, including analyzing account variations, obtaining explanations of business reasons for variation and reporting findings to management. Provided quarterly summary of accounting information for management review. Prepared monthly summary of underutilized leased property.

- Selected to research accounting matters for the Corporate Accounting Group through preparation of a quarterly summary of accounting-related information for management review. Report summarized new or proposed EITF issues, FASB and AcSEC exposure drafts or proposals, and new SEC rulings that affected FedEx Express.

—— **Education and Professional Accreditations**——

Bachelor of Science, Finance, University of Pennsylvania   1999
Certified Public Accountant (CPA)   2004
Certified Internal Auditor (CIA)   2006

Superior references available

Orlando Montoya

245 Green St.
San Mateo, CA 94401

ledgerdomain.smith@comcast.net

C: 415.555.9573

Experienced General Ledger Accountant
For global technology companies

Performance Summary
Strong general ledger experience supported by accounts payable background. Takes leadership role in systems conversions, process improvement, and establishing better vendor relations. Communicates well with team members, purchasing department, and operations employees.

Career Highlights
- Team Lead in successful $1\frac{1}{2}$ year conversion to global SAP Purchase to Pay module.
- Reconciled 18-month-old, $3.2M vendor discrepancy working closely with European offices.
- Eliminated significant past due invoice backlog, improved procedures, and rebuilt vendor relations.

Accounting Core Competencies
General Accounting

✓ Accounts Receivable	✓ Internal Controls	✓ Master Data Accounts
✓ Intercompany Accounts	✓ Bank Deposits	✓ Inventory Control
✓ Bank Statements	✓ Journal Entries/Accruals	✓ Month End Close
✓ Cost Center Budget	✓ Cash Applications	✓ Cashier – Cash Controls
✓ Fixed Assets	✓ Payroll Processing	✓ Staff Training
✓ Capitalized Assets	✓ Billing	✓ GAAP

Accounts Payable

✓ Account Reconciliations	✓ Procurement Procedures	✓ Credit Cards / Employee Expenses
✓ Sales/Use Tax Returns	✓ Full-Cycle Accounts Payable	✓ Systems Conversion (SAP)
✓ Invoice Discrepancy Resolution	✓ Vendor Relations	✓ Payment Monitoring Verification

Technical Skills

✓ Microsoft	Word, Excel, PowerPoint
✓ Applications	*SAP:* Vendor, Purchasing
✓ PRMS	Accounts Payable, Accounts Receivable, Vendors, Customer Masters, Journal Entries
✓ Payroll	ADP
✓ Other	MAS90, FAS Fixed Asset Software, T Rowe Price 401k system, Lotus Notes

Professional Experience

Intel, Mountain View, Ca   2004 – 2010
General Ledger Accounting Specialist   2007 – 2010

Balance Sheet: All accounts and subsidiary ledgers, including accounts payable, accounts receivable, fixed assets.
Intercompany: Invoiced and reconciled for both domestic and international company locations.
Month End Close: Prepared reconciling and recurring journal entries. Compared cost center budgets to actual.
Fixed Assets: Tracked construction-in-progress and capitalized assets in accordance with GAAP.
Accounts Receivable: Assisted all functions, including cash applications and reconciling customer accounts.

Special Project: SAP Implementation   2008 – 2010

Team Lead – **Purchase to Pay:** Managed two other staff for successful implementation of Purchase-to-Pay process for SAP conversion.
Master Data: Set up and implemented Master Data accounts, including vendor, material, product Information, record (PIR), and source listings.

General Ledger Accounting Specialist
Special Project: SAP Implementation *continued…*

Process Implementation and Documentation: Incorporated and revised existing purchasing and subcontracting processes into new system. Trained other team members.
Key User – General Accounting and Controlling: Resource for reviewing master data for general ledger set up. Assisted with GL account mapping for reporting and financial statement consolidation. Assisted users with cost center accounting. Assisted in transfer of accounts receivable and accounts payable to shared services department.

Accounts Payable Specialist   2004 – 2007

Full-Cycle Payables: Handled all aspects of accounts payable, including general ledger coding. Processed 100 checks per week, $2.5M per month.
Vendor Relations: Eliminated significant backlog for processing vendor and freight invoices that happened with job predecessor. Improved vendor relations by bringing payables up-to-date.
Process Improvement: Streamlined process for accounts payable invoices. Implemented effective Excel report to keep track of discrepant invoices.

ISYS MANUFACTURING, INC., Concord, CA   1998 – 2004
$50M manufacturer of electronic components for semiconductor industry
Accounting Clerk
Payroll: Processed full-cycle payroll for 130 salaried and hourly employees.
Accounts Payable: Performed lead role for full-cycle accounts payable with approximately 100 weekly checks.
Accounts Receivable: Handled full-cycle accounts receivable including billing, cash applications, labor applications, and general ledger entries.
Inventory Control: Tracked parts and finished goods inventory worth approximately $5M. Implemented improved procedures for shipping and receiving.

ORCHARD SUPPLY HARDWARE, Concord, CA   1996 – 1998
Cashier Instructor/Backup Customer Service
Managed front-end store operations. Trained and scheduled all cashiers.

Education

BS–Accounting, Phoenix   2004

Exemplary references available upon request.

Patricia Johnson

65 Winston Ct., Palmdale, CA 93550   Mobile (661) 555-9876   aaa_acountant@email.com

Internal Auditor/Financial Analyst/Staff Accountant

Performance Profile/Performance Summary

Detail-oriented problem-solver with excellent analytical skills and a track record of optimizing productivity, reducing costs, and increasing profit contributions. Well-developed team-building and leadership skills with experience in training and coaching coworkers.

Works well with public, clients, vendors, and coworkers at all levels. B.S. in Finance, graduating with honors concurrent with full-time, progressive business experience.

Core Competencies

➢ Research & Analysis	➢ Accounts Receivable	➢ Accounts Receivable
➢ Accounts Payable	➢ Journal Entries	➢ Bank Reconciliations
➢ Payroll	➢ Financial Statements	➢ Auditing
➢ General Ledger	➢ Artist Contracts	➢ Royalties
➢ Escalation Clauses	➢ Equipment Leases	➢ Licenses & Royalties
➢ Invoice Coding	➢ Invoice Coding	➢ Microsoft Office
➢ Peachtree	➢ J.D. Edwards	➢ Tracs

PROFESSIONAL EXPERIENCE

MAJOR HOLLYWOOD STUDIO, Hollywood, CA   2000–Present
Royalty Analyst—Music Group, Los Angeles, CA   2005–Present

Achieved fast-track promotion to positions of increasing challenge and responsibility. Process average of $8-9 million in payments monthly. Review artist contracts, licenses, and rate sheets to determine royalties due to producers and songwriters for leading record label. Ensure accuracy of statements sent to publishers in terms of units sold and rates applied. Research, resolve, and respond to all inquiries.

• Resolved longstanding problems, substantially reducing publisher inquiries and complaints.
• Promoted to "Level 1" analyst within only one year and ahead of two staff members with longer tenure.
• Provided superior training to temporary employee that resulted in her being hired for permanent, Level 1 position after only three months.

Accounts Payable Analyst—Music & Video Distribution   2002–2005

Processed high volume of utility bills, office equipment leases, shipping invoices, and office supplies for 12 regional branches. Assisted branches with proper invoice coding and resolved payment disputes with vendors.

• Identified long-standing duplicate payment that resulted in vendor refund of $12,000.
• Created contract employment expenses spreadsheet; identified and resolved $24,000 in duplicate payments.
• Gained reputation for thoroughness and promptness in meeting all payment deadlines.
• Set up macro in accounts payable system that streamlined invoice payments.
• Consolidated vendor accounts, increasing productivity and reducing number of checks processed.

Accounts Receivable Analyst—Music & Video Distribution   2000–2002

Processed incoming payments; received and posted daily check deposits, reviewed applications for vendor accounts; distributed accounting reports and ordered office supplies. Handled re-billings of international accounts for shipments by various labels. Promoted to permanent employee from temporary after 90 days.

Additional Experience: Billing Clerk/Accounting Clerk/Bookkeeper (*details available upon request*)

EDUCATION

CALIFORNIA STATE UNIVERSITY, Northridge, CA   2005
B.S. in Finance; Graduated With Honors • Completed Studies Concurrent with Full Time Employment

Computer Skills: Windows, Microsoft Office (Word, Excel, PowerPoint), Peachtree, J.D. Edwards, Tracs

Robert Smithson

123 Wellington Ave. 201.555.8956 branchmgr@email.com
West New York, NJ 07726

Branch Management/Customer Service ~ Finance

"Personable, competent, analytical, e-commerce savvy"

Performance Profile/Performance Summary

Results-oriented Finance and Banking professional with demonstrated ability to develop corporate growth, stability, and financial performance. Skilled analyst, strong organizational and communication skills, and proven leadership qualities. Comprehensive understanding of financial needs at all levels of business including: evaluation, analysis, financial data communication.

Recipient - Commerce Capital Markets Referral Award –2009

Core Banking Competencies

❖ Lending Policies, Practices	❖ Collateral Loans	❖ Unsecured Personal Loans
❖ Asset-based Loans	❖ Mortgage-based Loans	❖ Teller Operations
❖ Underwriting Criteria	❖ Compliance	❖ Loan Documentation
❖ Project Management	❖ Team Management	❖ eBusiness Management
❖ Customer Service Relations	❖ Problem Solving	❖ Communications
❖ Audit Compliance	❖ Branch Management	❖ Sales Management

Professional Experience

COMMERCE BANK, New Brunswick, NJ   2004 to Present
Customer Service Relations

Extensive knowledge of lending policies, practices, compliance, and underwriting criteria. Experienced processing collateral loans, unsecured personal loans, asset-based loans, and mortgage-based loans. Process all loan documentation, performing research activities as necessary.
Counsel clients in the selection of financial products in order to meet their financial planning and banking needs.
- Create and process client accounts providing excellent customer service.
- Sell bank products based on specific sales focus.
- Identify prospective clients and develop and implement presentations for clients.
- Originate and process consumer and mortgage loan applications.

Accomplishments
- Consistently meet and exceeded sales quotas and standards by cross-selling and up-selling bank products and services.
- Increased branch loan production volume.
- Sold a variety of loans by pulling CBA, creating loan worksheets, and making recommendations to lenders upon request.
- Ensured that loan policies and procedures were followed in accordance with audit guidelines.

Concurrent & Complementary Professional Experience

STAR FIRE AUTOGRAPHS, West New York, NJ   <u>1996 to Present</u>
Business Manager/Principal

Established and currently manage Internet and mail-order entertainment media business. Implemented strategic marketing programs, successfully retaining clients and achieving dominant market position. Instituted pricing structure after conducting extensive marketing research utilizing industry resources. Explored marketing and advertising opportunities adding value to new initiatives. Tracked data and improved business operations accordingly.

Accomplishments
- Grew annual revenues to 1200% over 15 years
- E-commerce competent
- Authored inventory item descriptions
- Managed customer service relations
- Implemented and sourced technology solutions
- Developed eMarketing strategies

Education & Professional Training

FAIRLEIGH DICKINSON UNIVERSITY, Madison, NJ
    BA - History, Minor - Politics

Commerce University Finance Training Courses

- ❖ Finance
- ❖ Customer Service
- ❖ Loan Underwriting
- ❖ Business Management
- ❖ Loan Products
- ❖ BSA/AML
- ❖ Bank Secrecy
- ❖ Consumer Lending
- ❖ Privacy Compliance
- ❖ Foreign Assets Control

Computer Skills

    Microsoft Office, Lotus Notes, Dbase, Basic HTML, ecommerce

References available on request.

Kanji Mosoui

29 Schubert Ave.   617.555.1831   finance_focused@gmail.com
Boston, MA 02108

QUALIFICATIONS FOR BANK OF AMERICA INTERNSHIP

- Committed to a career combining formal education in economics with practical work. Experienced with analysis for project management, including budgets, labor resources, and timelines.
- Prepared and delivered numerous presentations on project status to city and PG&E officials. Researched and presented options to property owners and investors for construction materials.
- History of taking on responsibility and successfully managing personnel for multi-million dollar project. Excellent communication with individuals, businesses, municipalities, and professional firms.
- Conversational Spanish.

Education

SAN JOSE STATE UNIVERSITY, San Jose CA

Masters, Economics	Anticipated Dec 2008
Bachelor of Arts, Economics	Graduated 2005

Professional Experience

CONFIDENTIAL, San Jose, CA   2006 – 2008
Installer of wet and dry underground utilities for new developers and municipalities
Project Manager

- Managed $3.6M project to install new underground dry utilities and new street lights on Main Street in Santa Cruz. Worked with city, PG&E, telephone and cable companies. Project took approximately 1-1/2 years for planning, execution, and completion. Averaged approximately 15 full-time crew, including both union and non-union.

Independent Contractor   2005, 2006
Davé Construction   2005
Residential and investment property new construction and renovation
Construction Manager/Project Manager

- Functioned as general contractor for construction of new $2M, 4,700 sq. foot residential property. Hired and managed approximately 300 subcontractors and vendors over the course of the project.
- Obtained building permits, and worked with general contractors and clients on architectural plans. Oversaw daily construction, and handled accounting, including paying all subcontractors.
- Worked with owner to convert 1,000 square foot home to 3,200 square feet. Same duties noted as above. Sale of home resulted in net profit of almost $400K for property owner.

Leadership Experience

PHI DELTA THETA, Davis, CA   2000 – 2005
Consecutively **Treasurer, House Manager, Vice President, President**

Excellent references available.

David Sedaris

143 MacArthur Blvd. 334.555.4957 rainmaker@earthlink.net
Montgomery, AL 36101

FUNDRAISING CONSULTANT/PUBLIC RELATIONS
Verifiable Record of Raising Significant Amounts of Money for Charitable and Public Causes

Performance Profile/Performance Summary

Early-retirement Corporate Executive, committed to providing expertise in communications to promote the public good. *Verifiable record of raising significant amounts of money for charitable and public causes,* plus an extensive network of contacts. Combines distinguished career building and leading successful company growth with extensive history of contributing efforts to charitable causes.
  - o Proven strengths in the fine art of communications and negotiations with the ability to establish confidence and trust, resolve conflicts, build consensus and motivate parties with divergent opinions toward common goals.
  - o Excellent listening skills with focus on a "win/win" philosophy.

Foreign Languages—Fluent in Spanish
Computer Skills—PC and Mac; Proficient on Microsoft Office Suite
Military—United States Army, Honorable Discharge

PROFESSIONAL BACKGROUND

DEEP SOUTH CONFECTIONS, Montgomery, AL 1982 to 2008
Managing Partner, Chief Operating Officer

Launched and directed activities of confectionary manufacturing company from start-up through 20 years of successful operations. Built business from initial capital investment of $10,000 to annual revenues in excess of $40 million. Established and nurtured key contacts with retail and wholesale operations on local, regional, and national level including major chain stores.
- Generated widespread goodwill for company through extensive, ongoing involvement with numerous community charitable organizations. Recognized by city for contributions.
- Sourced vendors and contractors and directed manufacturing operations in U.S. and abroad.
- Finalized sale of company to international conglomerate in 2007 to devote time to travel and community involvement.

Education
B.A. in Humanities, UCLA

Community Activities —Partial List
  - ➢ **Fundraising Chair**—Friends of Valley Glen Hospital
  - ➢ **Platinum Donor, Chair of Steering Committee**—Valley Glen Youth Association
  - ➢ **Member, Past-Officer**—Valley Glen Chamber of Commerce
  - ➢ **Member, Board of Directors**—Neighborhood Youth Industries, Inc.
  - ➢ **President**—Valley Arms Homeowners Association
  - ➢ **Fundraising Chair**—Friends of the Glen Wilderness Project

Activities
Los Angeles Marathon (annually since 1995), Golf, Tennis

Scott Simon

455 Roosevelt Rd.   313.555.2394   falseclaims@meritech.com
Detroit, MI 48201

INSURANCE ADJUSTER/INVESTIGATOR
Seasoned fraud squad detective poised to join the insurance profession.

Performance Profile/Performance Summary

Logical and analytical approach to identifying and resolving situations with high potential for conflict. Organized and creative, with solid approach to comprehensive information gathering.

Police-trained investigator, superior questioning and analytical skills, experienced in negotiations, able to develop trust and open communication.

Calm under pressure. Committed to applying a trained and seasoned detective's skills to the insurance profession.

Core Competencies

➢ Investigative Techniques	➢ Witness Questioning	➢ Legal Compliance
➢ Courtroom Representation	➢ Incident Documentation	➢ Negotiating
➢ Risk Assessment	➢ Report Writing	➢ Safety Principles
➢ Needs Assessment	➢ Conflict Resolution	➢ One-on-One Training

Professional Training

➢ Police Science	➢ Investigation Techniques	➢ Security
➢ Reconnaissance	➢ Surveillance	➢ Accident Investigation
➢ Photography	➢ Family Violence	➢ Child Abuse/Rape
➢ Crisis Evidence	➢ Public Relations	➢ Communication Skills

Police Service

Detroit, MI   2004 – 2009
➢ **Detective Fraud Squad**
Southfield, MI   2001 – 2004
➢ **Detective Serious Crimes**
Ann Arbor, MI   1995 – 2001
➢ **Officer Canine Unit**
Bad Axe, MI   1994 – 1995
➢ **Patrolman**

Education

➢ **Masters of Science, Leadership and Organizational Change**   2008
Michigan State
➢ **Bachelors of Science, Criminal Justice**   1993
Pfeiffer University, Charlotte, NC
➢ **Information systems security coursework**   2009
Stanly Community College, Albemarle, NC

Superior references available upon request.

VERSION 1

CHARLENE DeDARBY

2084 Van Ness Ave. #118 • San Francisco, CA 94105 • (415) 555-4367 • cdedarby@comcast.net

SENIOR ACCOUNTANT/ACCOUNTING MANAGER/FINANCIAL ANALYST

Performance Profile/Performance Summary: Results-focused Senior Accountant and Financial Analyst with 12 years' progressive experience—through numerous mergers and acquisitions—including 5 years as Accounting Manager for leading global company. Proven ability to combine "big-picture" strategic thinking with day-to-day policies and processes to deliver consistent, on-time, accurate results in support of organization goals.
Diligent in executing critical month-end closing process. Highly adaptable to change. Tech savvy; learns and implements new programs quickly. Works well with cross-functional/cross-departmental teams, as well as public and coworkers at all levels.

Core Professional Competencies: Project Management ~ Financial Analysis ~ Research ~ Accounting Processes ~ GAAP ~ Compliance ~ SOX ~ Expense Review & Control ~ Productivity & Process Optimization ~ Complex Account Analysis & Reconciliation ~ Fixed Assets Management ~ Trend Analysis ~ Variance Analysis & Resolution ~ Training & Supervision ~ Internal/External Client Relations ~ Change Management ~ Teambuilding & Leadership

PROFESSIONAL EXPERIENCE

A GLOBAL FINANCIAL SERVICES COMPANY • 1998— Present
$2T plus in assets and 200,000 employees

Accounting Manager II—Global Financial Services Company, San Francisco, CA (2008–Present)

Received promotion prior to acquisition by **************** in late September 2008. Overall responsibilities remained similar to Accounting Manager I position.

Selected Accomplishments

- Selected as primary accounting contact for project to determine disposition of outstanding customer rebate checks. Resolution reduced number of outstanding items > 90 days old from 130,000+ items to less than 60,000 and reduced reconciliation time 20%.
- Partnered with various areas to transition group's functions to **** following acquisition by ****, to reduce redundancies.

Accounting Manager—Global Financial Services Company San Francisco (2004–2007)

Promoted to newly created position, reporting to Senior Accounting Manager, and managing three staff accountants. Reviewed corporate expense analytics and variance analyses; oversaw balance sheet reconciliation process including cash accounts, fixed assets, various PPD accounts, and accrued expenses. Supervised processing of monthly accruals and reclassifications. Ensured on-time, accurate completion of key accruals including bonuses, workers compensation, etc.

Selected Accomplishments

- Oversaw variance analysis process for $1.5B credit card division—from initial identification and research— through collaborating with various business units on resolution.
- Participated in preparation and maintenance of SOX documentation and quarterly departmental testing.
- Researched tax code and identified division under-accrual that had resulted in $5M+ overpayment of taxes over 9 months; executed process that recaptured $1.2M+ per month.
- Created process ensuring timely and accurate completion of all business owner accruals and reclassifications.

Sr. Accountant—Global Financial Services Company, San Francisco (2000–2004)

Relocated to San Francisco and joined **** prior to acquisition by WaMu. Prepared expense analytics for $40M in income statement accounts. Reconciled various balance sheet accounts; compiled cost allocations.

Selected Accomplishments

- Participated in creating and performing expense analytics process for Marketing Group; identified millions of dollars in past over- and under-accruals.
- Converted poorly formatted *Accrued Expense* account to well-organized, easy-to-identify and -understand format that resulted in identifying and resolving $40M in excess accruals out of $100M total, dating back up to five years.

- Assisted management in determining correct accounting of third party partnership expenses.
- Reduced time required to prepare cost allocation database from five business days to half a day while increasing accuracy of data and reducing management review time from one day to less than two hours.
- Key person in standardizing, updating, and cleaning up fixed asset system comprising 35,000+ items. Worked with managers and key personnel across multiple departments in identifying owned vs. leased assets.

Accountant II—Global Financial Services Company, Northridge, CA (1998–2000)

Hired by **** to perform general accounting functions. Took over responsibility for reconciling, researching and clearing major GL account with average activity of $100M+ daily and up to $4B per month, three months after joining company. Reconciled GL accounts for company-owned loans.

Selected Accomplishments

- Reduced unreconciled items in key GL account from 12,000+ items to less than 4,000 within four months and fewer than 1,400 within one year; concurrently eliminated all items aged > 60 days.
- Reversed prior steady increase in number of unreconciled items.
- Gained support from another company group that led to improvement in fraud identification and paved the way for receiving payments of millions of dollars in loans.
- Recommended, and assisted in creating, process for communicating with branches and loan centers on outstanding un-booked loans; became trusted point of contact for branches and loan centers for resolving un-booked loans.

COUNTRYWIDE HOME LOANS, Simi Valley, CA • 1997 – 1998
Mortgage company with $200B in managed loans during this period

Investor Accounting Analyst

Joined company with responsibility for mid-month and special loans for end-of-month investors. Completed period close within one day and reconciliations within two weeks of closing.

Selected Accomplishments

- Reconciled 160+ bank accounts and prepared $350M in wire transfers monthly.
- Researched and cleared variances in <1 day for significant investor on monthly basis.

PAYPHONE SERVICES INC., Ventura, CA • 1996 – 1997
Regional business with 150 employees

Junior Accountant

Hired following college graduation to code accounts payable, rapidly assumed additional responsibilities. Prepared, processed, and posted journal entries to GL; prepared financial statements for two small companies including general partnership. Worked with outside auditors during due diligence process following company sale.

Selected Accomplishments

- Participated in determining best accounting method inventory valuation in computing sales and use tax.
- Assumed A/P functions for 5 out of 18 companies with minimal training.

EDUCATION

DeVRY UNIVERSITY, Pomona, CA
BS in Accounting

Computer Skills

Microsoft Office (Excel, Word, Access, PowerPoint, Outlook)
Visio, Macola, Peoplesoft for Government, Extensity (GEAC) SmartStream

VERSION 2

CHARLENE DeDARBY

2084 Van Ness St. #118   San Francisco, CA 94105   Senior_Accountant@comcast.net   (415) 555-5964

SENIOR ACCOUNTANT/ACCOUNTING MANAGER/FINANCIAL ANALYST

Performance Profile/Performance Summary

12 years' progressive experience—through numerous mergers and acquisitions—including 6 years as Accounting Manager for leading global company. Proven ability to combine strategic thinking with existing policies and processes to deliver consistent, on-time, accurate results in support of organization goals.
Diligent in executing critical month-end closing process. Tech-savvy multitasker; learns and implements new programs quickly. Works well with cross-functional/cross-departmental teams and colleagues at all levels.

Core Professional Competencies

✓ Project Management	✓ Research	✓ Accounting Processes
✓ Financial Analysis	✓ GAAP	✓ Productivity Optimization
✓ Training & Development	✓ Trend Analysis	✓ Analysis & Reconciliation
✓ Compliance	✓ Variance Analysis	✓ Fixed Assets Management
✓ Expense Control	✓ Leadership	✓ Process Optimization
✓ Change Management	✓ SOX	✓ Int/Ext Client Relations

PROFESSIONAL EXPERIENCE

A GLOBAL FINANCIAL SERVICES COMPANY   1998–Present
$2T plus in assets and 200,000 employees
Accounting Manager II   2008–Present

Received promotion prior to acquisition by *************** in late September 2008. Overall responsibilities remained similar to Accounting Manager I position.

Selected Accomplishments

- Selected as primary accounting contact for project to determine disposition of outstanding customer rebate checks. Resolution reduced number of outstanding items > 90 days old from 130,000+ items to less than 60,000 and reduced reconciliation time 20%.
- Partnered with various areas to transition group's functions to **** following acquisition by ****, to reduce redundancies.

Accounting Manager   2004–2007

Promoted to newly created position, reporting to Senior Accounting Manager, and managing three staff accountants. Reviewed corporate expense analytics and variance analyses; oversaw balance sheet reconciliation process including cash accounts, fixed assets, various PPD accounts, and accrued expenses. Supervised processing of monthly accruals and reclassifications. Ensured on-time, accurate completion of key accruals including bonuses, workers compensation, etc.

Selected Accomplishments

- Oversaw variance analysis process for $1.5B credit card division—from initial identification and research—through collaboration with various business units on resolution.
- Participated in preparation and maintenance of SOX documentation and quarterly departmental testing.
- Researched tax code and identified division under-accrual that had resulted in $5M+ overpayment of taxes over 9 months; executed process that recaptured $1.2M+ per month.
- Created process ensuring timely and accurate completion of all business owner accruals and reclassifications.

Sr. Accountant   2000–2004

Relocated to San Francisco and joined Providian prior to acquisition by ****. Prepared expense analytics for $40M in income statement accounts. Reconciled various balance sheet accounts; compiled cost allocations.

Selected Accomplishments

- Participated in creating and performing expense analytics process for Marketing Group; identified millions of dollars in past over- and under-accruals.
- Converted poorly formatted *Accrued Expense* account to well-organized, easy-to-identify and -understand format that resulted in identifying and resolving $40M in excess accruals out of $100M total, dating back up to five years.
- Assisted management in determining correct accounting of third party partnership expenses.
- Reduced time required to prepare cost allocation database from five business days to half a day while increasing accuracy of data and reducing management review time from one day to less than two hours.
- Key person in standardizing, updating, and cleaning up fixed asset system comprising 35,000+ items. Worked with managers and key personnel across multiple departments in identifying owned vs. leased assets.

Accountant II   1998–2000

Hired by **** to perform general accounting functions. Took over responsibility for reconciling, researching and clearing major GL account with average activity of $100M+ daily and up to $4B per month, three months after joining company. Reconciled GL accounts for company owned loans.

Selected Accomplishments

- Reduced un-reconciled items in key GL account from 12,000+ items to less than 4,000 within four months and fewer than 1,400 within one year; concurrently eliminated all items aged > 60 days.
- Reversed prior steady increase in number of unreconciled items.
- Gained support from another company group that led to improvement in fraud identification and paved the way for receiving payments of millions of dollars in loans.
- Recommended, and assisted in creating, process for communicating with branches and loan centers on outstanding un-booked loans; became trusted point of contact for branches and loan centers for resolving un-booked loans.

COUNTRYWIDE HOME LOANS, Simi Valley, CA   1997–1998
Mortgage company with $200B in managed loans during this period
Investor Accounting Analyst

Joined company with responsibility for mid-month and special loans for end-of-month investors. Completed period close within one day and reconciliations within two weeks of closing.

Selected Accomplishments

- Reconciled 160+ bank accounts and prepared $350M in wire transfers monthly.
- Researched and cleared variances in <1 day for significant investor on monthly basis.

PAYPHONE SERVICES INC., Ventura, CA   1996–1997
Regional business with 150 employees
Junior Accountant

Hired following college graduation to code accounts payable, rapidly assumed additional responsibilities. Prepared, processed and posted journal entries to GL; prepared financial statements for two small companies including general partnership. Worked with outside auditors during due diligence process following company sale.

Selected Accomplishments

- Participated in determining best accounting method inventory valuation in computing sales and use tax.
- Assumed A/P functions for 5 out of 18 companies with minimal training.

EDUCATION

DEVRY UNIVERSITY, Pomona, CA
BS in Accounting

Computer Skills

Microsoft Office (Excel, Word, Access, PowerPoint, Outlook)
Visio, Macola, Peoplesoft for Government, Extensity (GEAC) SmartStream

VERSION 3

CHARLENE DeDARBY

2084 Van Ness St #118 • San Francisco, CA 94105 • (415) 555-3020 • Senior_Accountant@comcast.net

SENIOR ACCOUNTANT/ACCOUNTING MANAGER/FINANCIAL ANALYST

Performance Profile/Performance Summary: Results-focused Senior Accountant and Financial Analyst with 12 years' progressive experience—through numerous mergers and acquisitions—including 5 years as Accounting Manager for leading global company. Highly adaptable to change. Tech savvy; learns and implements new programs quickly. Works well with cross-functional/cross-departmental teams, as well as public and coworkers at all levels.

Core Professional Competencies: Project Management ~ Financial Analysis ~ Research ~ Accounting Processes ~ GAAP ~ Compliance ~ SOX ~ Expense Review & Control ~ Productivity & Process Optimization ~ Complex Account Analysis & Reconciliation ~ Fixed Assets Management ~ Trend Analysis ~ Variance Analysis & Resolution ~ Training & Supervision ~ Internal/External Client Relations ~ Change Management ~ Teambuilding & Leadership

PROFESSIONAL EXPERIENCE

A GLOBAL FINANCIAL SERVICES COMPANY • 1998–Present

Accounting Manager II—Global Financial Services Company, San Francisco, CA (2008–Present)
Accounting Manager—Global Financial Services Company, San Francisco (2004–2007)

Reviewed corporate expense analytics and variance analyses; oversaw balance sheet reconciliation process including cash accounts, fixed assets, various PPD accounts, and accrued expenses. Supervised team of three in processing monthly accruals and reclassifications.

- Partnered in transitioning group's functions to **** following acquisition by ****, to reduce redundancies.
- Oversaw variance analysis process for $1.5B credit card division—from initial identification and research—through collaborating with various business units on resolution.
- Participated in preparation and maintenance of SOX documentation and quarterly departmental testing.
- Collaborated on transfer of assets following acquisition of **** (2005)

Sr. Accountant—Global Financial Services Company, San Francisco (2000–2004)

Prepared expense analytics for $40M in income statement accounts. Reconciled accounts; compiled cost allocations.

- Identified millions of dollars in past over- and under-accruals.
- Resolved $40M in excess accruals out of $100M total, dating back up to five years.
- Assisted management in determining correct accounting of third party partnership expenses.
- Reduced time required to prepare cost allocation database from five business days to half a day while increasing accuracy of data and reducing management review time from one day to less than two hours.
- Streamlined fixed asset system comprising 35,000+ items.

Accountant II—Global Financial Services Company, Northridge, CA (1998–2000)

Performed general accounting functions. Reconciled, researched, and cleared major GL account with average activity of $100M+ daily and up to $4B per month.

Early Experience
Investor Accounting Analyst—COUNTRYWIDE HOME LOANS, Simi Valley, CA • 1997–1998
Junior Accountant—PAYPHONE SERVICES INC., Ventura, CA • 1996–1997

BS in Accounting; DEVRY UNIVERSITY, Pomona, CA
Computer Skills—Microsoft Office (Excel, Word, Access, PowerPoint, Outlook); Visio, Macola, Peoplesoft for Government, Extensity (GEAC) SmartStream

Sun Huynh

52 Tiger Lilly Drive
Sunnyvale, CA 94087

(408)737-9398
quality.engineer@gmail.com

Software Quality Assurance Engineer
Performance Summary

QA engineer with in-depth knowledge of complex wired and wireless technology. Superior testing skills with outstanding analysis, programming, and debugging capabilities with the ability to identify critical software defects before market release. Backed by two promotions within four years and receipt of MVP award within last two years. MS in Computer Science.

- ✓ Performs test plan creations, manual and automated product testing, troubleshooting failures, and tracking with defects.
- ✓ Strong interpersonal and communication skills with the ability to work with cross-functional departments, including software developers.
- ✓ Performs product validation automation by creating test scripts and investigating script failures.
- ✓ Experienced with layer 2 and layer 3 networking protocols.

Professional Skills

* Software Testing Methodologies	* Network Protocols	* White Box & Black Box Testing
* Test Plan Creation	* Problem Isolation & Recreation	* System Testing
* Test Beds	* Complex Test Scenarios	* Functional & Design Test Reviews
* Automation Scripting	* Troubleshooting Skills	* Regression Testing
* Product Testing & Debugging	* Scalability & Performance Testing	* Root Cause Identification

Work Experience

Silicon Sun Networks, Cupertino, CA   2009–Present
Software QA Engineer (WLAN Team)   2012–Present
Manages deployment of wireless networking protocol APs on wireless network; drives each user's connectivity issues to fullest resolution. Uses agile development processes for test and validation. Performs manual and regression testing of next generation access. Leads test efforts for developing an innovative and unique Adaptive radio management technology.

- Created up to 500% faster network connections for smartphones, tablets, and laptops, resulting in vastly improved client and system performance.
- The network continuously optimizes client connections, keeping network capacity and performance consistent.
- Reduced help desk calls 30%.

Software QA Engineer (WLAN Team)   2009–2012
Performed manual and regression testing of next generation access points, controller, and switches. Performed problem isolation and recreation in complex test scenario failures. Designed functional and interoperability-level verification test from system specifications and product requirements. Executed functional, interoperability, and customer use test cases; tracked test case results.

- Achieved 2012 Q3 MVP Award by turning around a customer deal for high-density iPad performance competitive testing. Completed multiple rounds of testing under time constraints, resulting in a 30% improvement on streaming capabilities and lowering video stalling, outperforming Cisco and Ruckus. Emerged as a golden test case for TME and Aruba partners, leading to multiple customer wins.
- Accomplished ARM2.0/1.0 feature regression testing and test plan write-ups, building test beds on multiple releases with features including Spectrum Load Balancing Band-Steering, Mode-Aware ARM, Airtime Fairness, and PerSSID Bandwidth Management and Scanning.
- Performed high-density (HD) testing on a testbed with 200+ heterogeneous client devices, resulting in improved AP performance with high client density.
- Identified significant hardware issues in early life cycle on two new AP platforms crucial to the company's new initiative in the hospitality market, resulting in decreased hardware schedule risks.

Awards

Quarterly MVP Award Nominee, Q2 2013
Quarterly MVP Award, Q4 2012

Education

Cal Berkeley, Berkeley, CA   2009
Master of Science   Major: Computer Science GPA: 3.93

San Jose State University, San Jose, CA   2007
Bachelor of Engineering Major: Computer Science

Computer Network Skills

NX-OS and Cisco Nexus Switching: VLANs, Private VLANs, STP, Port-channels, Virtual Port Channels, Unidirectional Link Detection, Cisco FabricPath, Firewall, High Availability, SPAN, ERSPAN, Unified Fabric, Nexus 1000V, QoS, OTV, MPLS,
Layer 2: VLANs & Trunks, Inter-VLAN routing, Etherchannels, STP, High Availability
Layer 3: Routing basics, EIFRP, OSPF, Route filtering, BGP (Good concepts)
Extensive knowledge in 802.11 a/b/g/n/ac WLAN
Protocols: TCP/IP, UDP, ARP, DHCP, ICMP, 802.3, 802.1x, HTTP, FTP, TFTP, DNS, Syslog

Programming

TCL	C
Expect	C++
Shell Scripting	JAVA

Hardware

IXIA XM12 High Performance Chassis	Aruba Controllers
WaveTest 90/WaveTest 20	Cisco Catalyst 3560 & 3750 Switches
Aruba Corvina Switches	Lantronix Terminal Servers
Netgear Gigabit Series Switches	Access Points (APs)
Dell PowerEdge R620 Server	

Software Applications

IXIA: IxChariot, IxExplorer,	Testlink
IxLoad	SecureCRT
IxVeriwave	mRemote
3CDaemon	Winagents TFTP Server
iPerf	Backtrack
Wireshark	MIB Browser
Omnipeek Packet Analyzer	Linux Screen and VI Utilities
Bugzilla	

Operating Systems

Linux (Fedora, Centos, Ubuntu)	Apple MAC OS X
Cisco IOS	Windows Server 2000 & 2003
Aruba OS	Windows XP/7/8
Google Androids	Unix
Apple iOS	

Excellent references available on request

Georgia O'Keefe

734899 Lagos
Anaheim, CA 92801

C. 714.555.1234
H. 714.555.2345

hrmanagement@yahoo.com

Human Resource Management – Food Industry
Operations/Labor Relations/Staff Development

Performance Profile/Performance Summary

Dedicated HR manager experienced in industrial food service (world exposition food service management), restaurants, and catering. Proven leadership skills—able to recruit, retain, develop, and motivate employees to new levels of productivity. Communicates successfully and productively to any and all types of people. Excellent problem solver, strong team orientation, accomplished public speaker. *Expertise in boosting profitability by maximizing sales and reducing costs.*

Core competencies include

Recruitment	Selection	Performance Evaluation
Separations	Vendor/Supplier Relations	Promotional Programs
Training & Development	Payroll Audits	International Labor Law
Labor Policy Audits	Program Development	Policies & Procedures
Vendor Contracts	Work Policy Manuals	Contract Negotiations
Labor Relations	On Clock Productivity	Disbursed Management
Facilities Maintenance	Employment Contracts	Government Relations
Employee Manuals	Customer Service Systems	Overseas Location Recruitment

Professional Experience

World Exposition Services—*Costa Mesa, CA*   2003-Present

Food service logistics and restaurant operations for world fairs and expositions.

Director of Personnel, Labor, and Human Resources/General Operations

- 2008 Canadian National Fair Exposition
- 1986 World Exposition—Lisbon, Portugal
- 1998 World Fair Exposition—Biel, Switzerland
- 1992 World Exposition—Osaka, Japan
- 2002 French National Fair Exposition—Paris

Directed activities of all managers and assistant managers in supervision of multiple locations (8 in France, 10 in Switzerland) and up to 280 food service and facilities maintenance personnel, plus one beverage director to ensure full stocking and successful operating of all restaurants, bars, and food concessions. Reported directly to CEO.

Accountable for all phases of personnel management—hiring, staff development, evaluation, promotion, and separations. Created general employee contracts and work policy manuals. Controlled labor costs by optimizing staffing requirements according to customer visitations and by monitoring break times, clock-in/out accuracy, and on-the-clock productivity. Created working relationships with government officials in European Union.

Selected Contributions

- Initiated full-scale recruitment of host-country hotel school interns. Secured motivated general employees 20% below budget.

Cut labor costs from 27% to 20%, significantly increasing net profit to investors on gross of $8.5 million in 6 months of event operation.

Selected Contributions continued

- Streamlined staffing needs by reengineering food service stations, allowing employees to multitask. Discovered thousands of overpaid dollars by auditing every paycheck for inaccuracies.
- Increased sales in Mexican food concession. Designed innovative ticket system to reduce line wait. Simultaneously eliminated loss of impatient customer sales and boosted service capacity.
- Successfully interpreted and complied with all host country labor laws and regulations. Faced comprehensive labor policy audit by host country's top labor official. Passed with flying colors.
- Played key role in company meeting exposition revenue goals (grossed $11.25 million in 6 months with only 9 concessions) by facilitating open and productive communication with management-level and general employees.
- Conversant with Swiss labor laws, culture, and practices. Resulted in productive, lasting international business relationships.
- Participated in formulation of management structure, labor policies, employee handbook, management and employee training handbook, and operating guidelines in preparation for expo.

Gourmet Foods Inc, Costa Mesa, CA   2003
                                                                          1999-2001
                                                                          1995-1996

General Manager

Monitor customer service levels, employee performance, and labor costs. Track and evaluate daily sales. Responsible for prospective employee interviewing and hiring. Teach and facilitate communication skills. Supervise up to 50: concession managers, counter help, cooks, and cashiers for 4 locations.

Selected Accomplishments

- Launched innovative ongoing promotions.
  - Costa Mesa police and fire department discount program.
  - Home-meal and catering menu program.
  - "Daily Special" program.
- Improved customer service levels by retraining employees in the following areas: quick/personal attention to customers, cleaning without turning backs to customers, and interpersonal communication skills.

Zuara's Pizza, Costa Mesa, CA   1988-1995
Assistant Operations Manager

Promoted from positions as counter help/delivery to oversee operations of 4 stores. Supervised roughly 70, including store managers, counter help, cooks, delivery personnel, cashiers, and dishwashers. Ensured store cleanliness, product availability and timely delivery, and customer satisfaction.

Computer Skills/Foreign Languages

Internet (Netscape Navigator, Internet Explorer)
E-Mail (Outlook, Outlook Express)
MS Word, Excel
Conversational French

Veronica Kent

Placentia, CA 92870   (562) 555-9012   ronnie.kent@sbcglobal.net

Human Resources Generalist/Accounts Payable/Administrative Support
Flexible, disciplined, organized, and hardworking - the consummate small office professional

Performance Profile/Performance Summary

Top-performing human resources and accounts payable professional with over 15 years' administrative support experience. Skilled in all aspects of small office human resources: payroll, benefits administration, accounts payables, customer service, sales support, collections, administrative support, purchasing, facilities management, event planning, and compliance. Recognized for outstanding discipline, leadership, and going the "extra mile" to meet departmental and company goals. The "go to" person for diverse organizational challenges.

Core Competencies

- Human Resources
- Payroll Processing
- Benefits Administration
- 401k and Section 125 Plans
- Customer Service
- Employee/Vendor Relations
- I-9 and EEO Compliance

- Accounts Payables
- Invoice Discrepancies
- Payment Processing
- Purchase Orders
- Expense Tracking
- Journal Entries
- Auditing & Compliance
- Spreadsheets/Reports

- Administrative Support
- Collections
- Bank Deposits
- Internal/External Liaison
- Property Leases
- DMV Renewals
- Month/Year End, 1099s
- Event Planning

Technology Competencies

- Windows 98/2000/XP/Vista
- Word, Excel, PowerPoint
- Outlook

- Corel Draw Graphics
- Digital Photo Graphics
- ACCPAC Accounting
- QuickBooks

- ADP Payroll, Time and Attendance
- Purchasing Software
- Internet Research

Professional Experience

Airfonix Communications, Los Angeles, CA. www.airfonix.com   2007-2009
Airfonix specializes in engineering superior quality wireless audio products for the professional and semi-professional audio markets.

Administrative Support Generalist

- Serves as support for an Independent Sales Contractor, selling Airfonix products to distributors nationwide.
- Related experiences: administrative support, customer service, contracts and proposals, accounts payable/receivable, expense tracking, bank reconciliation and deposits, email and Internet research.

Standard Tel Networks, Huntington Beach CA. www.standardtel.com   1991-2006
One of the largest independent business communications providers in the United States with over 8,000 customers. Standard Tel Networks grew from a traditional voice and data communications integrations company to a premium provider of IP telephony solutions.

Human Resources Generalist/Accounts Payable Specialist
- Managed full range of human resources, including research and analysis.
- Administered benefits administration; experience includes maintenance of costs through negotiations, and the development/implementation of alternative benefit programs.
- General liability, worker's compensation, sub-contractor and payroll auditing and compliance.
- Processed payroll for medium-size company.
- Responsible for all accounts payable functions, including monthly and yearly closeouts.
- Liaison between internal and external.
- Processed DMV renewals for corporate vehicles.
- Managed petty cash accounts, processed bank deposits, and handled expense tracking and reports.
- Related experience: administrative support, accounts receivable/back-up, property building maintenance/facilities management for three facilities, sales support/marketing and purchasing activities.

Outstanding Accomplishments
- Reduced corporate liability, worker's compensation insurance costs by one-third; restructured liability insurance management programs to facilitate savings.
- Detected fraudulent activities from utility companies and enabled company to recover $14,000 in taxes and fees.
- Assisted in the implementation of company merger, by reorganizing company policies and procedures, vacation/sick-time, and payroll systems.
- Employee of the year nomination 1999 and 2000.

McDonnell Douglas Corporation, Long Beach, CA   1986-1990
A major aerospace manufacturer and defense contractor; The Boeing Company acquired McDonnell Douglas Corporation in 1997.

Administrative Assistant
- Coordinated daily quality control efforts between the internal planning departments and upper management.
- Collaborated and cooperated, as a key member of the "Quality Support Team," along with the production line and management team to contribute to the main business goal, "First Time Quality and Customer Satisfaction."
- Performed daily office duties such as filing, typing, data processing, research, and answering phones.

Education
- Fullerton City College, Fullerton, CA. *Continued Education,* fall 2010.
- Long Beach City College, Long Beach, CA. *Continued Education*, units 97, 1997-2000.
- Long Beach City College, Long Beach, CA. *Associate's Degree, General Business*, graduated 1985.

Personal
- St. Jude Cancer Center, Fullerton, CA; critical care support group volunteer.
- Snail's Pace, Fountain Valley, CA; coach and train beginning marathon runners.
- Eleven competitive marathons, seven half marathons, 10k and 5k competitive runs.

"Every day I am determined to make a difference with my presence;
we get more done and the day goes more quickly."

Andy Goldman

943 Hartford Pike
Baltimore, MD 13257

803.555.1209
compliance gold@yahoo.com

INTERNATIONAL TRADE COMPLIANCE

TACTICAL MANUFACTURING OPERATIONS • INTERNATIONAL LOGISTICS • AUDITING • GLOBAL TRADE • TRANSPORTATION MANAGEMENT

Performance Summary

Diversified management and leadership background featuring significant global trade compliance accomplishments. Talent for analyzing business data and identifying opportunities to improve operational efficiencies and reduce expenses within domestic and international marketplaces.
Ability to guide and empower cross-functional groups to resolve complex import and export issues and accomplish objectives. Creative problem solver who controls cost and minimizes risks while simultaneously driving desired results for bottom-line profitability.

Core Competencies

- Strategic Business Planning
- Contract Negotiations
- Business Reengineering
- Regulatory, Compliance & Auditing
- Import and Export Operations
- Research and Data Management
- Transportation & Logistics
- Project Management
- Reporting & Administration

PROFESSIONAL EXPERIENCE

INTERNATIONAL TRADE INC., Baltimore, MD   2000 to Present

Senior Consultant, Policy & Compliance

Focal-point leader and advisor for Trade Compliance Program across 120+ countries. Maintain knowledge of current import/export regulations, evaluate proposed regulatory changes, and write business impact and recommendation reports. Create manuals, guidelines, standard operating policies, internal control programs, and other tools needed for import/export compliance. Develop and conduct customs/export training programs for employees, customers, and third-party logistics providers.

Key Achievements:
- Discovered $1.5 billion in errors and other significant compliance deficiencies during international audit.
- Recognized as subject matter expert for development of numerous software applications. Automated and streamlined operations by at least 50% while simultaneously increasing global trade regulatory compliance.
- Conceived, developed, and implemented countless ideas for increasing Global Trade Compliance among numerous business units around the world, including immediate funding and IT resources. Successful in improving productivity and increasing due diligence for regulatory requirements.

AMERICAN FREIGHT CORPORATION, Lancaster, PA   1995 to 2000

Senior Transportation Analyst

Produced Request for Quotations for domestic and international transportation, freight forwarders, and other logistics services. Analyzed bid packages and participated in negotiations with carriers and logistics service contracts. Identified corrective actions for domestic and international shipments. Supervised and trained three staff members in export compliance, packaging, freight damage claims, and freight payment with full accountability for budget of over $4 million.

Key Achievements:
- Restructured and streamlined international transportation and logistics processes/procedures resulting in net savings of $8.3 million through initiatives with transportation and logistics impact assessments, import port-of-entry points, and port-of-export points.

Continued

266

Senior Transportation Analyst *continued*

- Slashed 5% on freight payments ($7 million) through efforts in auditing transportation/accounts payable.
- Played key role in leveraging global transportation, customs brokerage, and freight forwarding services.

ABC MANUFACTURING COMPANY, South Ridge, RI   1990 to 1995

Corporate Transportation Manager

Full P&L accountability for receiving, raw material inventory, and shipping departments. Managed, prepared, and submitted applications to U.S. Government agencies for approval of import and export licenses. Hired, trained, and supervised staff of 22 in raw material inventory, receiving, shipping, importing, exporting, regulatory compliance, and freight payment. Negotiated and managed contracts for domestic, international transportation, customs brokers, freight forwarders, and other logistics services.

Key Achievements:

- Saved $500,000 in immediate refunds and reduced all future duties by more than $2 million annually through initiating reclassification of company's imported products with United States Customs Office.

- Instrumental in streamlining operations, optimizing transportation and international activities along with implementing legal measures to comply with United States import and export regulations.

- Successfully classified products according to harmonized tariff schedule numbers, assigned Export Control Classification Numbers, and assured compliance to country-of-origin marking requirements, NAFTA regulations, and Valuation Rules for imported and exported merchandise.

EDUCATION

Master of Business Administration—University of Southern Florida (3.7 GPA)
Bachelor of Science, Finance—The Pennsylvania State University

CERTIFICATIONS

Certified United States Export Compliance Officer (CUSECO)—International Import-Export Institute
Certified in Transportation & Logistics (CTL)—American Society of Transportation & Logistics
Licensed United States Customs Broker—Department of Homeland Security/Customs & Border Protection

PROFESSIONAL AFFILIATIONS

Chairperson, American Society of Transportation & Logistics (AST&L)
Member, Institute of Internal Auditors (IIA)
Member, International Compliance Professionals Association (ICPA)

MBA Finance

Morgan, CA 95037

Ben Solee

(408) 555-3219

BS Chemical Engineering

streamline@ameritech.com

Operations Management
Information Technology • Process Improvement • Financial Services

From "Hail to the Chiefs," article *Technology Today*
"[The company President] wanted [to hire] so*meone who understood not only computers but
also business and people – a management-level leader who could sell the changes to the staff,
handle outside consultants, and make sure the company's choices positioned it for growth."*

They Hired Ben

Performance Profile/Performance Summary

Operations Management Executive with a solid background in operations, business development,
information technology, staff training/development, change management, project management, and
turnaround situations with large and small organizations in multiple industries. Results-oriented, decisive
leader with proven success in streamlining operations, reducing costs, and boosting profits. Thrives in
fast-paced, growth-oriented, highly competitive environments. MBA Finance, BS Chemical Engineering.

Core Competencies

• Visionary Leadership	• Technology Integration	• Product Info & Education
• Operations Management	• Business Development	• Turnarounds
• Process Restructuring	• Market Identification	• Strategic Alliances
• Project Management	• Strategic Planning	• Staff Development
• Customer Service	• Finance	• Sales

Professional Experience

AT &T – Ferris, CA/Kavesh and Tau – Morgan, CA | 1999 to Present
Project Manager/Process Improvement Manager

Act Consultants, Inc. – Jordan, CA | 1996 to 1999
CIO/Vice President of Operations & Technology

Resource Management Group, Inc. – Temple, CA | 1995 to 1996
Vice President/Client Administrative Services

Northwestern Life – Jarod, CA | 1993 to 1995
Business Manager/Agent

Apple Computer/Marketing & Services Division – Long Beach, CA | 1982 to 1993
Project Manager/Systems Engineer

Education & Training

University of Southern California – Los Angeles, CA
MBA in Finance & Marketing ♦ BS in Mechanical Engineering

Professional Certifications: American Society of Pension Actuaries ERISA Consulting
Exams (Completed four exams; *first person in company history to pass all exams on first try*)
Registered Representative, Series 6 & 63, Life & Disability License
Certified Financial Planner Classes, UCLA (Completed two classes)

Community Leadership
Alumni Mentor, University of Southern California – Los Angeles, CA (1995 to Present)

Carl Hiaasen

Detroit, MI 49610   231.555.2347   hioctance@juno.com

FUEL DISTRIBUTION SYSTEMS SUPERVISOR, FOREMAN, OR SYSTEMS OPERATOR
*Training & Leadership • Refueling Point Inventory
Management & Control*

Performance History
Respected and loyal petroleum operations supervisor with vast knowledge of petroleum operations. Expertise in supervision of pipeline and pump station operations, petroleum supply storage facilities, water supply and distribution systems, supply point and terminal operations, pipeline systems, water supply operations, and laboratory tests.
Track record of performance, leadership, training and development of staff, maintenance activity supervision, and property accountability. Exceptional technical skills.

Core Competencies

Strategic Planning	Safety & Compliance	Fuel Systems Inspections
Preventive Maintenance	Petroleum Storage	Pipeline & Pump Station Operations
Water Supply & Distribution	Terminal Operations	Laboratory Tests
Pipeline Systems	Employee Relations	Maintenance Management
Property Accountability	Logistics	Team Building & Leadership
Operational Analysis	Administration	Aviation
Dangerous Environments	Safety	Organization & Time Management
Policies & Procedures	Training	Field Construction Management

—————— PROFESSIONAL EXPERIENCE ——————

U.S. ARMY   1984-3/2008
Afghanistan   2006-8/2008
PETROLEUM OPERATIONS PLATOON SERGEANT

Supervised, trained, advised, inspected, and maintained responsibility for the health, morale, discipline, and welfare of 10 non-commissioned officers and 41 enlisted soldiers in petroleum operations at four separate locations in Afghanistan. Coordinated daily training requirements to meet unit refueling goals. *Group issued over 2.9 million gallons of aviation-grade fuel with no safety issues and no damage to equipment or environment.*

Selected accomplishments
- Reorganized four mismanaged areas into highly effective centers. Maintained an operational readiness rate above 97% on all ground vehicles. Responsible for more than $8M of property.
- Assisted Platoon Leader in daily platoon functions, overseeing all training, including convoy operations, and providing battle-focused training and counseling.
- Directed construction of new living quarters for personnel.
- Served as the go-to person, continually sought out by leaders, subordinates, and peers throughout the organization for technical and tactical advice and expertise.
- Experienced zero accidents for entire period, due to stressing of the importance of safety.
- Developed a Soldier Study Board to encourage and assist staff in attending and passing boards.
- Awarded the Bronze Star for meritorious service.

Evaluations
"Concerned, caring leader of the highest caliber … instilled confidence in his soldiers"
"Among the best … a unique NCO whose technical knowledge and experience are above his peers'"
"Demonstrated unlimited potential … continue to assign to tough positions of increased responsibility"

U.S.ARMY

National Training Center, Ft. Irwin, California   2001-2005
PETROLEUM DISTRIBUTION TRAINER

Trained, coached, and observed platoon leaders, NCOs, and enlisted soldiers in the doctrinal employment of Forward Arming and Refueling Point (FARP) assets. Conducted post-action reviews and debriefings for up to 10 units per year. Monitored and incorporated changes in operational policy and procedure. Scheduled and coordinated painting and maintenance overhaul of all team vehicles.

Selected accomplishments
- Rapidly assessed soldiers' operational and organizational strengths and weaknesses and provided complete programs for improvement.
- Coached and mentored new distribution platoon leaders. Provided quality post-action reviews in one-on-one leadership format, as well as 3/5 platoon, small-group format.
- Recognized for high degree of self-motivation and initiative, for providing exceptional leadership and training guidance, and for continual willingness to go the extra mile.

U.S. ARMY

National Training Center, Ft. Irwin, California   2000-2001
PETROLEUM PLATOON SERGEANT

Shouldered responsibility for maintaining equipment valued in excess of $3M, including nine fuel tankers, nine tractors, two HEMTTs with trailer, a tanker aviation refueling system, two cargo trucks with tank and pump unit. Accounted for supplies received, stored, and issued. Supervised, trained, and developed 16 soldiers and junior non-commissioned officers.

Selected accomplishments
- Managed and directed a driver's training program which continuously qualified 100% of assigned personnel regardless of rank or MOS.
- Maintained accurate accounting of all bulk fuel issued.
- Ensured platoon received highest ratings during Aviation Fuel Inspections.
- Received an excellent performance rating as acting First Sergeant leading up to the Division Capstone Exercise.

** ** **

Additional experience as a Sergeant of a Support Platoon assigned to an attack helicopter cavalry squadron in South Korea, as Section Sergeant in a FORSCOM Petroleum Supply Company, as Supervisor in a refueling platoon, and as Section Sergeant and Fitness Trainer.

———————————————— **EDUCATION & CREDENTIALS** ————————————————

Graduate, Petroleum and Water Specialist ANCOC – Quartermaster School, Fort Lee, VA 1999
Graduate, Petroleum Supply Specialist Course BNCOC – Quartermaster School, Fort Lee, VA 1993
Graduate, Petroleum Supply Specialist Course – Quartermaster School, Fort Lee, VA 1987

Professional Development:

- Specimen Collection
- Inventory Management
- Artillery Leadership
- Hazardous Materials
- Train The Trainer
- Bus Training
- Environmental
- Leadership Development

Meritorious Service Medal, Army Commendation Medal, and Army Achievement Medal.
Received Certificate of Training Excellence, three Certificates of Achievement,
Certificate of Appreciation, the Order of the Condor Award, and the Order of St. Michael medal

Adolph Gottlieb

87 Liane Court
Swinburne, NY 11785

Cell: 917.555.9274
buy_right@ameritech.com

PURCHASING MANAGEMENT

Performance Summary

SENIOR OPERATIONS MANAGER offers extensive hands-on experience and a consistent track record in large-scale domestic and international capital projects, **fostering growth** and **delivering strong and sustainable gains**. A **self-starter** with a proven ability to conceptualize and implement **innovative solutions**. Applies **cutting-edge technologies** to update processes/systems.

Highly effective leadership and motivational skills support the development of cohesive teams (union and non-union) in the achievement of strategic goals. **Extensive experience** partnering with influential business leaders.

Core Competencies

✓ Business Planning	✓ ERP/MRP	✓ Project Management
✓ Quality Assurance	✓ Financial Analysis	✓ Process Reengineering
✓ Contracts Administration	✓ Influencing Skills	✓ Supplier/Vendor Management
✓ Cost Containment	✓ Negotiation Skills	✓ Systems Implementation
✓ Efficiency Improvement	✓ Logistics Management	✓ Warehouse Management
✓ Dun & Bradstreet	✓ Purchase Soft	✓ Visio
✓ Accpac	✓ EDI	✓ RAL

Career Highlights

- **Reduced operating costs by $500,000 per year** by outsourcing in-house printing department.

- Provided comprehensive capital procurement services for the **$300 Million construction and start-up of two printing facilities. Increased waste recycling revenues by $545,000 per year.**

- Directed **operating budget of over $180 million** during construction and operations of the **Famous World Exhibition**.

- Initiated the development and implementation of a **budget-tracking and -reporting system in support of a $90 million capital project**; completed **90 days ahead of schedule and $1 million under budget**.

- In security operations, **reduced in-house theft and drug and alcohol abuse by 99%, while reducing costs $100,000 per year**.

- Streamlined warehouse management procedures, enhanced **inventory planning and control** practices; **trained and coached warehouse crew**.

- Established **fully integrated logistics management function,** consolidating inventory, warehousing, and distribution.

Professional Experience

NEWSPAPER COMPANY   2001 to 2010

Manager, Procurement and Security

- Established processes and procedures, and **centralized purchasing and inventory management** via first-ever electronic system in the southern newspaper system, **reducing costs by $500,000/year.**

Manager, Procurement and Security *continued*

- Introduced new technologies resulting in **increased efficiencies** and **cost-savings;** technologies included fax services and color scanning, which increased turnaround in ad presentation and makeup and **saved $125,000/year.**
- **Reduced annual operating costs by $500,000/year through offshore purchasing and vendor partnerships.**
- Successfully **sourced national and international vendors, negotiated and administered contracts,** and executed **procurement strategies** on several large-scale capital projects: Development of a new $60 million facility; $97 million development project for implementation of new printing processes.
- **Directed international sourcing and managed logistics,** which included customs documentation and inspections.
- Served as **Project Manager in the design of a waste management system**, providing detailed specifications and managing project activities; **generated a significant increase in revenue**.
- **Overhauled the Security function**—outsourcing, modernizing equipment, establishing and training contract staff on new procedures and roles; significantly reduced costs, and nearly eliminated all incidence of theft.
- **Initiated and implemented the "pay in advance" system**—now used internationally among all newspapers—which contributed to a significant increase in revenue.
- Managed sale of assets from old facilities, building deconstruction, and **seamless relocation of 900 employees.**

WORLD EXHIBITION   *1984 to 1988*

Manager, Site Operations Procurement

World Exhibition's 6-month World Fair exhibition is orchestrated and attended by over 70 countries, each with its own on-site pavilion. Managed comprehensive procurement services for construction and start-up of operations. Held signatory responsibility for all purchases, and spearheaded profitable vendor partnerships.

- **Hired and established a procurement team** and **introduced new technology**, which facilitated shared communications and increased procurement and material-handling efficiencies. Successfully managed procurement activities throughout liquidation and site deconstruction.
- **Orchestrated first-ever buyback contracts** for heavy equipment and machinery utilized by the Exhibition, regaining a full 50% of the initial purchase price; negotiated and received free maintenance, providing additional cost savings. **Negotiated service contracts** for site equipment and operations.
- **Demonstrated creative problem-solving skills**, which enhanced operations ability to provide ongoing entertainment, while significantly reducing operating costs.

Associations
North American Newspaper Purchasing Association
American Society for Industrial Security
School Institute: Business/Marketing Management Diploma

Saul Poundstone

Oklahoma City, OK 73198   (405) 555-3953   topops@verizon.net

---

OPERATIONS MANAGER ~ PRODUCTION SUPERINTENDENT ~ QUALITY MANAGER
Special Expertise in Chemicals/Petro-Chemicals/Energy/Utilities

Performance Profile/Performance Summary

Senior Industrial Operations & Maintenance Manager with ten years' experience in corporate and military sector, including six years' operating and/or supporting nuclear submarine operations. Track record of consistently performing beyond the requirements of the position. Additional roles including formalized training and development, technical document development, and quality management system auditing. Six Sigma Green Belt, ISO 9001 Quality Management System Internal Auditor.

Outstanding communicator, leader, and team-builder; established and delivered training programs; coached and mentored; experienced in union and non-union environments. Exceptional technical and technology skills. BS in Applied Technology; MBA in progress.

Core Competencies

➢ Project Management	➢ Strategic Planning	➢ Operations Management
➢ Teambuilding	➢ Quality Management	➢ Recruitment & Selection
➢ Process Improvement	➢ Leadership	➢ Maintenance Management
➢ Safety Audits	➢ ISO 9001	➢ Lean Manufacturing
➢ Negotiations	➢ OSHA	➢ Profit Optimization
➢ Budgets	➢ SPC	➢ Productivity Management
➢ Policy & Procedures	➢ P&L	➢ Training & Development
➢ Labor Relations	➢ Collective Bargaining	➢ Process Development
	➢ Six Sigma Green Belt	

Professional Experience

CHEVRON, Oklahoma City, OK   2005 to Present
Shift Operations Supervisor   *Polypropylene refinery operation*

Direct team of up to 20 at 3 units—reaction, extrusion, and product loading, with responsibility for meeting planned production targets with no negative environmental impact. Ensure personnel and equipment safety standards are met. Contribute to continuous improvement and ensure plant remains ISO 9001 certified. Perform and report on scheduled audits.

Representative Accomplishments

- Achieved injury-free operations, contributing to overall refinery goal of 0.33 recordable injury rate.
- Completed ISO 9001 Quality Management System Internal Auditor Certification.
- Identified and resolved solutions for non-conformances.
- Designed and formalized training programs, reducing qualifying time and improving union relations, including:
  - Training program for new shift operations supervisors; authored 400+ page manual
  - Operations training for QA Laboratory
  - Training program for reaction area operators with program for extrusion and product loading by YE 09
- Streamlined multiple-unit operating manuals and SOPs, authored control center reference manual to ensure ISO 9001: 2000/FDA compliance, and optimized consistency of operations and quality across all shift teams.
- Collaborate with engineering to rewrite production procedures for product changes, unit start-ups/ shut-downs, including product change process that reduced downtime by 50%.

Professional Experience continued

UNITED STATES NAVY   1999 to 2005
Assistant Leading Petty Officer/Maintenance Supervisor   Norfolk, VA (2003–2005)
Oversaw maintenance of 200 nuclear-related items required for aircraft carriers and submarines; ensured adequate supply levels.

Electrical Division Member, USS Montpelier   Norfolk, VA (1999–2003)
Operated ship's nuclear reactor and performed maintenance on submarines electrical/electronic systems. Maintained internal and external audit records for ship's reactor and secondary plant IAW Naval Nuclear Propulsion standards. Served as divisional training coordinator; achieved 10% improvement in exam scores and reduced qualification time average of 3 months.

Concurrent Professional Experience

S&S Vacation Rentals   2007 to Present
Property Manager. Acquired and manage rental properties, ensuring low vacancies through creative promotions. Oversee maintenance and administrative personnel.

Education & Training

BS in Applied Science & Technology; Concentration in Nuclear Engineering Technology
OKLAHOMA STATE; 2009
MBA in Progress, OKLAHOMA STATE

NAVAL NUCLEAR POWER SCHOOL—**Major in Nuclear Power Operations**
Electricians Mate A School—Achieved Highest GPA, 3.8/4
Nuclear Power School—Achieved Highest GPA in Section, 3.7/4
Nuclear Power Training Unit—1st Operator Qualified

Certifications
Six Sigma Green Belt
ISO 9001 Quality Management System Internal Auditor

Professional Development

Practical Distillation: Quality; Operations; Principles and Practices; Business Ethics (2009)
Polypropylene ISO Quality Management (2009)
Process Safety Management (2009)
Labor Relations (4 hours; 2005)
Quality Management System Auditor (2008)
Preventing Operating Incidents Training (2007)
Taproot Incident Investigation Training (2007)
Managing Safety Performance (2007)

Military
United States Navy; Honorable Discharge
Served onboard USS Montpelier as nuclear electrician/operator
Operated nuclear reactor and performed maintenance on ships' electrical and electronic system
Awards: Submarine Service Pin, Navy Achievement Medal

Computer Skills
Proficient with Macs and PCs. Microsoft Office (Word, Excel, PowerPoint, Outlook, Project) Vision.

Anneke Tso

2423 Fairfax Court
West Bloomfield, MI 48322

Cel: 248.555.5254   expertsourcer@aol.com

Director of Recruitment
Process Reengineering/Project Implementation/Organizational Growth and Turnaround

"I offer process development, service delivery, and enhanced profits."

Performance Profile/Performance Summary

Talented and forward thinking senior recruitment leader with proven track record of success turning around company performance by distilling and managing processes, enhancing organizational structure, and developing skilled self-managed teams.

The "go-to" person for diverse organizational and process-related challenges. Confident and passionate individual with a mission to create "best in class" recruiting departments through comprehensive utilization of marketing tools and cutting-edge sales practices.

Recruitment Competencies

Project Implementation	Strategic Planning	On-boarding/Referral Programs
Process Reengineering	Sales and Marketing	Role Competency Design
Training and Development	Recruitment Metrics	Workforce Planning
Turnaround	Financial Analysis	Strategic Planning
Disbursed Management	Sourcing Channels	Proposal Generation
CRM	Advertising	Tracking Systems
Sarbanes-Oxley	Performance Metrics	Contracts
AP	EEOC	OFCCP

Professional Experience

A & E CORPORATION, *Bloomfield, MI*   2006 to Present
Leader in Recruitment Process Outsourcing
Recruitment Process Manager

Sourcing strategies to support the strategic, operational, and business plan for the company. Influence senior business executives on strategy, resources, hiring forecasts, and capacity planning. Establish and oversee maintenance of effective candidate sourcing channels and both internal and external resume tracking systems to speed the process of identifying qualified candidates and tracking effectiveness and efficiency metrics.

- Assist with proposal generation, implementation, training, and daily oversight of key account service delivery teams, overall delivery of key account results, and the management and nurturing of client relationships to deliver the highest caliber client results.
- Provide timely feedback to management and clients regarding workload and accomplishments, ensuring accuracy of data and timely, thorough completion of assignments.

SMITH & WILLIAMS CONSTRUCTION, INC., *San Francisco, CA*   2004 to 2006
Top 100 Design/Builders in the nation
Vice President, Recruiting

230-person corporate recruiting function. Report directly to CEO. Provided strategic direction and tactical follow-up on all levels of recruitment process redesign.
- Managed the internship program and volunteered to represent student construction organizations establishing a future flow of qualified construction management majors.
- Improved the "candidate experience" by instituting full life cycle recruiting at the company.
- Spearheaded company-wide skills matrix to aid in succession planning and resource management.
- Partnered with IT to create and launch career site to meet OFCCP and EEOC compliance requirements.
- Orchestrated a comprehensive multi-prong employee retention process overhaul.
- Established a 30-60-90 new employee review process, introduced buddy system, and re-engineered new hire on-boarding procedures, reducing communication breakdowns and ensuring employees' complete preparedness for first day of employment.

START UP AIR, *Dulles, VA*   2002 to 12/2004
A low-cost airline based in D.C.
Recruiting Manager

Hired to develop and implement recruiting function for a start-up airline to support 2000 hires. Assisted with the creation and management of a $1M advertising budget. Presented detailed and comprehensive reports and analysis on staffing metrics including attrition, program results, time-to-fill, and recruiter performance. Implementation of Sarbanes-Oxley narrative.
- Exceeded 2004 headcount targets by 20%, employing 2000 external and 500 internal employees.
- C-level approval for the implementation of an applicant microsite, which significantly increased the performance of the baggage handler screening process.
- Rebuilt recruitment and selection cycle for AAP, EEOC, and OFCCP compliance. Conducted quarterly internal audits to ensure compliance.
- Created a robust Employee Referral Program (ERP) that propelled referrals to 13% of total hires resulting in lower cost-per-hire for hourly airport employees.
- Implemented legally defensible behavioral interviewing with recurrent training for hiring managers, resulting in a significant reduction in EEOC claims.
- Designed and implemented a Service Level Agreement (SLA), greatly impacting the time-to-offer metric by eliminating communication disconnects. Time-to-offer on corporate hires went from 65 days to 30 days.
- Influenced two major internal departments to utilize in-house recruiting function rather than headhunting services, resulting in a savings of approximately $300k in 2004.

TNET COMMUNICATIONS, *Dulles, VA*   1999 to 2003
Voice, data, converged, and managed services
Staffing Manager
Responsible for 37-market telecommunications corporate, technical, and sales recruiting efforts for 1200-member organization. Engaged external agencies and internal recruiters in a massive hiring effort for top performers in sales arena, meeting the business objective of 300 hires in a timeframe of 3 months and dramatically impacting sales for the last quarter.

Staffing Manager *continued*

- Introduced SLA to firmly establish the recruitment strategy, reducing time-to-offer by 5 days. Significantly reduced time-to-offer to 27.01 and time-to-start to 40.01 after the initiative implementation completion.
- Successfully established solid customer service best practices and hired 700 sales employees.
- Reduced offer turnaround to a 5-day administrative cycle from a 2-3 week cycle.
- Implemented technical pre-screen process to eliminate unqualified candidates to meet OFCCP and EEOC guidelines.

MANPOWER   *1996 to 1999*
Global staffing company
Recruiter
Utilized both traditional and non-traditional search resources and techniques to identify and target top talent professionals including cold-calling, advertising, networking, and professional associations.
- Sourced, reviewed, and screened resumes for a variety of technical and corporate positions.
- Conducted preliminary IT candidate interviews and arranged for subsequent interviews with hiring managers and clients.
- Expanded growth of business by initiating direct placement contracts and placements service.

"Recruitment is the lifeblood of success. I know the challenges, the problems, and their solutions. I deliver."

277

Ted Hughes
MBA

Chicago, IL 60185   630.555.1837   supplychain_goto@ameritech.net

Supply Chain/Logistics Management
"21 years with world leader, from the loading dock to the negotiating table"

Performance Profile/Performance Summary

MBA with 20+ years of progressive growth with **UPS** in Supply Chain/Logistics Management, streamlining operations across a wide range of industries. Proven record of delivering a synchronized supply chain to optimize ROI and manage risk. Excellent negotiation and relationship management skills with ability to inspire teams to outperform expectations.

Core Skills

Supply Chain Mapping	Cost & Process	Facility Re-design
Contingency Planning	Competitive Analysis	Risk Management
Distributive Computing	Budget Management	Labor Relations
Recruitment	Training/Development	Organizational Change
Project Management	Haz Mat Compliance	Order Consolidation.
Order Process Automation	Demand Response Model	Vendor/Client Negotiations
Supply Chain Process	Financial Logistics Analysis	Inventory Planning, Control &
Costing		Distribution

Supply Chain Strategy: 500+ supply chain initiatives, negotiating agreements from $5k to $27M. Implemented technology and processes changes to reduce redundancies and staffing hours, improving both efficiency and productivity. Industries: automotive, industrial manufacturing, consumer goods, government and defense, healthcare, high tech, and retail.

Logistics: All modes of transportation; Ocean, Air Freight, LTL/TL, Mail Services, and Small Package.

Project Management: Implemented complete $1.2M redesign for 11 new UPS Customer Centers. Managed vendor and lease negotiations, developed budgets, training, and sales structure. All 11 centers operational, on-time, and on-budget.

Project Cost, Process, and Reorganization Impacts

➢ Reduced transportation expense by 15%, increased production levels by 25%, reduced inventory by 15% and staffing by 20%.
➢ Improved service levels by 30%, reduced damage by 45%, shipping process automation reduced billing function staffing hours 50%.
➢ Sales force realignment and reporting structure increased sales calls by 20%, reduced travel mileage 23%, and head count by nine; total annual cost savings of $920k.

Professional Experience

United Parcel Service (UPS), Addison, IL	**1986–Present**
World leader in supply chain services	
DIRECTOR/AREA MANAGER – SUPPLY CHAIN SALES	**2005–Present**

Leads a cross-functional sales force of 18 in consultative supply chain management services to Chicago-area businesses.

Continued

DIRECTOR/AREA MANAGER – SUPPLY CHAIN SALES continued

Directs development of integrated supply chain management solutions across all modes of transportation, closely mirroring client business plans. Mentors team in Demand Responsive Model, a proven methodology to quickly align internal and external resources with changing market demands, situational requirements, and mission critical conditions. Manages $100M P&L.

Accomplishments

➤ Implements over 100 multi-million dollar supply chain integrations per year with 14% annual growth on 8% plan.
➤ Develops future organizational leaders; four staff members promoted through effective mentoring and development.
➤ Choreographed a supply chain movement from the Pacific Rim for a Global fast food chain to deliver 300k cartons to 15k locations all on the same day. Utilized modes of Ocean, TL, air, and ground services, allowing for a national release synchronized to all locations on the same release date.
➤ Designed and implemented an automated reverse logistics program for a nationally recognized health food/supplement distributor. Automated returns process to reduce touches and costly staffing hours. Eliminated front-end phone contact using technology and web automation.

MARKETING MANAGER   **2004–2005**

Fast-tracked to streamline sales processes, increasing performance. Performed analysis of sales territory, historical data, operations alignment, reporting structure, and sales trends to devise solutions. Managed and coached area managers in business plan development and execution of sales strategies. Delivered staff development in cost reduction strategies and compliance requirements. Accountable for $500M P&L.

Accomplishments

➤ Drove $500M+ in local market sales. Grew 2004/2005 revenues 12% and 7% respectively.

RETAIL CHANNEL/OPERATIONS MANAGER   **2002–2004**

Charged with underperforming business unit turnaround. Managed development and implementation of new retail strategy across northern Illinois. Re-branded UPS Customer Centers and The UPS Stores. Performed vendor negotiations and collaborated with nine regions to support additional implementations.

Accomplishments

➤ Key revenue-generating initiatives across multiple channels: 65% growth in discretionary sales. Several strategies adopted across the national organization.
➤ Re-engineered inventory for over 1,000 locations, reduced lease expenses by 45%; inventory levels by 40% by SKU development, order process automation, and consolidation.
➤ Implemented new retail sales associate structure in 1,100 locations; scored highest national service levels by mystery shoppers.
➤ Selected as Corporate team member on Mail Boxes Etc. acquisition integration.

Continued

PROJECT MANAGER   2001–2002

Selected to support several underperforming business areas. Managed key segments of district business initiatives and compliance measures for 1,000 drop-off locations. Staff of 16; negotiated vendor and lease agreements.

Accomplishments
> ➢ Rolled out and managed on-going Hazmat compliance program for all locations.
> ➢ Generated $6M in sales through cross-functional lead program and increased participation from 20% to 100%.
> ➢ Attained Union workforce sponsorship of support growth program through careful negotiations and persuasion.

SENIOR ACCOUNT MANAGER   **1999–2001**
$2.8M in growth on $1.1M plan
ACCOUNT MANAGER   **1997–1998**
$1.3M sales on $500K plan.
SERVICE PROVIDER   **1994–1996**
378 hours under plan first year with zero accidents or injuries.
SUPERVISOR OF PACKAGE OPERATIONS   **1994**
Managed 65 full-time service providers. Performed post-routine analysis, operating strategy development, compliance, payroll, service failure recovery, and new technology implementation. Met 100% DOT and Hazmat compliance. Reduced post-delivery staffing time by 50% and missed pick-ups by 65%.
SUPERVISOR OF HUB OPERATIONS   **1988–1994**
100 union employees and staff processing 75k pieces per day involving 40+ outbound bays. Designed new management reporting format, reducing admin. time by 20% and improving load quality by 30%.
OPERATIONS DOCK WORKER AND TRAINING LEAD   **1986–1987**

Education

MBA
National Louis University, Wheaton, IL, *4.0 GPA*

BA, Business, Supply Chain Management
Elmhurst College, Elmhurst, IL, *3.84 GPA, Magna cum laude*

Additional Specialized Courses:
- Supply Chain Mapping, 20 Hours
- Financial Logistics Analysis (FLOGAT), 10 Hours
- Hazardous Materials, 20 Hours
- Labor Relations, 30 Hours
- Managers Leadership School, 100 Hours
- Supervisors Leadership School, 100 Hours
- Managing from the Heart, 30 Hours

"I know supply chain from the ground up. Let's talk."

Bill Root

Lubbock, TX 79424   Cell: 913-555-9532   financeguru@earthlink.net

SENIOR FINANCE MANAGEMENT EXECUTIVE

Performance Profile/Performance Summary

17+ years' progressive experience, CFO for Global Division of Wal-Mart. MBA in Finance; Graduate of Wal-Mart Financial Management Program; Green Belt Certified. Executive Board Member for Several Asian Financial Services Companies.

Senior-level finance executive/CFO with track record of directing and re-engineering large-scale corporate finance functions. Strategic analyst, forecaster, and planner with proven risk assessment credentials. Consistently effective in optimizing ROI, protecting assets, and ensuring strong bottom-line performance. Goal-driven leader.

Core skills

Corporate Finance Management	Acquisitions & Divestitures	Financial Forecasting & Modeling
Corporate Reorganization Affairs	Financial Analysis & Reporting	International Financial Affairs
Cost Reduction & Avoidance	Risk Assessment Management	Banking & Investor Relationships
Senior Executive Collaboration	Team Building & Leadership	Multi-Location Operations Leadership
Regulatory Compliance/SOX	Policy & Procedure Implementation	Budget Planning & Administration

PROFESSIONAL EXPERIENCE

WAL-MART   *1989 – Present*

Progressed through increasingly responsible positions and challenging assignments over 17-year period, demonstrating ability to generate quantifiable results on national and international scale.

Global Financial Planning & Analysis Leader – Wal-Mart Insurance (2004-Present)

Currently lead financial reporting and forecasting functions for $10 billion Revenue Insurance division with $40 billion in assets. Supervise local and international (India) team. Work hand-in-hand with CFO and CEO on mission-critical objectives and serve as primary point of contact to Corporate Finance organization. Create reports for BOD Audit Committee and CEO reviews. Assist top-level senior management in key strategic communication and presentation activities.

Challenges: Bring heightened visibility to key business information within complex, restructured organization. Improve financial reporting methods (previously lacking insightful analysis) to provide better view for senior management and Board into financial health of large operations.

Selected Contributions & Accomplishments

FINANCIAL FORECASTING & REPORTING

Built Center of Excellence team that took charge of financial reporting for $100 million in expenses, leading to significant improvements in cost control and immediate benefits to business operations.

MERGERS & ACQUISITIONS

Led successful forecasting improvements through design and development of new modeling tools; instituted new SG&A reporting infrastructure for ~$800 million cost base. Played key role in supporting largest re-insurance transaction in history (Wal-Mart Insurance sale to Swiss RE), performing due diligence functions to facilitate process. Provided value-driven

EXECUTIVE MANAGEMENT SUPPORT

recommendations and support to Chief Financial Officer and Chief Executive Officer, including preparation of strategic communication and presentation materials for delivery at Board of Directors and other key meetings.

CEO – Wal-Mart Hong Kong 2002 – 2004

Hand-selected for return to top leadership position following previously successful management tenure with Wal-Mart Capital Hong Kong, overseeing team of 150-160. Held full P&L responsibility for Consumer Financial Services Operations ($600 million in assets, $200 million in revenues) consisting of Mortgage, Personal Loans, and Automobile Financing divisions. Functioned as Capital's Lead Representative to Hong Kong Monetary Authority and Finance House Association of Hong Kong. **Challenges: Engineer turnaround for underperforming business affected by heavily saturated financial services market in Hong Kong and SARS epidemic, with continual downsizing initiatives.**

Selected Contributions & Accomplishments

NEW BUSINESS DEVELOPMENT

Transformed Hong Kong's mortgage strategy by strengthening operations and launching new product introductions, generating 30% growth in asset base as a result. Achieved $1.5 million cost savings through several productivity improvement solutions, including outsourcing and rationalization initiatives, leading to fulfillment of turnaround goals. Chief Executive Officer – Wal-Mart Finance Indonesia/Malaysia (2000-2002).

Promoted to hold full P&L accountability for Finance Indonesia, directing multi-branch platform with 800+ team members. Directed Credit Card, Personal Loans, and Automobile Financing divisions. Served as Board member for several Asian leading financial services businesses.

COST REDUCTION & AVOIDANCE

Challenges: Reverse 5-year history of declining profits as operations emerged from Asian economic crisis of late 1990s. Restructure commercial debt. Drive improvements for low employee morale.

Selected Contributions & Accomplishments:

OPERATIONS TURNAROUND

Met turnaround objectives by leading Indonesian business to 1st profitable year in 5 years by growing credit card/personal loan revenues and customer base over 150%.

BUSINESS DEVELOPMENT

QUALITY ASSURANCE

Launched Visa co-brand credit card with largest bank in Indonesia that became #1 Visa-issued card in Indonesia during 2001.

Utilized Six Sigma processes to improve operations through collection auto dialers, application scanning, and system migration to Vision+.

Education

Masters of Business Administration in Finance
New York University – New York, NY (1997)
Bachelor of Science in Information Technology

Professional Development

Financial Management Program (FMP)

Information Management Leadership Program (IMLP)
Six Sigma Green Belt Training & Certification
Financial Analysis for Business Development

Chang Apanya

San Francisco, CA 94109   415-555-2349   techmarketing@gmail.com

New Business Development • Product Marketing
Secure electronic commerce

Performance Summary

Accomplished Senior Executive with a strong affinity for *technology* and a keen business sense for the application of *emerging products* to add value and expand markets.

Proven talent for identifying *core business needs* and translating them into *technical deliverables*. Launched and managed cutting-edge Internet programs and services to win new customers, generate revenue gains, and increase brand value.

Unique combination of technical and business/sales experience. Articulate and persuasive in defining the benefits of e-commerce technologies, differentiating offerings, and increasing customer retention. Highly self-motivated, enthusiastic, and profit-oriented.

Professional Competencies

Sales & Marketing	Business Development	Strategic Initiatives
Business Planning	Project Management	Strategic Partnerships
Contract Negotiations	Relationship Management	Emerging Products
E-commerce Technologies	Increase Brand Value	Customer Retention
Secure E-commerce	Internet Services	Smart Card Technology

Technical Competencies

E-Commerce	Encryption Technology	Payment Products
Firewalls	Smart Cards	Stored Value
Digital Certificates	Network Security	Internet Security
Dual and Single Message	Payment Gateways	Financial Systems
Authorization	Clearing & Settlement	Java
Key Management	Public Key Infrastructure	RF communications

Professional Experience

ABC Credit Card Corp., San Diego, CA   2007 to Present

E-COMMERCE AND SMART CARD CONSULTANT

- Developed strategic e-commerce marketing plans for large and small merchants involving Web purchases and retail transactions using a multifunctional, microcontroller smart card for both secure Internet online commerce and point-of-sale offline commerce.
- Combined multiple software products for Internet and non-Internet applications: home banking, stored value, digital certificates, key management, rewards & loyalty program.
- PCS/GSM cell phone, and contactless microcontroller with RF communications without direct POS contact.

E-COMMERCE AND SMART CARD CONSULTANT continued

- Consulted on business and technical requirements to define new e-commerce products and essential deliverables for ABC Credit Card, valued at $2.5 M, supporting and enhancing Internet transactions.
- Analyzed systems relating to the point-of-sale environment in the physical world and at the merchant server via the Internet for real-time authorization, clearing, and settlement.
- Managed projects including the requirements management system for electronic commerce products affecting core systems: authorization, clearing, and settlement. Provided expertise about business and technical issues regarding SET and the Credit Card Payment Gateway Service.

Communications Technology Corporation, Miami, FL   2000 to 2007

MANAGER OF WESTERN REGION CHANNEL PARTNER

- Developed and maintained business relationships with Fortune 500 customers using client-server software for applications and contracts involving:
  - o E-commerce and smart card technology for a variety of Internet/intranet products.
  - o EDI, stored value, digital certificates, key management, perimeter defense with proxy firewalls, secure remote access.
- Negotiated an exclusive contract with one of the largest government and commercial contractors in the industry, projected to generate $2-4 million over a 24-36 month period. Contract includes secure remote access, telecommuting, secure health care applications.

Avanta Corp. Miami, FL   1995 to 2000

SENIOR SOFTWARE ENGINEER/SOFTWARE INSTRUCTOR

Managed a software engineering group of 53. Developed in-house program that saved over $150,000 in training costs for state-of-the-art communications system software development.

- o Designed new programs and trained software engineers in object-oriented analysis and design using UML. Solutions were implemented in C++ in a UNIX environment.
- o Developed and maintained C and C++ communication software in a UNIX environment.
- o Created curriculum and course materials that reduced overall training costs by more than $150,000.
- o Coordinated and presented software training programs.

Education & Credentials

B.S., Electrical Engineering, University of Miami, Emphasis: software engineering, Minor: Psychology, President of the Sigma Sigma Fraternity

Top Secret Security Clearance with Polygraph.

APICS   **Chris Eisenstein**   CPIM & CSCP

MBA in Finance & General Management

San Mateo, CA 95008   415-555-0606   chriseisenstein@juno.com

Electronics Manufacturing Management

"Chris is a strategic thinker, respected as a role model of integrity—he sets a good example for others to follow. Chris not only recognizes opportunities but takes decisive action to make the most of them. He knows how to get things done through channels."

Performance Profile/Performance Summary

15+ years of electronic manufacturing services management experience involving operations, finance, supply chain, project and materials management.
Includes 6 years' managing cross-functional teams and customer relations. Skilled at evaluating complex issues, identifying key issues, creating action plans, and guiding execution. APICS-certified: CPIM and CSCP.

Core Competencies

- ✓ Revenue & Profit Increases
- ✓ Cost Reduction & Cost Avoidance
- ✓ Process & Efficiency Improvement
- ✓ Customer Relationship Management
- ✓ Contract Development & Negotiation
- ✓ Team Building & Leadership
- ✓ Materials & Supply Chain Management
- ✓ P&L Management
- ✓ Metrics Management & Analysis

PROFESSIONAL EXPERIENCE

High-Tech Circuits, Inc., San Mateo, CA   1998-Present
Business Analyst, Business Unit Financial Analyst   2006-Present

Perform extensive analysis and reporting for a business unit group of 300+ employees. Key actions and accomplishments include the following:

- Revitalized the Time Clock project, which was behind schedule. Established close interaction with offsite project manager and completed assembly, installation, and testing ahead of schedule. Recognized for contribution to efficiency improvement and more effective plant operation.
- Compiled and updated quarterly customer QBR reports using Excel pivot tables and Access database information. In addition, generated and reported quarterly bonuses for employees.

Business Unit Manager   2003-2006

Managed a challenging $25 million/year account and approximately $18 million of materials to maintain profitability. Major areas included forecasting, contract negotiations, supplier performance, financial management, and HR issues. Developed and coordinated activities of cross-functional teams. Key actions and accomplishments included the following:

- Spearheaded revision and execution of full manufacturing contract within 4 months versus expected 6-12 months.
- Grew revenue 330% in fiscal year 2006.

Business Unit Coordinator   2001-2003

Managed accounts valued at $12 million per year. Interacted with customers to ensure high satisfaction. Contributed to cost-reduction and efficiency improvements that included developing Excel macros to use purchasing and inventory data more efficiently and an Access database to track ECN changes and impact.

Master Planning Supervisor   1996-2001

Established rules, procedures, tools, and techniques to move plant from prototype to volume production. Managed master scheduling for multiple programs, as well as work cell material management and metrics. Key actions and accomplishments included the following:

- Achieved smooth transfer of $30+ million program to another facility through detailed material transactions and planning.
- Reduced excess inventory by $400,000 and increased inventory turns 20%.
- Originally earned promotion from Master Planner position within less than a year.

Previous positions: Master Planner; Accounting Manager

Peterson Laminate Systems, Phoenix, AZ   1997-1998
Production/Scheduling/Inventory Manager

Served as a member of Plant Leadership Team and as High Performance Work Team coach for Shipping department. Additional actions and accomplishments included the following:
- Participated in Kaizen event that promoted continuous improvement and elimination of waste by initiating changes that included reducing product travel from 5,000 to 2,000 feet.
- Contributed to $500,000 inventory reduction and 98% on-time shipping record.

EDUCATION, AFFILIATIONS & CERTIFICATIONS

Master of Business Administration-Finance & General Management
Boston University, Boston, MA
Bachelor of Science-Accounting
Northeastern University, Boston, MA

Professional Affiliations
Member, American Production & Inventory Control Society

Certifications
Certified in Production & Inventory Management (CPIM): earned in less than one year
Certified Supply Chain Professional (CSCP): earned in less than 6 months

Application Competencies
Access; Visio, SAP, ERP Word, Excel (including pivot tables and macros), PowerPoint etc.

Exemplary professional and personal references available on request

WARD BUKOWSKI

3467 Jane St NW • Andover, MN 55304
Home (763) 555-9887• Cell (763) 555-4578 • managesrsults@comcast.net

ENGINEERING MANAGEMENT

Performance Profile/Performance Summary

Results-focused Engineering Leader merging sound technical skills with strong business acumen and management capabilities to lead technical projects and personnel in fast-paced environments.

- Proven ability to identify market needs, conceive new product development opportunities, and manage full-cycle projects that have driven millions of dollars in new revenues.
- Skilled communicator, leader, and team-builder, committed to recruitment and development of top talent.

Core Competencies

✓ Strategic Planning	✓ Project Management	✓ Product Design & Development
✓ International Operations	✓ Cross-Functional Management	✓ Training & Development
✓ Recruitment & Selection	✓ Mentoring	✓ Quality & Safety
✓ Profit & Productivity Optimization	✓ Cost Containment	✓ Presentations
✓ Disbursed Management	✓ Acquisition Integration	✓ Team Building
✓ Warranty Cost Containment	✓ Injection Molding	✓ Casting & Stamping
✓ Precision Machining		

PROFESSIONAL EXPERIENCE

INDUSTRIAL FLUIDS INC, Minneapolis, MN   1994–2009
Held positions of increasing challenge and responsibility for supplier of technology, equipment, and expertise for industrial and commercial fluids management.

Director of Engineering   2007–2009

Oversaw all areas of engineering in Lubrication Equipment Division. Developed, managed, and directed cross-functional team of 30+, including product development groups in Minnesota and China, technical assistance group, and technical publications group. Held $4M budget responsibility.

- Mentored, coached, and monitored progress of entire staff to achieve performance objectives and individual accountability.
- Instituted disciplined approach to product development, resulting in multiple successful product launches with significant reduction (20%) in warranty expense.
- Led effort and partnered with product development stakeholders on creation and implementation of divisional worldwide 5-year product plan with projected revenue increase of 50%.
- Conceived and received approval for ROI-based accelerated product development plan with 23% increase in engineering team.
- Identified product opportunity in un-served market with potential incremental sales of $10M.
- Actively involved in acquisition and integration of industrial lubrication company with projected revenue of $4M.

Product Engineering Manager   2001–2007

Managed engineering group of 12 in Applied Fluid Technologies Division, responsible for development of fluid-handling products for sealant and adhesive, industrial, automotive, and protective coating industries.

- Orchestrated large cross-divisional projects, including development of a pneumatic motor platform that is the core component of $40M in product revenue.
- Led numerous cross-functional design teams from concept development through product launch phases, concurrent with managed continuing product support.
- Communicated across multiple levels of management, including providing updates to executive management on project progress.
- Participated in developing relationships with universities and technical schools, resulting in hiring of top candidates.

Continued

Project Engineer (Industrial Fluids continued)   1996–2001

Oversaw numerous new-product development teams from concept development through product launch phases, ensuring rigorous quality and safety standards were exceeded. Gained valuable experience translating customer requirements into product specifications and ultimately launching products that exceeded customer's expectations.

- Selected by VP of Engineering to lead development of a breakthrough electronic paint proportioning system that exceeded forecast with $4M in sales.

Senior Designer   1994–1996

Designed and documented fluid handling equipment for industrial and automotive industries. Active member of design team responsible for the timely and accurate completion of projects. Gained extensive experience in product design on Pro/ENGINEER software, utilizing numerous manufacturing processes such as precision machining, injection molding, casting, and stamping.

Previous Experience as Senior Designer with Honeywell Inc.

EDUCATION AND TRAINING

BS, Mechanical Engineering
UNIVERSITY OF MINNESOTA

Diploma—Engineering Drafting and Design Technology
DUNWOODY COLLEGE OF TECHNOLOGY

Professional Development

Fundamentals of Marketing (Carlson School of Management)
Fundamentals of Project Management (Carlson School of Management)

Professional Affiliations

Member— American Society of Mechanical Engineers

References available on request.

Farad Judeah

1234 Ocean Road   Wilmington, NC 28402   (910) 555-6377   globalwisdom@email.com

International Marketing
Market & Product Strategist/Business Developer/Negotiator

Performance Profile/Performance Summary

20+ year track record driving revenue growth and market share. "C" level relationship builder. Delivers strong and sustainable revenue gains. Increases business unit performance, and negotiates the deals that guarantee success.

Contracts with

- *Xerox*
- *Microsoft*
- *Boeing*
- *The Gap*
- *EDS*
- *Oracle*
- *Nordstrom*
- *Sun*
- *Visa*
- *Nortel*
- *Fuji*
- *AMD*
- *Bank of America*
- *Lockheed Martin*
- *Morgan Stanley*
- *Apple*

Core Competencies

- Strategic Planning
- Global Practices
- CRM
- Reseller Channels
- P&L Responsibility
- Budgets
- National Accounts
- A/R & Bad Debt
- Contracts
- Product Management
- Contract Negotiations
- Sales Management
- Pricing Models
- Packaging
- Market Strategy
- Hands on Sales
- Business Development
- Program Development
- Recruitment & Selection
- Market/Product Strategies
- Global Account Management
- Process Re-engineering
- Global Account Development
- Product Re-engineering
- Acquisition Management
- Business Unit Re-engineering
- Lost Account Recovery
- International Markets

Accomplishments

- Conceived and coordinated the global account management process; grew market share from 7% to 100% and revenue from $330,000 to $6M per month. First pre-paid international contract, allowed company to accelerate into international markets achieving $1+ billion in revenues.
- Business unit turnaround, successfully recovering 60% of lost accounts plus new business to increase revenues by $5+ million in the first 12 months.
- Revitalized dying product with International Reseller Channel, extended product life by 2 years.
- Designed and implemented National Accounts Program. Increased revenue from $12M to $27M per month.
- Led the company's new technologies market development (VPN, Web Hosting), securing sales in excess of $15M within 6 months.

Professional Experience

Software Company, Inc. Philadelphia, PA   2006 – Present
Vice President, Business Development and Alliances

- Recruited to drive the product development process and expand market reach through the implementation of an international reseller channel and strategic business alliances.
- Negotiated contracts with Fuji Xerox, Xerox, Accenture, and Lockheed Martin capturing $10M in potential revenue.

Vice President, Business Development and Alliances *continued*
- Managed the renegotiation of two existing alliances that will net the company at least $2M over the next 12 months.
- Established a new technology relationship with Open Text, extending the company's reach in the Life Sciences market.

International Telecom, Inc. Nashville, TN   1997 – 2004
Regional Vice President National Accounts

Full P&L, $20M operational budget, 250+ personnel, mandate to build a national account program during a 15-company acquisition period; consistently exceeded all business objectives.
- Managed the best corporate A/R and bad debt levels, achieved outstanding customer retention level of 94%, and managed corporation's lowest employee turnover rate of 10%.

- Developed and implemented a National Account Program, expanding revenues within the first year from $180M to $260M.

- Averaged a 21% annual internal revenue growth and was selected to the President's Club from 1998 through 2003.

ABC Telecom, Inc Los Angeles, CA   1995 – 1997
Executive Director – Global Accounts

Promoted to manage the Western US team of 139 sales and support staff (5 direct reports) and to oversee 35 national accounts.
- Managed and negotiated $750M in contracts, including BofA, Visa, Microsoft, The Gap, Sun, Apple, Oracle, AMD, and Nordstrom. Grew market share from less than 15% to 48% in two years.
- Averaged 122% of revenue target each year.

ABC Telecom, Inc. Los Altos, CA   1992 – 1995
Branch Manager

Recruited to grow and manage the Bank of America account, successfully leading a team of 39 cross-functional members.
- Grew annual sales and revenue from $3.6M to $80M within two years, attaining 100% market share.
- Spearheaded largest commercial sale in ABC history, valued at $400M, successfully converting the entire Bank of America network to ABC in less than 6 months while maintaining 100% customer satisfaction.

BS&S, San Francisco, CA   1986 – 1992
Field District Manager

Consistently exceeded quota, averaging 112%, and made President's Club every year while in sales/sales management positions.
- As staff member for the President of BS&S Information Systems, was responsible for revenue and issues for all national accounts west of the Mississippi, approximately 200 accounts, achieving 109% of the revenue quota.

BS&S Headquarters, New York, NY   1983 – 1986
National Account Management

Negotiated and implemented the largest state government equipment contract, valued at $20M.
- Named to Management Development Program (top 2% of all management personnel), recognized for superior executive and leadership potential.

Education

Bachelor of Arts, New York University

Career Development: Intensive 18-week BS&S account management and product training seminar.

" I know business, I know people, and believe I'm getting the hang of sales too."

Yasuo Kuniyoshi MBA

Dallas, TX 75207   214-555-2375   alwaysonbrand@comcast.net

Online and Brand Marketing Communications

Performance Summary

20+ years' experience in brand marketing: international, corporate, and entrepreneurial cultures. Practical problem-solving skills, and a deep well of experience to meet the challenges of this fast-paced function.

Project-planning and management experience in high-stress scenarios where failure is not an option and the wrong decision could deliver substantial client loss.

- Consultative approach to assess client needs and provide "turnkey" solutions and programs that meet strategic goals.
- Strategic business sense, an uncompromising work ethic, and a burning desire to create consistently successful marketing solutions.
- Loyal support from clients, partners, managers, and business owners.
- Deep expertise in branding, management, and positioning product lines.
- Marketing messages that drive revenue and bring unique product "stories" to the community.
- MBA – Marketing

Core Skills

✓ Branding	✓ Needs Assessment	✓ Product Positioning
✓ Product Stories	✓ Strategic Rollouts	✓ Brand Development
✓ Brand Creation	✓ Project Planning	✓ Media Relations
✓ Brand Establishment	✓ Sales & Pricing	✓ Investor Sourcing
✓ Training Materials	✓ Sales Materials	✓ SEO
✓ Event Planning	✓ Event Promotion	✓ Charity Fundraisers
✓ Social Networking	✓ Distance Learning	✓ MarComm

Performance Highlights

Communications

- Built a packaged employee communication strategic rollout plan for *Montgomery General Hospital*, partnered with senior internal HR leaders and directed launch timeframe for new employee subscription benefit (*PepPods*, an online emergency preparedness and personal home record system).
- Sourced and secured a $1 million investor for *Zigzag.net*. Marketed online learning management system to military and law enforcement professionals.
- For *Nation's Bank*, developed an interactive kiosk concept for banking clients to receive instant product and service information during peak periods. Praised by customers nationwide during rollout.

Marketing and Events Planner

- Created and launched the *AT&T* "*No More Excuses*" multimedia cell phone campaign, the most successful January campaign in company history.

Continued

Marketing and Events Planner *continued*

- For *Mercy Health*, lined up stimulating children's entertainment musicians and artisans, food and health screening vendors and launched direct mail campaign to the *Mercy Health Plan* members, resulting in an impressive 900-person turnout. Located creative team to design mascot *Percy*'s character costume.
- Organized and launched a hugely successful *White Glove Car Wash* charity grand opening event, and donated a portion of the proceeds to the *Make a Wish Foundation*.

Multi Media Marketing Strategist

- Created the *Magistar* public corporate identity, including the marketing language on the corporate website, trade show participation strategy, and public relations presentations.
- Established strong rapport with *TMC Labs* editor who agreed to conduct an extensive product evaluation and testing, resulting in a rave product review for *Magistar* in the *Internet Telephony*.

Gifted Leader

Developed a turnkey fundraising program for immediate online client use complete with a fundraising micro-site, fundraising, sales and pricing procedures, and training and sales support materials such as scripts and FAQs.

Improved the volume and quality of traffic to *ActiveMedia* client web sites from search engines via "natural" search results, raising their resulting online rank, and improving their click through numbers.

Professional Experience

THE RIVER BANK GROUP – Reston VA	2001 – Present
Marketing Consultant	
MAGISTAR - Reston VA	1999 – 2001
Director, Brand Marketing	
NATIONS BANK/BARNETT BANK, INC - Jacksonville FL	1997 – 1998
Advertising Project Manager	
URBAN DESIGN, INC - Philadelphia PA	1994 – 1995
Director of Marketing	

Education

MBA Marketing Communications	2000
Phoenix	
Online Faculty at UNIVERSITY OF PHOENIX	2002 – Present

Develop and deliver online undergraduate courses in Marketing, Integrated Marketing Communications, Management and Organizational Behavior.

Excellent professional references available.

293

Walter Stuempfig

Los Angeles, CA 90001   322.555.8584   multimedia_production@sbcgloabal.net

---

MULTIMEDIA MANAGEMENT

Multimedia Communications & Production ♦ MIS Management
"A rare combination of technology management and creative multimedia skills."

Performance Review

Uniquely qualified management professional for a digital media technical production position with a distinctive blend of hands-on technical, project management, and multimedia communications experience. Offers a skill-set that spans interactive digital technologies, broadcast, radio, and print media.

Proven leader with an ability to identify talent, building and motivating creative teams that work cooperatively to achieve goals. Highly articulate, with excellent interpersonal skills and a sincere passion for blending communications with technology.

MIS Capabilities

- Systems Management
- Systems Configuration
- P&L
- Vendor Management
- Multimedia
- Technology Acquisition
- Resource Planning

- Needs Analysis
- System Testing
- Budgets
- LAN/WAN
- Network Security
- System Maintenance
- Recruitment & Selection

- Strategic Planning
- Systems Upgrades
- Project Management
- Telecom Integration
- Workflow Applications
- Technology Integration
- Performance Reviews

Multimedia Management Capabilities

- Multimedia
- Account Management
- Multimedia Production
- Corp Communications
- Photographers
- Scriptwriters
- Musicians

- Television
- Client Relations
- Creative Design
- Cross-Functional Teams
- Videographers
- Graphic Designers
- Talent

- Radio
- Market Research
- Multimedia Communications
- Multimedia Presentations
- Copywriters
- Artists
- Animators

PROFESSIONAL EXPERIENCE

LaRoche Investments, Inc., Los Angeles, CA	1989 – Present
VICE PRESIDENT OF MIS	2000 – Present
ASSISTANT VICE PRESIDENT OF IT/CORPORATE COMMUNICATIONS	1995 – 2000
CORPORATE COMMUNICATIONS OFFICER	1991 – 1995
ASSOCIATE	1989 – 1991

Advanced rapidly through series of increasingly responsible positions with U.S. division of European investment group. Initially hired to manage market research projects, advanced planning and execution of corporate communications projects, and in 1995, assumed responsibility for spearheading the introduction of emerging technologies to automate the entire company.
Current scope of responsibility is expansive and focuses on strategic planning, implementation, and administration of all information systems and technology. Lead technical staff members, manage budgets, select and oversee vendors, define business requirements, and produce deliverables through formal project plans.
Manage systems configuration and maintenance, troubleshoot problems, plan and direct upgrades, and test operations to ensure optimum systems functionality and availability.

Continued

Technical Contributions

- Pioneered the company's computerization from the ground floor; led the installation and integration of a state-of the-art and highly secure network involving 50+ workstations running on 6 LANs interconnected by V-LAN switching technology.
- Defined requirements; planned and accelerated the implementation of advanced technology solutions, deployed on a calculated timeframe, to meet the short- and long-term needs of the organization.
- Orchestrated the introduction of sophisticated applications and multimedia technology to streamline workflow processes, expand presentation capabilities, and keep pace with the competition.
- Administered the life cycle of multiple projects from initial systems/network planning and technology acquisition through installation, training, and operation. Saved hundreds of thousands in consulting fees by managing IS and telecommunication issues in-house.

Business Contributions

- Created and produced high-impact multimedia presentations to communicate the value and benefits of individual investment projects to top-level company executives. Tailored presentations to appeal to highly sophisticated, multicultural audiences.
- Assembled and directed exceptionally well-qualified project teams from diverse creative disciplines; collaborated with and guided photographers, videographers, copywriters, scriptwriters, graphic designers, and artists to produce innovative presentations and special events.
- Performed market research and analyses to determine risks and feasibility of multiple investment projects valued at up to $150 million. Developed and recommended tactical plans to transform vision into achievement.

Schwarzer Advertising Associates, New York, NY   1986–1988
DIRECTOR OF ADVERTISING
Rainbow Advertising, Brooklyn, NY   1984–1986
ADVERTISING ACCOUNT EXECUTIVE
WFDX-TV, WFDX-FM, WKLU   1978–1983
PRODUCER

Early career involved a series of progressive creative and account management positions spanning all advertising mediums: multimedia, television, radio, and print. Worked directly with clients to assess complex and often obscure needs; conceptualized and developed advertising campaigns to communicate the desired message in an influential manner.

Achievement Highlights

- Designed, wrote, produced, and launched advertising campaigns that consistently positioned clients with a competitive distinction. Developed a reputation for ability to accurately intuit and interpret clients' desires and deliver results.
- Recruited and led creative teams consisting of graphic designers, artists, musicians, talent, cartoonists, animators, videographers, photographers, and other freelancers and third-party creative services to develop and produce multimillion-dollar advertising campaigns.

EDUCATION & TRAINING

A.A.S, Broadcast Production, Russ Junior College, Boston, MA, 1974
Continuing education in Marketing Research and Broadcast Production, 1984 – 1986
The School of Visual Arts, New York, NY

Mary Sanders

111 East End Ave.   Elmhurst, NY 12509   (516) 555-1234   shop2drop@company.net

Assistant Buyer

Merchandise Buying/Coordination
"Consumer-connected, profit-oriented"

Performance Profile/Performance Summary

Wholesale/Retail Buying	Information Systems	Product Distribution and Tracking
Product Merchandising	Vendor Relations	Sales Analysis & Reporting
Inventory Replenishment	Order Management	Regional Marketing Campaigns
Commodities Buying	Promotional Calendars	Product Launches
Employee incentive	Retail Merchandise Buying	Vendor thru Retail Communications
Distribution	Sales Analysis	Accounting Discrepancies
Monthly Promotions	Sales Books	LAN

Professional Experience

London-American Commodities, Valley Stream, New York   7/2007 – Present
Assistant Buyer/Sales Analyst

Report directly to London-American's Director of Sales, providing support in areas of commodities buying and merchandising activities that reach annual sales volumes of $3 million for the division.

- Collaborate with multiple buyers to facilitate the marketing efforts of new products, and development of promotional calendars, product launches, and employee incentive programs.
- Maintain open lines of communication between manufacturers, sales teams, vendors, and warehousing personnel to expedite product orders, distribution, and problem resolutions.
- Reported directly to the Senior Buyer of Steinway Bedding in charge of day-to-day retail merchandise buying and merchandising activities impacting bedding sales across 37 Northeast locations.
- Successfully trained 45+ Steinway employees on a complex LAN database management system.

Sales Tracking, Analysis & Reporting

- Perform LAC's weekly sales analysis activities on regional/local transactions, achieving a recovery of $1,800,000 from 1998 to 2004 resulting from identification and resolution of accounting discrepancies.
- Develop sales books reflecting product lines, monthly promotions, discontinued items, order forms, and transparencies utilized by sales teams and personnel throughout 26 store locations.
- Formulate price breakdowns and track sales levels to determine product volume adjustments, replenishments, and allocations with a demonstrated proficiency in internal networking systems.
- Researched, compiled, and recorded Steinway's historical data to develop innovative sales strategies through close examination of inventory and product availability, pricing, and store promotions.

STEINWAY BEDDING, Woodbury, New York   4/2000 – 7/2007
Assistant Buyer/Merchandise Coordinator
Similar duties

Education

Associates in Science, Business Management   1999
STATE UNIVERSITY *of* NEW YORK *at* COBLESKILL

"Dedicated and conscientious."

Anne Granger

Charleston, SC 29424   Tel: (843) 555-1323   calmandsteady@fastmail.com

Customer Service

Performance Profile/Performance Summary

Organized, goal-oriented, adept multitasker. Sharp awareness of omissions and inaccuracies, and prompt with corrective action. Self-starter, quick study, and team player. Professional phone manner, data entry and word processing, composition of routine correspondence. Knowledgeable in Property, Casualty, Insurance Law, and Health Insurance.

Professional Experience

Liberty Insurance Corporation, Charleston, SC   1999–2004
CUSTOMER SERVICE REPRESENTATIVE

Hired as data entry operator and advanced to customer service position in less than a year. Took over problem desk, which had been inadequately handled by 2 previous employees. Worked closely with underwriters, answering client inquiries by phone or email. Analyzed complex situations affecting insurance coverage. Recognized opportunities to increase sales and advised clients when coverage was lacking in specific policy areas.

Key Accomplishments

During major restructuring of company resulting in 70% staff reduction, assumed more than triple the normal account responsibility, from 450 to over 1500, while still in training. Simultaneously studied for insurance licensing course; passed exam on first try, with score of 95.

Liberty Insurance Corporation, Charleston, SC   1997–1999
Applications processing center for Mutual Surety Corporation
APPLICATIONS SCREENER

Screened homeowners' new lines of business applications, verifying coverage against individual state regulations. Filled in whenever needed for switchboard, typing, and clerical assignments.

Royal Guard Insurance Company, Middleton, SC   1988–1990
SUBROGATION CLERK

Started as receptionist and promoted shortly thereafter to handle various clerical assignments in Subrogation Department. Prepared paperwork for file with arbitration board. Kept subrogation ledgers up to date for auditors' review.

Education

Carolina State University — 65 credits in Business Administration   1986–1988
American Insurance Academy   2000
12-week course in Property and Casualty, Insurance Law, and Health Insurance

BRENDA FORMAN

45 Duquesne   Parlin, NJ 08859   732.555.3642   calm&helpful@juno.com

CUSTOMER SERVICE
SENIOR CUSTOMER SPECIALIST • BILLING • CREDIT
SHIPPING & DISPATCH • INVENTORY CONTROL

Performance Profile/Performance Summary

20+ years' customer service experience with high call volume and intricate inquiries. Outstanding reputation for maintaining customer service standards, excellent customer feedback. Known to go the extra mile for customers and colleagues. A dedicated, efficient, goal- and deadline-oriented employee. **Order Processing, Crediting/Billing, and Diversified Accounts expertise.** Skilled planner with the ability to analyze client needs and achieve objectives. Train and develop customer service staff.

Customer Service Competencies

- Pricing/Quoting
- Credit/Billing
- Cash Reconciliation
- Leadership/Supervision
- Sales Force Support
- Accounts Receivable
- Hi-Volume
- Trade Shows
- Cycle Counting

- Order Processing
- Shipping/Receiving
- Expediting Deliveries
- Inventory Control
- Tracking
- Billing
- Written Reports
- Export Customers
- Return Authorization

- Diversified Accounts
- Troubleshooting Accounts
- Manufacturing Processes
- Special Attention Order Entry
- Customer Service Observations
- Training & Development
- Client Admin Orientation
- Back Order Reports
- UPS Call Tags

Software Competencies

- ✓ Orbit
- ✓ Retail Link

- ✓ Navision Financial
- ✓ EDI

- ✓ Trading Partners
- ✓ Word/Excel

Professional Experience

Edward Smith Inc., Cranbury, NJ   2003 - Present
Fine art supplies manufacturer
Senior Customer Service Representative, Trainer & Team Leader

Team leader, responsible for training and motivation of staff. Lead customer service meetings and prepare written reports of findings. Stand-in for supervisor as required.

- Discount and credit control.
- Order processing and ongoing interaction with sales management.
- Process all orders from *Wal-Mart*, our largest customer, through EDI system.
- Attend trade shows. Special orders. Export customers.
- Handle customer requests and orders, via Internet, phone, and fax, enter into system; edit order, and bill customers. Monitor through purchasing, warehouse.
- Online order processing systems: Orbit, Navision Financial Program, Trading Partners, Retail Link, Word, and Excel.

Edward Smith Inc. continued
Senior Customer Service Representative, Trainer & Team Leader

- Print back order reports on a weekly basis.
- Work with potential new clients and their representatives regarding administrative work.
- Responsible for the issuance of all return authorization numbers and UPS call tags.
- Research credits and input to system.

Roll Industries, Cranbury, NJ   1993 - 2003
Shipping/Receiving Coordinator/Customer Service Representative

Responsible for a wide range of shipping/receiving and customer service functions for this Fortune 500 carpet manufacturer. Handled an extremely high call volume. Processed orders, answered customer inquiries, tracking inbound/outbound shipments; expedited deliveries and set up delivery schedules. Prepared UPS shipments and participated in cycle counting and quarterly inventories.

- Attended trade shows and expedited special attention orders.
- Coordinated with and supported sales representatives in the field. Performed cash receipt reconciliations and resolved customer complaints, disputes, or discrepancies.
- Received Employee of the Month Award out of 300 people.

Continental Life Insurance, Plainfield, NJ   1986 - 1993
Customer Service Representative

Responsible for pricing/quoting customers, answering phone inquiries, processing orders, and expediting deliveries along with troubleshooting accounts.

Childcraft, Plainfield, NJ   1985 - 1986
Customer Service Representative

Responsible for pricing/quoting customers, answering phone inquiries, processing orders, and expediting deliveries along with troubleshooting accounts. Position required ability to work in a high-pressure/fast-paced environment.

~ LETTERS OF RECOMMENDATION AND REFERENCES UPON REQUEST ~

SCOTT KELLY

Woburn, MA 01801   (781) 555-3957   ScottKelly3@hotmail.com

RETAIL ~ SALES & MANAGEMENT
"Extensive knowledge of the wine and beverage industry."

Performance Profile/Performance Summary

Successful retail manager with 18 years of experience in Sales, Purchasing, Customer Service, Inventory Management, Merchandising, Staff Recruitment, and Supervision. Proven ability to increase sales and improve profitability through effective sales consultation, merchandising, purchasing, and inventory management. Demonstrate a high level of motivation and enthusiasm in all aspects of work.

o **Record of improving sales, successfully introducing new products, and growing customer base.** Expanded business for large volume - wine specialty - liquor establishment.

o **Excellent leadership skills.** Can communicate effectively with employees and motivate them to perform at their best. Can set direction for the team. Hands-on approach to training.

o **Established record of dependability and company loyalty.**

o **Experience in both general merchandising and specialty retail sales.** Extensive knowledge of the wine industry including suppliers, distributors, and consumers; extensive product knowledge.

Sales Management Core Competencies

❖ Sales	❖ Purchasing	❖ Customer Service
❖ Merchandising	❖ Staff Recruitment	❖ Inventory Management
❖ Purchasing	❖ Staff Supervision	❖ Inventory Management
❖ Cash Management	❖ Product Introduction	❖ Specialty Retail Sales
❖ Budgets	❖ Sales Forecasting	❖ Special-Order Purchasing
❖ Promotional Events	❖ Competitive Pricing	❖ Promotional Displays
❖ Security	❖ Training	❖ POS Technology

PROFESSIONAL EXPERIENCE

O'Leary's Discount Market, Woburn, MA   2003-Present

Manager (General Operations)

Direct the daily operation of a high volume liquor/wine specialty store, servicing over 1000 customers per week. Manage staff of 15 in the areas of sales and customer service, cash management, budgeting, sales forecasting, employee relations, merchandising, promotions, and security.

o Steadily increased revenues through strong focus on customer service, excellent merchandising, and teamwork.

o Trained staff in selling through increased product knowledge and food and wine pairing.

o Attracted new clientele to store through the development of a full-service wine department.

o Expanded product line. Increased sales and special-order purchasing by implementing specialized sales methods, such as promotional wine-tasting events.

o Competitive pricing, including regularly stocked hard-to-find selections.

o Participated regularly in trade tastings, shows, and vintner dinners, including Westport Rivers Vineyard, Nashoba Valley Vineyard, Prudential Center, and World Trade Center events.

Ames Department Stores, Boston, MA   1994-2002

Manager (Stock and Display)

Managed a staff of 12 in a large, national general merchandise store. Marketed and sold products; developed merchandise and promotional displays; maintained stock levels.

- o Increased profits through effective displays and merchandising.
- o Improved operations through effectively supervising daily staff assignments.

Beantown Gift, Boston, MA   1991-1994

Stock/Inventory Manager

Managed purchasing and supervised sales staff for a high-traffic specialty gifts store.

- o Expanded customer base by offering a wide range of attractive product displays and creating a welcoming atmosphere that increased the comfort level of patrons.
- o Supervised staff of three, ensuring quality of store display and product inventory levels.

Additional experience includes entry-level inventory/shipping-receiving position at Boston University (1987-1989).

Excellent references available on request.

Louise Bourgeoise

37 Riverside, Mahwah, NJ 07430   201.555.3896   servicemanager@aol.com

AUTOMOTIVE SERVICE MANAGER

Performance Profile/Performance Summary

23 years' customer service management experience with a proven track record. Decisive hands-on manager, able to lead service teams and administrative staff. Ability to increase employees' performance levels and develop rapport with diverse publics. Extensive knowledge of automotive warranty policies and procedures.

Core Competencies

- Customer Service
- Conflict Resolution
- Service Repair Analysis
- Operational Policies & Procedures

- Product Knowledge
- Teambuilding
- Franchise Establishment
- Warranty Policies & Procedures

- Problem Solving
- Warranty Expertise
- Safety & Quality
- Shop Utilization
- Supervision & Training

Professional Experience

KEASBY NISSAN & SUBARU, Keasby, NJ   2001 to Present
Service Manager

Manage both Service Departments while responding to client issues to ensure customer satisfaction. Direct reports include 35 staff: Service Advisors, Service Teams, Cashiers, Receptionists, Lot Attendants, and Detailers.

- Solve product issues for both departments while working with company representatives and senior management.
- Improve department productivity.
- Solve warranty issues.
- Monitor departmental budget, taking appropriate actions when required.
- Oversee implementation of new Subaru franchise, and obtain required certifications for service department.
- Achieved 2.2 hours per service order ratio for each customer.
- Eliminate expense and waste while reducing employee time-schedule loss.
- Repair order and team efficiency analysis, improving shop utilization and work in process ratios.
- Analyze monthly owner first reports for Nissan, and communicate findings with staff.

ESSEX COUNTY NISSAN, Stanhope, NJ   1987 to 2001
Service Manager

Direct reports included 13 staff: Service Advisors, Service Teams, Cashiers, Lot Attendants, and Detailers. Oversaw entire Service Department, ensuring complete customer satisfaction.

- Communicated with Nissan Service Representatives regarding product issues and warranty concerns.
- Improved departmental productivity, implementing several new programs.
- Conducted repair order and service department analysis.
- Increased service revenues and volume by 60% during first fiscal year.
- Maintained warranty expenses within manufacturers guidelines.
- Transferred to another location to manage larger department.

HAYNES NISSAN, Bloomfield, NJ   1984 to 1987
Service Consultant

- Handled and wrote over 20 customer service orders per day.
- Sold service and maintenance plans to clients.
- Coordinated service orders with technical staff, ensuring quality control through entire service process.
- Prepared final accounting of orders.
- Implemented first statewide service team model for dealerships.
- Transitioned to new organization after company purchase.

Richard Jagger

20 Redlights Road
Barstow, CA 92310

760.555.2541

skinsmooth@aol.com

Aesthetician

PERFORMANCE PROFILE/PERFORMANCE SUMMARY

An experienced, state-licensed professional, experienced in service-driven, team-centered spa environments. Consistently exceeds client expectations; recognized for a gentle, soothing touch and a pleasant attitude.

CORE SKILLS

- Facials
- Skin care
- Aromatherapy
- Acupressure
- Color Theory
- Body wraps
- Chemical peels
- Skin care
- Oriental massage
- Salt Scrubs
- Waxing
- Masks
- Multi-vitamin Treatments
- Lymphatic drainage
- Microdermabrasion

PRODUCTS

- Dermalogica
- Trucco
- Biomedics
- MD Forte
- Murad
- Jan Marini
- Skinceuticals
- Neo Clean
- Obagi
- Epicuren
- Bio Elements
- Magica

LICENSURE

- State of Arizona Aesthetician License
- State of California Aesthetician License

EDUCATION

HUDSON WILLIAMS DAY SPA, Palm Springs, CA   2003-2009
Aesthetician
NITA FOSHEE, Costa Mesa, CA   2001-2003
Aesthetician

PROFESSIONAL TRAINING

- Vitamin Therapy
- Health
- Wellness Therapies
- Aromatherapy
- Body Therapy
- European Skin Care Techniques
- Prescriptive Retailing

PROFESSIONAL EXPERIENCE

HUDSON WILLIAMS DAY SPA, Palm Springs, CA   2003-2009
Aesthetician
NITA FOSHEE, Costa Mesa, CA   2001-2003
Aesthetician

Working by appointment, provided comprehensive aesthetology services, from oxygen facials and anti-aging skin treatments to waxing, body wraps, and aromatherapy. Noted for customer service excellence and contribution to building a loyal customer base.

References available upon request.

Fairfax, VA 22033   Cell: 571-555-4959   Home: 571-555-2385   harringtonsam@aol.com

Chief Science Officer—Executive Director—Program Manager—Senior Scientist/Researcher

Biotechnology Enterprises—Molecular Research & Diagnostics Organizations

PERFORMANCE PROFILE/PERFORMANCE SUMMARY & DISTINCTIONS

- Professional with high-caliber general management qualifications ... strong orientations in finance and technology ... proven leadership talents. Led the startup of three biotechnology R&D organizations and turned around an existing test/surveillance laboratory.
- Accomplished senior-level scientist and recognized innovator in strategies, principles, methodologies, and processes for the biotech industry. Designed and developed numerous scientifically/commercially significant diagnostic reagents and assays.
- Professional experience spanning diverse clinical and technical settings; private biotech firms ... large R&D operations ... public health organizations ... hospitals ... academic facilities ... federally-funded homeland security projects.
- Effective in high-profile scientist executive roles, managing large organizations and overcoming complex business/technical challenges. Adept at communicating complex concepts to technical and non-technical audiences, and experienced maintaining impartiality in politically charged environments.
- Confident, assertive, diplomatic, and outgoing with exceptional communication and public speaking skills. Multicultural, bilingual professional—speak *fluent Arabic and English*.

MANAGEMENT COMPETENCIES

* Entrepreneurial Vision, Strategy & Leadership
* Financial Planning & Management
* Program & Project Management
* Training, Development & Supervision
* Team Building, Mentoring & Leadership

* P&L and Operations Management
* Budget Planning, Analysis & Control
* Process Design/Improvement
* Investments & Solutions
* Marketing, Communications & Public Relations

SCIENCE COMPETENCIES

* Molecular Diagnostics R&D
* Disease Investigation & Management—Infectious & Genetic
* Laboratory Management
* Quality Improvement & Assurance
* Advanced Laboratory Procedures & Technologies
* Homeland Security Strategies, Policies & Programs

* Molecular-Based Surveillance
* DNA Fingerprinting & Gene Banking
* Regulatory Affairs & Compliance—CLIA, CAP
* GLP, CQA, CQI
* Crisis/Emergency Preparedness & Response

PROFESSIONAL EXPERIENCE

State of Virginia, Fairfax, VA   1999-Present
Department of Health & Human Services, Public Health Laboratories (PHL)
STATE MOLECULAR BIOLOGIST   2004-Present

- Hold full P&L accountability for Virginia's only public health reference laboratory—infectious disease testing and surveillance services, bio-terrorism detection, prevention, and response—serving the state's 1.2 million citizens.
- Manage all aspects of business operations: strategic planning, budgeting, financial reporting, staffing, workflow, administrative affairs, internal/external customer service, quality and regulatory affairs.
- Provide technical and managerial oversight to six primary areas of laboratory operations: test development, disease surveillance, disease outbreak investigations: emerging infections, air-water-food-borne infections, and testing for bio-threat organisms/bio-terrorism.

STATE MOLECULAR BIOLOGIST – *continued*
- Manage $600K capital budget and $250K annual budget for operations. Lead a three-person management team and provide indirect supervision to seven technical and non-technical support employees.

DIRECTOR OF MOLECULAR DIAGNOSTICS—State of Virginia   2001-2004
- Put the State of Virginia "on the map" in the U.S. biotech industry. Distinguished the facility as one of the best labs in the nation, and one of the first public health organizations to receive federal funding for bio-terrorism testing and preparedness.

- Evolved a very basic laboratory operation into a dynamic scientific organization staffed with talented, highly trained professionals utilizing state-of-the-art technologies and contemporary methodologies to perform sophisticated testing/surveillance of emerging infections.

- Led an ambitious campaign to secure $600K+ investment in technology (state and federal sources). Achieved financial accountability and discipline throughout the organization in order to maximize ROI.

- Equipped the organization and prepared the staff to handle both routine and emerging infections (including potential bio-terrorism organisms) despite the challenges of operating under serious financial and staff constraints.

- Converted the test development strategy from a successive to concurrent approach. Reengineered laboratory processes and workflows, enabling completion of 80,000+ tests in FY 2001/2002.

- Designed and led intensive training and career development programs—trained/qualified four professionals in advanced molecular testing—and provided team coaching and one-on-one mentoring.

- Served as an effective representative/spokesperson for the organization to internal and external parties—scientific community, state/federal agencies (CDC, FDA, USDA, other public health laboratories), regulatory officials, media, and the public—and continue to advocate on behalf of the MDX/PHL and its activities, budgets, personnel, and projects.

Clinical Projects & Achievements
- Distinguished as the state's top-ranking science officer providing consulting, advisory, and leadership services on matters related to molecular diagnostics.
- Led the entire development cycle—design, validation, application, training, troubleshooting—of molecular diagnostics–based assays for rapid investigation, diagnosis, and surveillance of emerging/reemerging infectious diseases, including E. coli, Salmonella, West Nile Virus, and Noro Virus.
- Participated in validation of new rapid tests developed by CDC for BT organisms including anthrax, smallpox, and the emerging virus responsible for SARS.

Columbia University Medical Center (CUMC)—Mailman School of Public Health, New York, NY   1992-1998
Division of Molecular Diagnostics
PROGRAM COORDINATOR—DEVELOPMENT

Key member of a seven-person management team for a key division within this large, diverse health care conglomerate. 2nd largest medical center in New York and largest in northeastern area.

Medical center comprised of several regional hospitals and specialty institutions (including Columbia Cancer Institute and Starzl Transplant Institute). Managed the business, clinical, and technology aspects of test development. Led a team of 13 full-time technologists. Contributed to planning, development, and control of annual budgets of nearly $1 million for operations—including $200K for capital equipment.

PROGRAM COORDINATOR—DEVELOPMENT — continued

- Established the MDX developmental laboratories from the ground up—lab was a model followed by other laboratories throughout the U.S.—and provided the vision and operational framework for accommodating emerging technologies and future expansion.
- Developed/presented formal training programs—one-month courses in lecture and wet lab formats—to physicians on topics related to emerging/advanced molecular diagnostics methodologies, technologies, and applications.

Clinical Projects & Achievements

- Developed DNA fingerprinting method to distinguish between closely related isolates of Legionella pneumophila—causative pathogen for Legionnaire's Disease. Existence of this technique thwarted potential litigation (six-figure damage claim) by a former patient against the hospital.
- Developed test for identifying four most common gene mutations of Gaucher Disease among Ashkenazi Jewish populations. Delivered $110K+ per year in revenue from laboratory test fees.

The Methodist Dallas Transplant Institute (MDTI), Dallas, TX   1995-1998
SCIENTIST/CONSULTANT

Contributed expertise in molecular diagnostics to a multidisciplinary team of professionals—immunology, molecular biology, genetics, cell biology, and other disciplines—working clinical R&D activities for the oldest/largest comprehensive international organ transplant programs in the world (a division of the University of Texas Medical Center). Developed customized, specialty reagents utilized in research at the Institute.

Clinical Projects & Key Accomplishments

- Developed 2-hour assay—vs. existing test requiring 24+ hours—for detecting presence of low-level HCV in donated livers to be used in transplantation.
- Established custom oligonucleotide design and synthesis service. Generated $150K+ in annual revenue (commercial value exceeded $300K).

Applied Genetics Laboratories, Inc. (AGL), Melbourne, FL   1991-1992
PROJECT LEAD/STAFF SCIENTIST

Managed a five-year, $2.5 million project funded by the National Institute of Environmental Health Sciences (NIEHS) for R&D of early cancer detection/treatment methods. Provided technical and managerial oversight to all aspects of the project lifecycle. Tracked and controlled project budgets. Supervised four laboratory technologists.

Clinical Projects & Key Accomplishments:

- Designed and executed protocols for searching for TSGs in mice genome and detecting mutations enabling early diagnosis of cancer in humans.
- Participated in presenting annual project report to National Institute of Environmental Health Sciences in North Carolina.

Kuwait Institute for Scientific Research, Shwaikh, Kuwait   1985-1987
RESEARCH SPECIALIST. Department of Biotechnology

Established and managed Kuwait's first molecular genetics laboratory. Developed research strategies and managed projects. Provided consulting/advisory services on business and scientific issues. Built and led a team of 10 scientists, and hired/managed administrative support staff.

Research Projects & Key Accomplishments
- Distinguished as the only molecular biologist in Kuwait, and independently started and managed mission statement, business/clinical strategy, business/laboratory operations, policy/procedure formation, budget, staff, and equipment for this, the first molecular genetics laboratory in the country. Co-Principal Investigator on three-year, $480K+ project involving establishment of basic tools and methodologies for subsequent production of high-value compounds—single cell proteins—for use as animal feed supplements.

TEACHING EXPERIENCE

University of Virginia, Hampton, VA   2000-Present
Department of Microbiology
ADJUNCT ASSOCIATE PROFESSOR

Serve in a consulting role as a biotechnology subject-matter expert. Lead presentations to faculty and graduate students on topics related to molecular diagnostics, public health, and bio-terrorism. Provide advice on technical issues and made recommendations for academic/scientific programming.

Florida State University, Tallahassee, FL   1987-1991
RESEARCH ASSOCIATE
Supervised graduate students and taught undergraduate coursework in chemistry. Worked with senior scientists on projects.

Kuwait University Faculty of Medicine, Jabriya, Kuwait   1987-1991

LECTURER
Provided classroom and laboratory instruction in biochemistry and molecular biology to undergraduate students. Led/participated in scientific research with focus on rheumatic fever.

EDUCATION
Ph.D.—Medical Biochemistry, West Virginia University, Morgantown, WV, 1983
M.S.—Biochemistry, Duquesne University, Pittsburgh, PA, 1979
B.S.—Biochemistry, Kuwait University, Khaldiya, Kuwait, 1977

PUBLICATIONS—*a partial list*
- **Samuel Harrington.** Molecular Diagnostics of Infectious Diseases: State of the Technology. Biotechnology Annual.
- **Samuel Harrington,** Robert Lanning, David Cooper. Rapid detection of hepatitis C virus in plasma & liver biopsies by capillary electrophoresis. Nucleic Acid Electrophoresis Springer Lab Manual, Dietmar Tietz (ed), Springer-Verlag, Heidelberg (1998).
- **Samuel Harrington,** William Pasculle, Robert Lanning, David McDevitt, David Cooper. Typing of Legionella pneumophila isolates by degenerate (D-RAPD fingerprinting. Molecular and Cellular Probes, 9 405-414 (1995).
- John A. Barranger, Erin Rice, **Samuel Harrington,** Carol Sansieri, Theodore Mifflin, and David Cooper. Enzymatic and Molecular Diagnosis of Gaucher Disease. Clinics in Laboratory Medicine, 15 (4) 899-913 (1995).

PUBLICATIONS—*continued*

➤ **Samuel Harrington,** Robert W. Lanning and David L. Cooper. DNA Fingerprinting of Crude Bacterial Lysates using Degenerate RAPD Primers (D-RAPD). PCR Methods and Applications. 4 265-268 (1995).

➤ **Samuel Harrington,** Carol A. Sansieri, David W. Kopp, David L. Cooper and John A. Barranger. A new diagnostic test for Gaucher Disease suitable for mass screening. PCR Methods and Applications, 4 (1) 1-5 (1994).

➤ David L. Cooper, **Samuel Harrington.** Molecular Diagnosis: a primer and specific application to Gaucher disease. Gaucher Clinical Perspectives, 1 (3) 1-6 (1993).

PRESENTATIONS—*a partial list*

➤ **Samuel Harrington** and Krista Marschner. "A new, two-hour test for Bordetella pertussis using the SmartCycler," 103rd General Meeting of the American Society for Microbiology (ASM), Washington, DC, May 2003.

➤ **Samuel Harrington.** "Methods & Applications of DNA Fingerprinting Techniques," Five 1- and/or 2-week-long workshops presented at the University of Puerto Rico, 1997 through 2003.

➤ **Samuel Harrington** and Denise Bolton. "Development of a duplex real time RT-PCR test for surveillance of West Nile and Eastern Equine Encephalitis viruses using the SmartCycler," 102nd General Meeting of the American Society for Microbiology (ASM), Salt Lake City, UT, May 2002.

➤ D.K. Voloshin, A.W. Pasculle, S.P. Krystofiak, **S. Harrington** and E.J. Wing. "Nosocomial Legionnaire's disease: an explosive outbreak following interruption of hyperchlorination," Interscience Conference on Antimicrobial Agents and Chemotherapy, San Francisco, CA, October 1995.

➤ **S. Harrington.** "Genetic identification technologies: PCR and DNA fingerprinting," Second UN-sponsored Conference on the Perspectives of Biotechnology in Arab Countries, Amman, Jordan, March 1999.

➤ Bahr, G., **Harrington, S.,** Yousof, A., Jarrar, I., Rotta, J., Majeed, H. and Behbehani, K. "Depressed lymphoprolypherative responses in vitro to different streptococcal epitopes in patients with chronic rheumatoid heart disease," Conference on Infectious Diseases in Developing Countries, Kuwait City, Kuwait, March 1987.

PROFESSIONAL AFFILIATIONS

Member, Association for Molecular Pathology—AMP
Member, American Society for Microbiology
Member, Council of Healthcare Advisors, Gerson Lehrman Group
Consultant, INTOTA Corporation

DONALD T. THOMAS

2009 Churchill Drive
Aliso Viejo, CA 92656
donaldthomas@gmail.com

Ho Home: 949-555-9006   Mobile: 949-555-1234

SENIOR-LEVEL EXECUTIVE
FINANCE, CORPORATE STRATEGY & DEVELOPMENT
Expert in Leading & Partnering Corporate Finance with Enterprise Strategies, Initiatives, Transactions & Goals

---

Performance Profile/Performance Summary	Core Competencies
Strategic Finance Expert—Dynamic CFO with extensive experience and exceptional success in conceiving, planning, developing, and executing strategic and tactical finance initiatives that drive top-line performance and bottom-line results. Technically proficient in all aspects of finance and accounting functions, and expert in partnering corporate finance with enterprise strategies, initiatives, and objectives.	Vision, Strategy, Execution & Leadership
	Strategic Corporate Finance
	P/L & Performance Improvement
	Financial Forecasting, Analysis & Reporting
	Cost Analysis, Reduction & Control
Corporate Strategy & Development Specialist—Characterized as a rare visionary, strategist, and tactician. Consistent originator of bold, innovative business strategies that have extraordinary results on growth, revenue, operational performance, profitability, and shareholder value. Heavy transactions background including startup financing, industry rollup, merger of equals, acquisition, and sale.	Treasury, Tax, Internal Audit
	GAAP, SEC & Statutory Reporting
	Corporate Development & Strategic Alternatives
	Due Diligence, Deal Structuring & Negotiation
	Financial & Legal Transactions
Consummate Management Executive—Top-performer and valuable contributor to corporate executive teams. Extremely versatile with high-caliber cross-functional management qualifications, experience-backed judgment, and excellent timing. Outstanding role model. Talented team builder, mentor, and leader.	Growth Management & Business Development
	Organizational Design & Transformation
	Turnaround & Restructure
	Crisis & Change Management
Diverse Industry & Situational Experience—Public and private; small and Fortune 500; startup, rapid growth, turnaround, post-IPO, post-acquisition integration, bankruptcy—consulting services, real estate, hospitality, resort/vacation property, travel companies doing business in highly regulated industries in US, European, and global arenas.	Internet Strategies & IT Projects
	Team Building & Leadership
	Investor, Analyst, & Board Relations
	Executive Advisory & Decision Support
Extraordinary Personal Characteristics—Articulate, intelligent, ambitious, self-driven, and creative. Outstanding corporate ambassador to customers, industry groups, regulatory bodies, private investors, Wall Street analysts, board members, and other internal and external stakeholders. Speak conversational French and German.	

PROFESSIONAL EXPERIENCE

DTT Management Consulting, San Diego, CA   2007 to Present
Successful Management Consulting Firm—Significant Repeat Business and Value-Added Partner to Leading Consulting Firms (e.g., Alix Partners, PKF Consulting)—Retained by Startup, Small-Cap, and Fortune 500 in US, UK, and Asia

PRINCIPAL

Operate an independent firm specializing in the delivery of a full-range of consulting services—strategic business planning; strategic finance; corporate strategy, development, and financing; organizational design; operational and financial turnaround; marketing and market research and strategy. Identify and acquire new businesses and manage all aspects of the project lifecycle—from scope of work through provision of deliverables, follow-up and relationship management—for large-scale, long-term projects. Engaged by corporate clients representing a broad range of industry sectors—travel and tourism; hospitality; real estate development; marketing services; technology and Internet.

Management Successes
- Leveraged professional reputation contacts worldwide to build and grow a successful management consulting firm.
- Acquired significant repeat business and positioned the firm as a value-added partner to high-profile management consulting firms in the US and UK (e.g., ABC Partners, DEF Consulting).

Key Engagements

- **Turnaround & Change Management**—Retained (by principal consultancy group) to evaluate a key strategic business unit of a $500 million resort/vacation sales company in Chapter 11. Performed in-depth analyses of operations, identified deficiencies and risks, and presented recommendations for restructure and turnaround of call center operations, program management, inventory control, and member services functions. Engagement contract was extended to serve as Chief Business Architect during execution and post-C11 transition/recovery phases.
- **Operational Startup & Financing**—Retained by UK-based client of a $10 million marketing services business to advise and participate in creating a business plan, raising capital, and executing a startup in the global event management and incentives sector.
- **Corporate Strategy & Finance**—Retained by independent US resort developer to determine the viability and ROI of expanding into international markets. Analyzed business, financial, marketing, competitive intelligence, and geopolitical issues impacting the world tourism and hospitality sectors. Pinpointed key target markets, and authored business strategy and financial plan for launch of a luxury boutique hospitality brand.
- **Corporate Strategy**—Engaged in joint consultancy project with ABC Consulting in developing a full-scale corporate strategy plan for $500 million public hospitality company. Researched and analyzed internal and external organizations, market opportunities, competitive differentiators, business models, and challenges.

CDE Group, Ltd., London, England   1999 to 2007
Venture Capital-Backed Dot-Com Startup Operating in a Niche Sector—Fine Arts and Antiques Online Sales/Auction

MANAGING DIRECTOR

Held full P&L accountability—recruited by and reported to the investor group and Chairman of the Board—for an early-stage Internet company. Developed and executed strategy, managed finance and operations, directed sales and marketing, steered technology development, and managed relationships with internal and external stakeholders. Led a core team of three executives—Director of Sales, Director of Operations, Manager of Finance & Administration—and provided indirect oversight to team of 18 in sales, operations, IT, finance, and administrative roles.

Strategy & Leadership Successes

- Revised corporate strategy to leverage core competencies—a well-established network of dealerships and virtually unlimited source of product—and position the firm as inventory and distribution solution to another company.
- Conceived and executed viable exit strategy—vs. minimum requirement of additional 2+ years' investment to achieve breakeven—by identifying a buyer and negotiating sale of the company to a US-based business. Provided investors with ROI on their original investment/commitment of 660%+.

STUV Corporation, Inc., Orlando, FL   1997 to 1999
$500 Million Company—One of Largest Resort and Vacation Development/Sales Companies in US—in Rapid Growth Through International Expansion, Strategic M&A, Industry Rollup, and IPO

VICE PRESIDENT—BUSINESS DEVELOPMENT

Key member of the executive committee—retained in company's buyout of UK-based LSI Group—in charge of the strategic and tactical business development activities during period of dynamic growth and change. Crossed over functional lines to address product development, marketing, branding, sales, corporate communications, legal, and regulatory matters. Administered $10 million business development budget. Reported directly to the CEO/COO, led a team of five Director-level executives, and interfaced with Board of Directors, Wall Street analysts, and strategic alliance partners.

Strategy & Leadership Successes

- Led the company's single most significant post-IPO strategic initiative—conceptualization, development, and execution of transformation of the company's infrastructure, business model, product offering, and marketing strategy—without negative impact on sales, operational performance, or customer service during execution.
- Shifted the business model and organizational structure from a disconnected collection of resort properties—to a membership-based vacation sales company with an exclusive, points-based vacation product, and strong value proposition with single marketing message.

Business Development Results

- Credited with personal contributions to explosive growth—from $330 million in 1997 to $500 million in 1999—by spearheading the development and rollout of an innovative vacation ownership product and complementary offerings.
- Expanded market reach and brand recognition by initiating and leveraging relationships with high-profile strategic business partners—American Airlines, Time Warner, HSN, MemberWorks, and others in the travel, hospitality, and marketing services industries.

XYZ, Ltd., Lancaster, England   1994 to 1997
$65 Million, Privately Held Enterprise—One of Largest Vertically Integrated Vacation Ownership Companies in Europe—Specializing in Development and Management of Resorts, and Marketing and Sales of Timeshares and Travel Services

DIRECTOR—BUSINESS DEVELOPMENT (1995 to 1997)
CHIEF FINANCIAL OFFICER (1994 to 1995)

Held two key executive positions on the management team—both reporting to CEO (one of two principal shareholders)—following a major debt restructure, physical relocation, and preparation for sale. As CFO, managed all aspects of the corporate finance and administration functions (including treasury, tax, statutory reporting, and internal audit) for headquarters and 10+ overseas branches. Directed the preparation and analysis of financial statements, budgets, forecasts, desktop "dashboards," and other essential management reports. Hired, trained, mentored, and managed a team of 28 including three senior financial and accounting professionals.

As Director of Business Development, identified, created, and capitalized upon both innovative and traditional business opportunities. Conceived, developed, and managed strategic and tactical messaging, branding, marketing, sales, and relationship-building initiatives. Directed product development, positioning, and go-to-market strategies, and launched a series of breakthrough concepts and techniques—trial membership, incentive-driven referral program, customer/prospect profiling, direct-to-consumer sales, interactive multimedia presentations.

Strategy & Business Development Successes
- Key contributor to providing deep due diligence to ABC in its purchase of LMN Group—activities and relationships that led to recruitment to executive position with the acquiring company.
- Credited with personal contributions (strategy, finance, operations, business development)—to growth—from $40 million to $65 million—profitability—from 5% pre-tax margin in 1994 to 11% in 1997—and shareholder value—from $15 million to $55 million at sale of the company in mid-1997.

Finance & Operations Results
- Built and managed a best-in-class finance and accounting function. Managed the complete turnaround of the corporate finance organization to include new systems, technologies, processes, and personnel.
- Provided the executive team and stakeholders with comprehensive, meaningful decision support by restructuring virtually all financial reporting systems.

WXY Group, London, England   1987 to 1994
One of London's Largest Public Accounting and Business Consulting Practices—Professional Services for Entrepreneurial Public and Private Companies in Real Estate, VC Funding, Hospitality and Leisure Travel Sectors

Rapidly Advancing Levels of Seniority to:
MANAGER—CORPORATE FINANCE & INVESTIGATIONS DEPARTMENT (1992 to 1994)

Managed client engagements involving deep due diligence for numerous acquisition and funding transactions. Provided a full range of advisory services and functions including creating/opining on corporate development strategies, authoring business plans, preparing projection models, and performing operational and financial assessments. Developed expertise in fraud and litigation support, debt workout, and internal audit. Interfaced with firm's Partners, investment bankers, private investors, senior-level corporate executives, board members, industry specialists, and regulatory officials.

Key Engagements
- **Debt Restructure**—Contributed to restructure of £100+ million debt with complex asset security position.
- **Fraud Investigation & Litigation**—Provided support on several high-profile engagements including collapse of a private financial services firm (represented WXY as the client) and a Formula One motor racing team.
- **Corporate Recovery**—Contributed to financial and operational turnaround of several hospitality and leisure firms.

EDUCATION & CREDENTIALS

British Chartered Accountant—ACA (CPA equivalent), Institute of Chartered Accountants in England and Wales
G Mus (Hons)—Four year degree in Music (with honors), Royal Northern College of Music, Manchester, England
Training in Corporate Finance and Treasury, Association of Corporate Treasurers

PROFESSIONAL AFFILIATIONS

Institute of Chartered Accountants in England and Wales (ICAEW); American Resort Development Association (regular speaker and panelist at conventions) (ARDA); American Marketing Association (AMA); San Diego Chamber of Commerce; Association of Chartered Accountants in the US (ACAUS); American Real Estate Society (ARES); and Financial Management Association (FMA)

Professional Performance Commentaries
on
Liane McDonald
213.555.1237 • coolhand@sbcglobal.com

From last four years of annual performance appraisal reviews

"Liane stands out in her attention to the nuances of a complex operational infrastructure. Strong communication skills, tuned analytical mind, and a team player."

"She proactively seeks out seminars and webinars that keep her professional awareness on the cutting edge."

"If there's a problem, Liane is always the first to step up."

"A by-the-book type of employee, professional in her dealings with vendors and employees."

"A demonstrated ability to multitask and manage her time effectively based on departmental priorities. Unusual ability to make informed decisions on the details based on the imperatives of the big picture."

~ Elizabeth Myerson, VP Operations and immediate supervisor

From annual performance appraisal reviews at prior employer

"Liane has proven herself adept at accomplishing tasks with individuals throughout the company. She takes care to clarify issues and expectations for delegated tasks."

"Always ready to accept responsibility."

"Willing to work on projects that may not lie directly in her job responsibilities, but which impact the overall productivity of the department."

"Hardworking, ethical, and even-tempered."

~ Scott Driscoll, Director Operations and immediate supervisor

JANE ROCKHARDT

1251 Marsh Street, Apt # 476 •Salt Lake City, UT 84101
Home (801) 555-1049 • Mobile (385) 555-2423 • srprofessionalmgr@juno.com

---

Senior Software Architect
Solid Leadership – Software Architecture – Mobile Application Development – Internet Marketing

Professional References

Lead Software Architect   2008 to Present
MOBILE APPLICATIONS, SALT LAKE CITY, UT
Designed and developed iPhone application, iLogMiles, for commercial transportation
industry.
Reference: James Trautman, VP
Professional Relationship—Immediate supervisor

VP Information Technology
SALT LAKE FEDERAL SAVINGS BANK, SALT LAKE CITY, UT   2003 to 2008
Led technology department and created tech strategy for bank. Technology infrastructure,
including migration strategies for accounting and loan origination systems.
Reference: Renee Montaigne, President
Professional Relationship—Immediate supervisor

Software Developer
MORTGAGE PORTFOLIO SERVICES, DALLAS, TX   1999 to 2003
Designed, developed, and deployed mortgage lock platform using CGI and C++.
Reference: Corey Flintoff, President
Professional Relationship—Immediate supervisor

PAUL QUARN

98456 Patient Street, Apt. # 789 • Charlotte, NC 28277
Home (704) 555-1238 • Mobile (704) 555-9283 • plantmanagementpro@earthlink.net

SENIOR OPERATIONS/PLANT MANAGEMENT PROFESSIONAL

Continuous Improvement/Lean Six Sigma/Start-Up & Turnaround Operations
Mergers & Change Management/Process & Productivity Optimization/HR/Logistics & Supply Chain

SALARY HISTORY

UNITED STATES MARINE CORPS AIR STATION, Cherry Point, NC—2008 to 2010
Chief Operations Officer/*** Training School Officer in Charge**
Salary—$95,309

UNITED STATES MARINE CORPS AIR STATION, Futenma, Okinawa, Japan—2005 to 2008
********* **Maintenance Chief—General Operations Manager/Plant Manager**
Starting Salary—$64,484/Ending Salary—$97,500

UNITED STATES MARINE CORPS AIR STATION, Beaufort, SC—2001 to 2005
Plant Manager/Senior Operations Manager
Starting Salary—$49,507/Ending Salary—$64,484

UNITED STATES MARINE CORPS RECRUITING STATION, Jacksonville, FL—1998 to 2001
Recruiting Manager
Starting Salary—$42,545/Ending Salary—$49,507

INDEX